AF422294

Murder in The Medicine Bow

A Novel by James W. Murphy

Copyright © 2023

At this point, I'd like to thank a few people for their significant input into this work. Without their assistance and expertise, this work would not be the product it is:

First, I'd like to thank God, Jesus, and the Holy Spirit. Without their influence in my life, I would most likely not be where I am today. They have blessed our lives beyond measure.

My wife Jean, who has for the last God-given FIFTY years, has been my constant companion and friend. Her patience and support through the times I sat glued to a typewriter or keyboard, and her 'keep going' attitude encouraged me throughout the process, not only with this book, but the previous six novels. Thanks, babe! (15)

I interviewed two officers of the law, one a retired police chief, and one a retired sheriff's deputy, and received invaluable advice and insight into this piece of fiction. Gentlemen, my eternal thanks:

Don Hollingshead, Retired Captain, Laramie County Sheriff's Office, Cheyenne, Wyoming; 27 years

Jeffery C. Johnson, Retired Chief, Worthington, MA Police Department; retired Chief Master Sergeant, United States Air Force, Security Forces; 32 years (and he's a former US Marine! Semper Fi my friend)

The cover photo was taken by yours truly, however, thanks to the expert skills and artistic ability of Ann Lauwers, of *An Artist's View Photography*, the cover would not be what it is. Ann has now done the covers of all seven of my novels. Thanks Ann, and again, great job.

Table of Contents

Cast of Characters

MURDER IN THE MEDICINE BOW

Detective First Class Anita (Wilson) Bishop: Cheyenne Police Department (CPD) veteran of twenty years, and wife of Samuel 'Bish' Bishop. Thirty-nine years old, five feet six inches, one hundred fifteen pounds, strawberry blonde hair, blue eyes, unspeakable nails. Hair usually tied up in a bun. More often than not, found to be wearing jeans and cowgirl shirts, usually by Wrangler or Scully.

Detective Samuel 'Bish' Bishop: Medically retired, twenty-two year veteran of the CPD, and husband to Anita (Wilson) Bishop. Forty years old. Loves the gym, riding mountain bikes, jogging, and reading; a large man with muscles and large chest, hands like anvils and the beginning of a 'settling of muscle' as he liked to call it, around his waistline and under his chin. He has brown hair, no facial hair, sideburns to the bottom of his ear lobes.

Lucy Stone: Rookie Police Officer, CPD.

Frances: Secretary for Cheyenne CPD Chief, Jonathan Webster.

Jonathan Webster: Chief, Cheyenne CPD

Amanda: Secretary for Captain Daryl Carlisle, CPD, Chief of Detectives

Michael 'Mike' Hicks: Detective, CPD, Donaldson's partner

Peter 'Pete' Donaldson: Detective, CPD, Hicks' partner

Andrew 'Andy' Nelson: Patrolman, CPD, rookie

Constance 'Connie' Dominguez: Patrolman, CPD, rookie

Clint James: Patrolman, CPO, rookie

Thomas 'Tom' Alton: Patrolman, CPO, rookie

Markel: Detective First Class, Chief of Photographic Evidence Lab; CPD drone pilot

Jeanne Best: Director, Laramie County Emergency Management Agency

Timothy Dalton: Patrolman, CPD; second sniper for Detective Wilson's team

Willie J. Smith: Patrolman, CPD; spotter for Patrolman Dalton sniper team

Michael Norman: Crime Scene Team (CST) Chief Detective

Malcolm Arceneaux – Patrolman, CST photographer, and assistant

Nathaniel (Nate) Adams, Officer SWAT Team One, Cheyenne Police Department

Trudy Gleason – Girlfriend of Nate Adams

Joshua Akins – Medicine Bow National Forest Ranger, rookie.

Judson Thomas – Medicine Bow National Forest Ranger Chief.

Al Tomlinson - Sheriff, Albany County, Wyoming

Roberto Salinas – Son of Enrique Salinas; heir to the Salinas crime syndicate

Daniel Flores - Special Agent with the FBI

MURDER IN THE MEDICINE BOW

Chapter 1

The midnight blue Jeep stopped several yards from the cabin nestled in the trees, then backed into a spot seemingly made for it in the tree line. The man got out as did the woman. The woman gazed at the man with a questioning look.

"Other than the realtor, you're the only other person that knows about this place now," medically retired Cheyenne, Wyoming, Police Detective Samuel 'Bish' Bishop said with a sly smile. "I bought this property some twenty years ago. The realtor doesn't know about the cabin. Now, you and I are the only people that know about it," he explained looking at her and her amazed countenance. Sam was a large man, looking somewhat gaunt however. He had had a near-death experience from a bullet wound to the abdomen in which he lost half his liver and several pints of blood before the doctors in the Cheyenne trauma center saved him. The wound took him out of his more than twenty-three year stint as a police officer and detective with the Cheyenne Police Department (CPD). He was now medically retired on a full pension. He also received a small disability pension.

Mrs. Detective First Class Anita (Wilson) Bishop, almost out of breath, whispered, "It's beautiful, Bish. Why did you keep this a secret all these years?" Anita is forty years old and looking somewhat haggard herself after Bish's ordeal knocking on death's door and their subsequent wedding, which the governor of Wyoming officiated no less. She was now over her twenty-year mark with the CPD herself, and had, after *The Rescue of the Ladies of Cheyenne* as the operation had come to be known, was promoted to Chief of the Detective Division. She now had seven detectives working with her.

"You know all those times I called in for an extended weekend…?" he asked.

"Yeah?" she questioning, returned.

"I was coming out here and building this cabin," he murmured. "This is my retreat…my castle of solitude…my palace in the arboretum. This is where I come for my quiet time, to unwind if you will."

"Most fitting for that," the new missus said in awe taking in her surroundings, eyes wide.

"Come on then, let me show you the cabin," the tall man said. Bish had lost almost seventy pounds since being wounded. He had spent several months in rehab, and was now well on his way to recovery. After the governor-officiated wedding, the pair had been whisked away in a private aircraft to the island nation of Barbados, where they had spent an all-expense paid honeymoon together - a time in their lives they would never forget and be forever be grateful for. A very rich father of one of the abductees paid for the works as a very generous thank you and wedding gift for the pair.

Together they climbed the stairs onto the porch. He gently grabbed her shoulder stopping her from going inside, stepped forward, opened the door, and then swept her off her feet and carried her into the one-room enclosure. He sat her down and with a wave of his hand said, "Here you go."

"You're still in recovery. You shouldn't be picking me up. What if you'd undone something they fixed during your surgery?" referring again to his recent severe wounding in a gunfight. He almost died from the blood loss. Both detectives along with their entire team, which included six rookies, took on a force of thirty hired professionals employed by one Enrique Salinas, also known as el Jefe, the Boss. Salinas had been abducting two-year-old girls since the sixties, and doing horrific things to them. The operation, or rescue, resulted in one other officer being wounded and one other tragically killed in action.

"I'm fine, really," Bish, told her.

She shook her gaze away from him and looked the room over quickly and replied, "Well, I'm not going to say it needs a woman's touch because for what this is used for, it's perfect…it's really perfect."

"You haven't seen anything yet. Wait till tomorrow and I take you on a tour of our forty acres. You're gonna love it."

"Forty acres…that'll take all day'"

"Pretty much; I'll save the best for last, and then we'll come back here and I'll make dinner – trail fare."

"So, for tonight it's the rest of this Burger King stuff, huh?"

"Fraid so, honey. I can make you some tea here in just a bit."

"One more question."

He looked at her and said, "Shoot."

"What's with the faucet in the stew pot over there?"

He chuckled then explained, "That's the hot water tank."

"I don't get it; how do you get hot water in there?"

"Simple. Come on and help me unload the Jeep."

The newlyweds went out and unloaded the Jeep. He carried two six-gallon jugs of water after he'd slung his Kelty *Expedition II* backpack onto his shoulders, and practically bounded up the cabin steps.

"I'm going to make a fire if you would get the last water jug outta the Jeep, please," he said.

"Sure," she replied and turned to leave.

Bish started the fire quickly, adding a few larger logs to the mix, filled the stew pot with water and set it on the fire to get hot. Once the fire was going well, he swung a framed, iron grate over to the fire and set their BK dinner out to heat – two burgers and fries. They would be hot again soon.

After finishing their lovely BK dinner, they sat out on the front porch, she with a rum-n-coke and he with a tumbler of scotch. Since the damage to his liver was so great from the shooting incident, he wasn't supposed to drink, but between his surgeon and himself, they had made a pact that a double shot of good scotch once in a while was acceptable. He was not to overdo it when it came to drinking alcohol.

"Tomorrow, we'll head west, and then cut north, then east and I'll take you to the south last. You're gonna really love the territory to the south, I guarantee it."

"That's swell," she answered, then added, "I'm wondering where we sleep…"

"I have some rollout mats and sleeping bags for that," he told her. "Believe it or not, they're quite comfortable."

"Hmmm, that's one thing I'll probably have to change, the sleeping arrangements that is, as I would want something just a bit more comfortable for my taste."

"Well, let's just go and find out how comfortable those mats can be," he retorted with a demure grin on his face.

*****

The smell of burning wood, cooking bacon, and perking coffee woke Bish. He leaned up on one elbow and saw Anita busy at the fireplace.

"You know, I've never seen a more beautiful site out here," he said with a big smile.

She, startled, exclaimed, "Lordy, boy, you just scared me outta my skin!"

"Oops, sorry there Mrs. Bishop didn't mean to scare you."

"No problem, just wasn't expecting you to do that. You've been out nine hours."

"Guess I needed the sleep. Probably 'cause of loading and unloading the Jeep, huh."

She tossed a sheepish smile over her shoulder his way and said, "Probably not that. And by the way, those mats aren't too bad. But I'm still gonna get something better."

"They are nice. I've slept many a night on these things out here and always had a good night's sleep."

"Come on, cowboy, get dressed and I'll have breakfast ready when you are."

"Yes ma'am." Bish climbed out of the sleeping bag, dressed, went outside, relieved himself, and brushed his teeth. He never shaved when he was at the cabin, waste of water.

Back inside, he went to the fireplace and asked, "Might I kiss my bride this morning?"

Anita stood, spatula in hand, and gave him a passionate kiss, then went back to cooking their breakfast.

He watched her, shook his head, and asked, "Hey, how do you know how to cook over an open fire like that?"

"My dad…we camped a lot and hunted a few times and we cooked like this every time. I really enjoyed those outings with him." She became quiet after telling him that, reflecting on her times with her mother and father and how much she missed them and the adventures.

✳✳✳✳✳

Breakfast had led to another romantic episode for the two. Afterwards, they dressed for the day of hiking and sightseeing, he throwing his Kelty *Expedition II* backpack on leaving the cabin and turning to the west, they began their day. As they moved along, both kept quiet, enjoying the sounds of the Medicine Bow National Forrest, which surrounded his property on three sides. They paused at an opening in the trees and he pointed out Sheep Mountain to the east.

"That thing is ten miles long from north to south, and five miles wide at its widest point. It rises almost ten-thousand feet, and there is a trail over there going up the steep northwest face. The trail is just over eleven miles and takes about five or six hours to complete - its quiet rugged and not for beginners."

"We'll have to go do that when you're better," Anita said. "Maybe get to the top and camp for the night. Would that be possible?"

"Sure, because most of the mountain is part of the Medicine Bow National Forrest and one can tent camp just about anywhere on it. I don't know of any restrictions for camping on the mountain, but we'll stop in the ranger's station and ask just to be sure."

"Where's the ranger station?"

"Just west of Centennial, and they have *beau coup* information on the Medicine Bow."

"I think I'd like that trip," Anita commented, still looking at the mountain some five miles or so in the distance to the east.

"Wait 'till you see that in the winter all covered with snow. It's a sight. Come on, let's get going."

Both turned back to the west and were soon at the western boundary of their property. "This is the western border. Not much to see 'cept the trees. Come on, we're going north now." Turning north, they hiked to the northwest corner of the property. From there, he pointed out the village of Albany, Wyoming, about a half-mile to the northwest, and said, "That's the closest neighbors."

They turned east and hiked until reaching the northeast corner, and broke for a rest and some water. They sat, again looking at a vista of Sheep Mountain, and talked about what they would do for the rest of their lives. She would continue with the CPD until she felt it was the right time to retire. Bish was and always would be supportive of her decisions when it came to her career.

"So, what are you going to do when your recovery is complete?" she asked him.

"I've been giving that some thought, and I feel since my mind is so agile, I think I'm going to start writing. You know about my book collection so you know too, that I'm well read. I believe I can write a good story."

"Will you write fiction or nonfiction?"

"Fiction to begin with; I might attempt a nonfiction piece later on."

"Why fiction if I can ask?"

"Our experiences and training as police officers gives us a very clear grasp on people. We can spot a fake right off and know with a fair amount of certainty when someone is lying. I think that experience and training gives me an edge on writing and designing my characters. I've written a few short stories already and think they're good."

"Have you let anyone read them yet?"

"No, too…uh…embarrassed I guess."

"Silly. You should let me read them. I'll give you an honest opinion. We should be able to do that with each other, give honest opinions."

"Yes, I agree with you my lady. But I'm not sure I'm ready to let anyone read the stories just yet. Scary letting someone else read them."

"Scared? You…oh, come on Bish - you're the bravest man I know. And I love you."

"I just don't want the disappointment of a rejection I guess."

Anita picked up a stick and began scratching at a small patch of dirt in the leaves and quietly said, "You wrote them so you must be proud of them. If I read them, I bet I'll be amazed by what your mind has produced. I bet they'll be wonderful stories."

Bish looked at her and a small smile crept onto his face. He came to a kneeling position and began placing all their lunch trash into his pack. The pair stood, folded up the blanket they'd set out and placed it into the pack. Bish donned the pack and pointed to the south.

"You're gonna love this," he said, smiling. "Come on."

They hiked for another fifteen minutes then came to the cliff near the 'bottom land' as he called it since it was near the creek that ran through his property. He heard Anita take in a breath, turned to look at her, and saw her eyes wide as she looked at the cliff and creek.

"I like coming here and looking for stones," he began. "Sometimes there'll be a small land slide and new rocks will become visible. Those rocks on my windowsill…this is where they came from."

"I love the sound of the creek," Anita almost whispered, her voice so low. "This is beautiful and wonderful."

"Last time I was here - remember right before the rescue – I saw a bull moose right over there," he said, pointing.

"Was it big," she asked, wonder written on her face.

"Pretty big, so I eased off towards that way," he said pointing again, "and got well away from him. We looked at each other for some time, and then he turned and went to the south. That made a swell memory."

"This place is beautiful what with the cliff, the brook and the noise it makes, the birds…it's so calming," Anita said.

"I've sat in here for hours doing just that, listening and watching. You're right, it is calming."

The two stood there listening and watching. He tapped her on the shoulder and indicated she should follow him. Together, they hiked around to the east of the cliff, began the climb up, and at about the twenty-five foot level, he showed her the 'shelf' as he called it, a five-foot wide shelf in the cliff face. He pointed for her to sit down after he'd spread their small blanket. Together they sat, listening and watching, for almost an hour.

Bish looked at his wife and said, "Come on. We need to head back and get dinner going and then police up the cabin since we've got to go back tomorrow."

"I don't want to leave," she said, continuing to watch, listening to the sounds and animal action below them.

"I know exactly what you mean. But, come on, we need to get back."

She stood and he gathered the blanket, folded it, and put it back in the Kelty. Together they made their way back to the cabin. He started the fire and made sure the water tank was full.

"How 'bout you make the salad…I'll get the potatoes going and get the steaks ready to grill," he said.

"I can do that," she answered.

He washed the two potatoes he'd brought, wrapped them in aluminum foil, and then placed them on the grill. He took the small steaks out of the cooler, opened the packages setting the meat on a paper plate. Bish was well known for his steaks and he pulled out a bag of seasoning. He sprinkled a small amount onto each piece of meat and set it aside for the seasonings to permeate.

"Salads ready," Anita announced.

"Spuds should be ready in about a half-hour. Want to sit on the porch?"

"Sure; have any more of that wine?"

"I believe we do," Bish answered and poured two glasses.

They retreated to the porch and sat quietly, listening to the birds and the wind in the trees. It was a perfect moment for the couple. They had been sitting quietly for close to ten minutes when a doe with a small fawn stepped out of the forest thirty yards away or so. Bish slowly turned his head and looked at Anita and her eyes were huge, taking in the rare scene. The fawn could not have been more than three or four months old, still spotted. The little critter's ears twitched, trying to hear danger. Mom was calm, so no need to fear. It was another wonderful moment. They watched as the ruminants walked to the north and out of sight.

"That was worth remembering," Bish commented.

"Yes, indeed it was," Anita, agreed. "I've never seen anything like that. They didn't run."

"As long as you keep still and quiet, they'll hang around like that."

Bish got up and went inside to check the baking potatoes. They were near perfect so he placed the steaks onto the grill. They sizzled, the good sign the grill was hot enough. He smiled since he so much enjoyed a steak cooked on a wood fire.

Anita came in a few moments later, refilled their wine glasses, his with water, and then set the small table. She lit the one candle and set it on the table also. She pulled and folded two paper towels, their napkins, and placed them on the plates.

"Four minutes," Bish announced.

"Ready; I've poured me more wine, you some water, and set the table," Anita told him.

"I'm ready for this after that hike today."

"I am too, and I'm going to sleep very well tonight after that hike. The property is beautiful and I'm happy you've showed it to me. I'm still rather surprised you kept it secret all these years."

"I probably will sleep like a log myself. Not so much a secret. I suppose I would have told someone if they'd asked. It's just a pleasant place to come for some quiet time. That's why I think I can write. I just might make a few improvements out here that'll include electricity. That way, I can come out here and write some on my computer."

"You know, I think you're right about that. A few improvements and some power would do this place nicely. Not too many. Just a few since it's already perfect."

"Soups up," Bish said, placing the medium-rare steaks on the paper plate. He turned and set them on the table, then pulled Anita's chair out and seated her, then himself. He bowed his head and said a prayer for their dinner and thanking the Lord for allowing him to have the peaceful surroundings and the beauty that went with it.

*****

After dinner, they sat on the front porch, drinking water and watching for animals again. Anita kept giving him sideways glances every now and then, and he couldn't take it any longer and said, "Okay, what's the matter? You keep looking at me. What'd I do?"

"Nothing!" she exclaimed. "Honestly, nothing. I was just wondering what you might put together for a first novel that's all. You have my interest piqued now. So tell me, what will be the *crème de la crème* for your first book?"

20

"I was considering a murder mystery," he answered flatly.

"'Cause you're a cop…?"

He gave her a glance and said, "Yeah, write what one knows about, you know?"

"Ah."

"What?" he asked looking at her.

"Have you done any research yet or written notes, you know, put some ideas on paper yet?"

"No."

"Well, tomorrow, when I've gone to work, you should get started. You know, write some ideas down, start thinking about characters, places, events, the 'how was it done' and the rest of what goes into a good murder mystery. You've done murder investigations - you'll know what to put on paper."

He was looking at her, thoughtfully, and figured she had a good idea, "I'll do just that," he said.

The two had moved into his apartment as they decided they really didn't want to move the over three thousand books he had lining the shelves in his library, a converted bedroom. In that room, his desk faced a gabled window on the west side, giving him an unobstructed view to the west. He could see prairie and mountains. Bish thought of the spot as his place to contemplate Psalm 46:10, "Be still and know that I am God." He often sat and read his Bible there and included Mark 6:31, Habakkuk 2:20, Zephaniah 1:7, and Zechariah 2:13 that were all similar to the Psalm passage about contemplating God.

*****

The newlyweds arrived home a bit after two in the afternoon, unpacked the Jeep and after placing their dirty laundry in the washing machine, got a bottle of water out of the fridge and sat in the living room.

"That was a nice experience which I hope we'll have more of pretty soon," Anita said, taking a swig of water.

"I'm glad you liked it, and you can bet your sweet bippy we'll be going out there as often as you wish," Bish told her, also taking a swig of his water.

"Any ideas for dinner?" she asked.

"Something with chicken sounds good," he answered.

"That does sound good, especially after those steaks yesterday. I know a recipe for a chicken enchilada casserole, how does that sound?"

"Perfect. I have a new jar of salsa in the fridge and some nacho chips. Want me to defrost a chicken in the nuke box (his term for a microwave)?"

"Yes. You have any green chilies in the freezer?"

"Just so happens, my lady. I'll get them, too."

The pair jumped up and went their ways, he to the freezer and she to the kitchen where she got out a large stew pot, half filled it with water and set it on the stove top on high heat to boil. She found an onion and chopped it into quarter-inch cubes, and placed them in a frying pan with a healthy chunk of butter. Once the butter melted, she stirred the onions, and then sprinkled a heaping tablespoon of brown sugar on top, stirring that in well.

Bish came in with the chicken and chilies, handed her the chilies, and he opened the chicken package and gently placed the bird into the steaming water.

"I'll get outta Dodge now," he said and turned for the living room.

"Good plan," she said with sarcasm. "I'll let you know when it's ready."

She chopped the chilies and added them to the onions simmering in the pan, the aroma permeating the apartment and making Bish's mouth water. She looked in the fridge and found a bag of Mexican style four-cheese mix and brought it out. She next found a can of Campbell's *Cream of Chicken Soup* and another of *Cream of Mushroom Soup*, opened both, and added them to the mix in the pan. She brought that mixture up to a simmer, and then let it sit on low heat.

The chicken was close to being done, and once it was, it would be cooled until she could handle it, then she would peel the meat from the bones. This would be chopped finely and added to the pan on the stove.

After everything was ready and to her liking Anita put the casserole together and slid it into the oven to heat. She cleaned up the kitchen and went out to sit with Bish.

"Should be done in just a bit," she told him.

"Mouth's watering something fierce," he told her with a smile.

"I think you'll like it."

✶✶✶✶✶

And he did - two helpings worth then said, "Man that was great. Where did you get that recipe?"

"My mother and I don't know where she got it. Good stuff, huh?"

"Indeed. I'll do the dishes," he said getting up, giving her a kiss, and collecting the soiled dishware, taking it into the kitchen.

"You wash, I'll dry?" Anita suggested following him.

"Sure."

The two lovebirds washed the dishes, splashing each other with soapy water and laughing at the additional mess they were making. It took another half-hour to wipe up all the water and together, they collapsed on the couch and snuggled. The apartment became quiet after that.

The phone ringing made the pair jump the sound was so unexpected. Anita was the one who jumped up to answer the thing. Neither liked the phone anymore. It more often than not was the harbinger of bad news.

"Hello?" she said answering the thing. "Yes, this is Detective Bishop. Yeah…yeah…okay," she ended with sadness in her voice.

She looked at Bish and said, "We have a murder, north end, drug involvement, and domestic. I gotta go." The domestic meant there was a lot of shouting and who knows what between spouses or significant others.

Bish jumped up and went to the closet, took her coat out and waited for her while she tied her shoes. She grabbed her bag, gun, and badge from the Parson's table and headed for the door, stopping long enough to take her coat from, and giving Bish a kiss.

"Not the way I planned the rest of the evening," he solemnly commented.

She smiled, gave him another kiss, and said, "Hold that thought…" and turned for the door.

Bish stood there alone, gazing at the door, and suddenly realized he was worried about Anita. She was a cop going to a murder scene and that always meant unknown dangers. His face became blank as he turned back to sit on the couch. *Now I know what cop spouses feel like. It ain't good,* he thought.

Chapter 2

"Over here, boss," Detective First Class Peter Donaldson called out to Anita. She closed her car door and, after dipping under the yellow and black 'Crime Scene' tape, walked over to where he was standing with two patrolmen.

Chief of Detectives Anita Bishop nodded at the patrolmen and asked. "What'a we got, Pete,"

"We gotta dead guy and a spazed out female over in the cracker box," he said pointing to the ambulance, "and a mess inside. Drugs everywhere – meth, weed, and some kind of pills, maybe meth or fentanyl – and trash everywhere so watch where you step. The woman is stoned near as I could tell and scared outta her mind – she was backed into a corner in a fetal position quivering when we found her. She wasn't much help when I tried asking her questions. Other than that, it's all hunky-dory."

"What kind of weapon?" she asked him.

"Unknown, probably a handgun of some sort," he commented. "Looks like a nine-millimeter, but we couldn't find any brass lying anywhere what with the mess that's in there."

"Who's in there now?" she asked Donaldson.

"Crime scene folks from the Department of Criminal Investigation (DCI) are giving it the once over," he answered. "I told them to search for brass."

She gave him a weak smile and headed for the home. She stopped several yards from the front door and took the time to look…at everything. It was a typical post-World War II 1950's home, probably a two bedroom, one bath affair. There were two windows up front, one a picture window, the other probably a bedroom or an office. It had a carport not a garage. Hedge in the front along with two cottonwood trees. Grass a bit high, but otherwise looked reasonably kept.

Anita pulled her paper booties out of her bag, put them on, a pair of black latex gloves, a dust mask, and entered the home. She stood in the entryway, looked to her left – it was a living room – the mess was horrendous according to her standards. Empty pizza boxes, empty bags from fast-food establishments, along with empty soda cups and cans, and beer cans and bottles, littering the place. The walls were dirty with hand and fingerprints everywhere. A six-inch diameter hole was in the far wall where obviously someone punched the spot.

To the right was another wall some three feet away. It, too, was dirty with hand and fingerprints. She could see a smattering of used drug bags among the litter. She didn't see any brass. She moved to her right and angled towards an opening in the wall that obviously went to the kitchen. There, she found a typical low-income galley kitchen, also dirty beyond measure. The sink was full of dirty pots, pans, and dishes. A washer/dryer combo was in the far corner, a pile of dirty clothing nearby.

The stove was almost directly to her left, the top with burned who knew what all over it. The cabinets all had filthy fingerprints around the handles. Several had no doors at all. A small table to her right held bags of drugs - marijuana, and what looked to be heroin. A plate held what looked to be a meth cake, probably a half-mil worth. She shook her head, disgusted at both the mess and the drugs.

"Hey detective how's things?" the Crime Scene Chief Detective Michael Norman asked as he walked back into the kitchen. He was covered head-to-toe in a protective suit, the only thing not covered were his eyes.

"Not bad Mike; how ya doin'?" she asked.

"We gotta real mess here, kid. You want the low down?"

"Yep, let's have it."

"Body is back in the bedroom on the left. Appears as though he'd just turned to do something when whoever shot him, hit 'em once in the back of the head with what looks to be a nine-millimeter - circumference of the hole makes it a nine I think.

Powder burns and burnt hair around the wound site so a close shot. He's face-down in there. I figure he never knew what hit him but he did know who shot him. We cannot find any brass, anywhere, so that brings up two hypotheses: first, the shooter had a revolver or secondly, he or she policed brass, in other words a professional making this shot, not just some random shooting during a robbery. My gut says it was a hit. The woman was freaking out when we got here so we haven't processed her yet. She's out in the ambulance."

"Yeah, I saw her. Go on."

"There's prints everywhere – the guy and the woman – plus a few extra we'll have to run. Other than that, you've seen it all."

"What makes you think he knew who it was that killed him?" Detective Bishop asked.

"The guy was relaxed. He had no sweat, wasn't tied up or otherwise in any distress. Probably turned to get something off a little table in there and that's when whoever popped him."

"What was on the table?"

"When we got here…nothing but dust and the dead guy's prints," Mike answered.

Anita gave a little turn of her head, not comprehending the statement. "Let's go look." The two detectives went to the back bedroom where the murder had taken place.

"You can see it took place here as the body hasn't been moved – no drag marks or blood smear – and you can see just a small amount of blood splatter spreading out from the head in the direction of the fall. There's the table," Detective Norman said, pointing.

"Clear to walk around?" she asked him.

"Sure, go ahead. We've already photographed and taken video of everything. If you feel a piece of what may be brass underfoot, sing out and we'll come running."

She gave a small grunting sound and moved around the body to the small bistro table in the corner. As said, nothing was on it. She stooped down and gazed at the top, looking for imprints - nothing. She then looked underneath and again, nothing.

"We swabbed it. Did a big 'X' in the middle," Norman volunteered.

"Run that one quickly," she ordered.

She pulled a pencil and began moving trash around, looking underneath papers, cups, discarded napkins, sports magazines, and dirty socks. Nothing interesting so she stood up and moved to the far corner of the room, turned and looked at the space from a different viewpoint. She still didn't see anything out of what would be considered ordinary for the room or the residence.

"What about the closet?" she asked.

"A few garments hanging up - nothing special. Shelf is clear...dusty. Pockets were all empty," he answered.

"Guy was dead before he hit the floor," she said pointing at the head. "His face hit flat. Bet his nose is broken."

"We're ready to turn him if you want...we were waiting for you," Norman offered.

"Got clearance from the coroner?" she asked.

"Yep."

"Let's do it."

Norman moved over to the body's left side and knelt. He reached over and pulled the body towards him, letting it settle onto its back. There was no exit wound. The eyes stared into nothingness and the nose was definitely fractured.

"Malcolm!" Norman yelled. "Cameras in here please."

Malcolm Arceneaux, patrolman and photographer, came into the room with his cameras hanging all over it appeared. "Yes, sir?"

"We turned the body over. Film it all and video, please," Norman ordered.

"On it," Malcolm said, bringing a camera up and began shooting as Norman moved out of the way. "Looks like something in the left shirt pocket, chief."

Norman knelt next to the body again and pointed for Malcolm to get some close-ups of the shirt pocket, then reached in with his gloved hand and pulled out a folded piece of paper, Malcolm shooting photos through the whole process.

"Malcolm, if I may ask..." Anita said to the patrolman shooting photos.

"Sure," he answered.

"Where are you from?"

"Lake Charles, Louisiana," he answered. "Why do you ask?"

"I hear a little bit of French accent and wondered if you were from France or Quebec – I never figured on French/Cajun," she responded, smiling.

"Yeah, my folks were that indeed. Dad's family was Cajun and moms French. My mother's mother was from France."

"So what brought you to Cheyenne, Wyoming?" she asked.

"After graduating Louisiana State University, I left - too many bugs, snakes, gators, and too much humidity and heat for me. Saw an ad on the net y'all needed a photag and here I am. I'm happy. Y'all got a few snakes and a few mosquitos, but otherwise, it's a nice place here in Cheyenne. I like the Medicine Bow, too," he ended, referring to the Medicine Bow National Forrest to the west.

She smiled and said, "I like it too." She went into a faraway look then, reminiscing about the past weekend with Bish at the cabin. *And the cabin is my new comfort zone* she thought to herself.

"What are you thinking about?" Malcolm asked her.

"H...huh...what?" she stammered.

"You're face – you had a faraway look on your face when I mentioned the Medicine Bow. What came to mind?"

"Oh, I've had some of the best times of my life in the Medicine Bow," she answered tranquilly. "Have you been over near Centennial and taken the pass over to Saratoga or Encampment?"

"No, not yet, I've been meaning to, but haven't gotten over there yet," Malcolm replied.

"You'll love it. The drive through the pass on Highway 130 is spectacular. If you're a fisherman, there are a lot of small lakes up there worth the time to fish, and plenty of space to camp out."

"I'm free this weekend so I may just take a trip over and look around. Thanks for the minds-eye vision you've given me. I'll take my fishing gear along, too. Is there a place to climb?"

"You're a climber?"

"Yes ma'am."

"Plenty of spots to climb, both technical and free climbing in the Snowies," she answered.

"You climb?"

"I've jumped a rock or two, especially out west in the Tetons, plenty of nice climbing out there."

"I gotta get the maps and make a few trips. You're making my mouth water just seeing your eyes light up talking about it," he said with a big smile.

"Well, make sure you take a partner. There's some rough and dangerous country out there, both the mountains themselves and the bear threat. One must be careful out in the Tetons."

"Noted; well, thanks for the chat, I need to get back to it," he ended and began taking more photos of the scene.

Anita looked at Norman, who was unfolding the paper taken out of the shirt pocket of the body, and read what was on it.

He looked up at her and said, "It's an address, here in town, over on Fourteenth Street. No name, just the address."

"Have your team print it, please," she asked.

"Sure will," Norman, answered placing the slip of paper into a locking evidence bag. He noted the date, time, location, his name, Anita's name as witness, then signed the bag and placed it into a basket of evidence.

Anita went back to just looking around. She would move from one point in a room to another, stand there and look at everything, then change positions and do it again. She did that in every room.

She looked up and saw Norman and Arceneaux packing up and asked, "Did you video every room?"

"Yes, ma'am, I did, and from every corner," Arceneaux said giving her a thumb up.

"How soon with the film be uploaded on the net?" she asked, referring to the police net where she could view evidence photos and videos.

"Wednesday, I should say, ma'am," he answered with a smile.

"Thanks," she said and then went back to looking around.

✶✶✶✶✶

Anita had been at the scene for almost three hours and was getting tired, both physically and her eyes were burning from so much intensive staring. She blinked her eyes several times, left the building and stopped in the front yard and stretched then removed all her protective material. She noted the ambulance had departed and asked a patrolman if they'd taken the female to the emergency room and he told her they had. She signed out of the scene with the scene commander and departed for her office. She would make Detective First Class Peter Donaldson the lead detective on this case and would ask him to interview the woman if and when she was coherent.

Anita had turned onto Dell Range Boulevard, and stopped by the City Brew Coffee stand for an iced coffee and a half-bagel. Pulled out from there and turned onto Converse Avenue heading south. She pulled into the underground parking garage for the police station and rode the elevator to the fourth floor where her office was.

Detective Michael Hicks stood and said, "Howdy, boss, how was the trip?"

"Delightful, Mike, how are you?" she responded.

"Doing great ma'am; how's Bish doin'?"

"Crabby as ever and always complaining," she complained herself.

"I bet. What's he gonna do now that he's retired?"

"He says he's going to write a book - a fiction book of some kind. He's supposed to be moving a few things around in his library to help him with that tomorrow. I'll see when I get home if he's already started."

He chuckled and said, "I'm guessing you've been at the murder scene?"

"Yeah, but more like a hit than just a murder," she answered.

"How so?"

"One in the back of the head – nine-millimeter by the looks of the hole and no exit wound so looks like either a hollow point or a frangible round. Understandably cut the medulla since there was little or no blood, and the little bit of splatter came from the initial wound site. Landed face first as the nose was broken with no bloodletting – you know how those can be."

"Yeah."

"No brass to be found so either the shooter had a revolver or policed up his or her brass; looks to be a professional hit. Drugs involved, a bunch of it lying around. The place was a mess, what with all the trash, dirty dishes, and dirty clothes everywhere. They're pulling every piece of trash out of the room where the murder occurred to make sure they haven't missed the brass, but I bet a cup a joe that they won't find anything."

"Wow, this one sounds like it'll be a tough nut to crack. Think it'll go cold?" Mike asked.

"Just might. Still haven't heard what the woman has to say. I'll wait to hear that."

"What woman?" Mike asked.

"Oh, sorry, there was a very stoned and distraught woman sitting in an ambulance when I got there. They've since taken her to the ER. Caucasian, mid-twenties, blonde, slender, probably an addict by the looks and sounds I heard."

"Drugs…wish I could twitch my nose and make it all go away," Mike mused.

"That would be nice, but I'm afraid we live in the real world my friend and we'll have to take what God gives us," Anita responded. She turned and went to her desk, flicked on her computer and sat down.

The few detectives in the room for a Sunday afternoon were either looking intently at their computer screens or on a telephone with someone. She was happy to see the team working so hard. It seemed they always did so, and she was very satisfied with their level of work ethic since it meant she didn't have to supervise much.

She was proud of her team. Their conviction rate was the best in the state. Capital crime was a rare thing in Cheyenne, Wyoming, and she knew it was because of the work of her team and others. It just didn't pay to commit such a crime in Laramie County, much less Cheyenne. Her team or the sheriff's office team would get the criminal. Wyoming still had the death penalty, but rarely used it and hadn't since 1992.

She pulled her notes from the murder scene, and thought to herself, *this just may be the next execution in Wyoming.* The crime was obviously premeditated and fell under Federal law 18 USC § 924, "murder committed by the use of a firearm during a crime of violence or a drug-trafficking crime," and Wyoming law 6-2-101, which this most likely was due to the large amount of drugs on-hand and the other paraphernalia lying about used in dividing the drug into smaller, sell-able amounts. They obviously received shipments at that place, and then processed it for sale and distribution.

Tomorrow she would know just what all the drugs were found on the scene. She had seen the marijuana and meth, but the CST might find more. The cakes of meth and the amount of weed verified it was an occupied structure for distribution so proving that will be the easy part of the case. They have the woman on trafficking charges at least. Time would tell if they added any other charges.

Anita began typing her findings into her computer, creating an unchangeable log so other detectives could access if necessary. Pete certainly would. She typed for almost an hour, reviewed her work making two spelling corrections, and then saved the document. It now could not be changed without a court order. She sent an email to Pete and the Captain, letting them know it was ready for review.

She sent an additional email to Pete, telling him to check the airport for incoming and outgoing flights for the past two weeks and to review the airport security films if he suspects someone coming in that was or could be suspect. Whoever it was probably drove in from who knew where, possibly Denver. She immediately brought Enrique Salinas to mind and just as quickly shook her head and drove him out.

Enrique Salinas, otherwise known as el Jefe, the Boss, was the orchestrator of an abduction ring that specialized in taking two-year old females, storing them in an underground facility, and training them to bear his children when they reached 'the age'. He was killed along with several of his henchmen in a combined CPD, Sheriff's Department, and State Patrol raid more than a year earlier. That is where Sam Bishop was wounded in action and almost died. His wound was what prompted his medical retirement from the CPD. Anita hated to think of Salinas or the action that almost took Bish's life.

*****

A week later and nothing new had come in on the murder case. The woman was no help at all, as she was too burnt out by the drugs she had been using. It would be a miracle if she cleaned up enough to live a normal life again.

They still had not found any brass at the murder scene, even after cleaning the entire place. They did, however, find a hidden compartment in the floor of the second bedroom that held over three-hundred thousand dollars, and another kilo of heroin. That prompted a visit by the Drug Enforcement Agency (DEA), much to the chagrin of Anita Wilson. At least all they did was ask questions.

Interestingly enough, the DEA gave the team some useful information. The heroin came from a distributor they had been watching in Denver. They knew this by the distinctive lime-green wrapping used to contain the drug. They also said the meth cakes found on the site most likely came from the same source, and they would follow those leads to Denver.

Anita and Pete were sitting in the squad room discussing the case. "This one has me stymied," Pete told her. "Other than what the DEA shared, I got nothin' new, Boss."

"Mike from DCI said this one might go cold," Anita said. "All we can do is continue digging and hope for a break. Maybe someone saw something and will come forward with the information and tell us. Who knows…?"

"I don't think we've ever run into one like this," Pete said. "I'm thinkin' the killer came from Denver, since that's where the drugs came from."

"That does make one wonder doesn't it?" Anita posed.

"Yeah, did they kill the guy 'cause he was scalping a little off the top, or was it just because of bad business?" Pete returned.

"You check the bank accounts?" Anita asked.

"Sure did. Nothing to be proud of - the guy had a bit over three grand and, surprisingly, the girl had seven bucks in a credit union. Checked for offshore accounts and nothing came from that. Unless they were using a false name, we got nothing from that. No deposit boxes either."

"Seven bucks, huh? I'm surprised she had an account somewhere. Most don't. What about cars or other homes?"

"Nah, nothin' there either - neither had passports. He graduated from East and her, from Central. Both were born right here in River City. She had a part-time job at a Taco John's over on the west side, and he had a sheet full of odd jobs. Both had priors, she for prostitution two years ago, and he for a B&E over on Kennedy Drive and another for possession of two ounces of weed in 2020. As far as friends go, we interviewed a few and didn't really get anything at all. Girl's parents moved to San Diego, California. The guy's parents have passed. Blank walls all around it seems."

"Well, keep at it. Something just might pop up," Anita told him. She got up, refilled her coffee cup at the pot, then sat at her desk contemplating her brew and thinking about the murder. She finally gave a small snort and set her coffee mug down and began the rest of her day.

Chapter 3

Bish woke with a start, actually sitting up in the bed with his arms out, palms attempting to will the bullet from hitting him again. He was unsuccessful as usual. He was drenched in sweat, chilled to the bone, and quivering.

Sunlight seeped into the bedroom and lay in straight lines of yellow streaking across the floor. Anita had shut the window and the blinds allowing Bish to sleep in mostly darkness after she'd left for work. He squinted at the streaks of almost scalding light rising from the floor and took in gulps of air until his heart returned to a semi-normal rate.

He shook his head, wiped his face with the damp sheet, and then rubbed his face with his hands. He slid out of the bed and went into their bathroom, turned on the cold water in the shower and let the cold fluid calm him even further. He stood there, hands on the shower wall, letting the coolness of the water cascade over his back.

Fifteen minutes later, he stepped out of the shower, dried himself, brushed his teeth, looked in the mirror and gave a harrumph and skipped shaving. He had some work to do in his library. He slipped on some fresh workout shorts, donned an old tee shirt, and lastly, his moccasins.

First things first – he did have his priorities – so he scampered down the stairs going into the kitchen and started a pot of coffee. While that perked, he opened the fridge and took out a bag of sesame seed bagels, opened it and took out one of his favorite breakfast foods, cut it in half and placed it in their toaster oven to heat. He opened the freezer, took out a pack of pre-cooked sausages, taking two out and placing them on a paper plate for the task, placed that in the nuke box and punched in a minute-and-a-half, and then hit start.

The three would be ready just about the same time, with the sausages being first, then the bagel halves, and lastly the hot coffee. The coffee was a blend of his favorite *Folgers* brand and a bag of *Beyond Black* from the *Black Rifle Coffee Company*. He would take a three-pound can of coffee, pour in the *BRCC* bag and mix, pouring it all into his coffee canister. He used three scoops every morning to brew his joe.

The nuke box dinged so Bish pulled out the piping hot sausage patties, setting them aside. A moment later, the toaster oven dinged so he pulled out his mildly toasted bagel and added a bit of butter to the crispy halves. He placed them on another, larger, paper plate, and then set each sausage patty on top. Sometimes he would add an over-easy egg on top of each, but he was in a hurry this day.

The coffee ready, he took out a non-spill mug, removed the top, poured in the steaming hot brew, and screwed the lid back on snugly. He took his coffee, his bagel with sausage, and stepped out onto the back porch where they had a small bistro table and two chairs on the deck. He set his breakfast on the table and sat down, and started his day with a prayer of thanksgiving for everything the Lord, His Son Jesus, and the Holy Spirit did for him on a daily basis. He said Amen, and took a bite of his bagel-n-sausage breakfast. The coffee was great.

He used forty-five minutes of his morning on his breakfast. Afterwards, he refilled his coffee mug and went back upstairs to his library, where he spent the rest of the morning moving books, shelves, his desk and computers around to suit his new direction in life – being a writer.

The desk, now centered on the window faced out to a view of the Rocky Mountains. His two computer screens on one of each of the far right and left corners of the desk. Between the two screens, he had a dictionary, thesaurus, word divided speller book, two versions of the Bible, a concordance, and possibly one of his most favorite books, Webster's *The American Dictionary of the English Language,* 1828 edition by Noah

Webster. He enjoyed this dictionary immensely as it even quoted scripture from the *King James* version of the Bible.

To his right, book shelves held his reference, history, biographies, and non-fiction books about American history, books on the wars that America had been involved in, books by Winston Churchill, and other great statesmen, and books by the great generals – Grant, Lee, Jackson, Washington, Patton, Rommel, Schwarzkopf, Halsey, Spruance, and others. He used these frequently and knew he would use them even more as a writer.

He was once asked why he read about these men. His answer was always the same – "I can learn how to lead by reading about their victories and defeats, and how they handled themselves in times of crisis and peace." His father had taught him that saying, "Son, read about the good and the bad. Both will serve you well and help you to become a better man." That always reminded him of a verse in Proverbs chapter eighteen, verse fifteen, "The heart of the discerning acquires knowledge; the ears of the wise seek it out."

His father's, not to mention the Bible's, wisdom had served Bish well over the years. He was a good supervisor with the CPD when he had the opportunity to lead, and earned the respect of those under his leadership by being fair and impartial. Bish felt he was a good Christian man and used his Christianity to the fullest in his daily life, even in the way he led others – he considered it a major portion of his discipleship as a Christian. The Bible teaches us to be like Christ, and in Ephesians, Paul even tells us to 'be imitators of God'. For a mere human, that is a tough assignment since we're all sinners and as such, failures. However, Jesus was the only sinless man to walk the earth, and because of his sacrifice on the cross, those that believe in Him are forgiven of their sins, just like John 3:16 says, "For God so loved the world that He gave His one and only Son, that whoever believes in Him shall not perish but have eternal life." Bish knew the Bible also said that the greatest thing one can do for another is to give his life for that person. It often made him wonder why God allowed His Son to die in the horrible manner He did for us.

Bish shook his head as contemplating what God does was too much to handle sometimes, and looked to the other side of the room. Those shelves held his fiction novels – Clancy, Cussler, Coonts, Sandford, and Patterson - were just a few of the authors and his favorites to say the least. He thought how wonderful it might be to write a book of the caliber of those successful authors – he shook his head again.

Looking up, he gazed out the window. The vision looked out over a few homes of his neighborhood, but more importantly, he could see the mountains to the west, those Wyomingites called the "foothills of the Rocky Mountains." They were mountains and ranged from seven to nine-thousand feet in elevation, above sea level. He had climbed most of those he could see from his library window.

He could just make out the gold of the Aspen leaves dotting the mountainsides. It was Autumn. Snow would be coming soon. He gave a slight shiver, smiled at the thought of snow on the ground, and pitied those that would have to travel in it to work. His smile became a contemptuous sneer as he thought about those folks trudging through the white stuff. He would be warm and comfortable with a steaming mug of coffee, writing at his desk.

"Yes, I will be comfortable," he said aloud.

Music - he needed music in his workspace. He jumped up and went down the stairs into the garage. There, he had an old stereo system he used once in a while. In his library, working on his writing skills, it would come in handy. This system could play radio, CD's, cassette tapes, or vinyl albums. He unhooked the speakers and carried them upstairs first and then back down to the garage for the system. He made room for the large, box-like affair on a small end table, ran the wiring for the speakers to the top shelves on each side of his desk so he could get the full effect of the music, hooked up the speakers to the wire, and went back to the unit.

After plugging it in, he turned on the radio and found his favorite station, FM 103.3, *KRAN The Range*, a Country music radio station that served Cheyenne. The station was actually located on the local Air Force base, but was heard by all in the Laramie County listening area. Bish loved it, as it was a conservative station, even having Sunday church services broadcast. It also broadcast a lively hour of Bluegrass music on Sunday mornings. He really enjoyed that.

His favorite station tuned in, Bish went back downstairs and picked through their albums. He selected Pink Floyd, Journey, Grand Funk, Steppenwolf, James Gang, Chicago, and even a few from Black Sabbath. He liked the music from Black Sabbath, but not the lyrics so much.

Back upstairs, he opened the turntable, and picked his favorite vinyl album of all time, Pink Floyd's *Dark Side of the Moon*, cleaned the track grooves with a velvet brush and cleaning fluid, set it on the turntable, and hit the button for the arm to activate. He went over and sat in his chair. As the heartbeat began, he was looking out of the window at the mountains beyond, closed his eyes, and enjoyed the music. He remembered when his father said he'd bought the album in the early seventies and the day his dad gave it to him. He still had the poster and the stickers that came with the album, and knew what he had, an original, was worth some big bucks to collectors. He made a decision to order a CD of the album and set the original aside for safekeeping. But for now, he would enjoy the wonderful sound.

When the music ended, Bish got up, replaced the vinyl album in its protective cover, and slid the album in between two large books about American Government. He grabbed his coffee mug and went back downstairs for another mug of joe. He went back out on the back patio and sat down to enjoy some sunshine. He'd had a pleasant morning. His one big chore was done to his satisfaction and he listened to some great music as well.

For the afternoon, after a small lunch, he would clean out the garage, a chore he had not done for a few years and would take most of the afternoon.   He would have to watch the clock as Anita would be home for dinner around five, unless something happened. He had KP tonight and he was planning to make his chicken cordon bleu crescent ring with white sauce along with fresh green beans for their dinner.   He would add a bottle of Napa Zinfandel wine. It would be a nice relaxing evening for the two.

✳✳✳✳✳

The garage had been a headache and would take another day to finish up. It was a mess and he promised himself that he wouldn't leave it for years before the next clean up. He at least got rid of all the trash lying about, and had swept the floor. It would still need to be mopped as it had several years' worth of winter's residue left behind.

It was three o'clock and he needed to begin dinner. After cleaning up, he moved into the kitchen and began gathering the ingredients for their evening meal. The cordon bleu crescent ring was a time-consuming meal to put together, having to cook the chicken and vegetables first, then making the sauce, and then putting it all together with the bread dough.

He was always being inventive with his dishes, and this night would be no different as he mixed fresh corn off the cob, green and red chopped peppers, onion, and green onion flakes to place in the center of the crescent ring. It would be a nice meal.

Everything was ready by ten till five. He had always been one to clean as he cooked or baked so the kitchen was already cleaned up, used dishes cleaned and put away, and the counter tops wiped down with a disinfectant giving the kitchen a medicinally clean smell.

Bish set the table out on the back patio as the weather was cooperating and remained pleasant. He had placed the wine in the freezer for a quick chill. He took it out, wrapped it in a kitchen towel, and set in into a bucket of ice to keep it chilled, setting it next to the table in the shade.

Everything was ready. Only thing left was to have Anita arrive so he sat on the patio and waited, and waited. At five-fifteen, he checked the dinner dish in the oven making sure the breaded portion was not getting too crispy. It was fine, so he turned the oven down to the warm setting and closed the door.

Back out on the porch, he wondered if he should go ahead and pop the cork on the bottle of wine, but thought better of it. He would wait until she pulled in.

At five-forty-five, his stomach began to growl. Every time he caught a whiff of dinner, he thought about going ahead and eating. But, no, he waited for his wife. He was actually becoming somewhat irritated when he heard a car pull up out front. Must be her. He stood up, popped the cork on the wine, placing the bottle back into the ice, and went for the front door to greet her.

She looked tired coming up the front steps, which to him was perfect as she could clean up some and then sit down to a great dinner. He opened the door for her, surprising her such that she actually took a step back, but relaxed when she saw his smiling face.

"Evening, ma-lady," Bish said with a bit too much flourish. "Your repast is prepared and the wine cooled ma-lady."

"What'd you do…?" she asked.

"Cooked dinner for you, that's all," he sheepishly answered. "Oh, and cleaned up the garage some. Oh, and moved the furniture around up in the library and redid all the books. It looks cool up there."

Her head turned to the side some and she gave him an almost unbelieving look, and then said, "I'll have to go up and take a look…later. I'm going to shower first and put some relaxing clothes on. I'll be back in twenty minutes."

"Sure, take your time," he answered with a smile. "I'll keep everything hot and chilled for you."

She turned and went up the stairs, cleaned up, changed into her 'grungies' as she called her relaxing clothing and tiredly went back downstairs. She could smell dinner and her stomach began to rumble with hunger.

"We'll be dining out on the back deck this evening - here, you start with this glass of wine, and I'll bring your dinner out to you. The table is already set out there."

She took the wine and turned for the back door. Outside, she found their bistro table set with a light blue tablecloth, a red rose in a bud vase, the bucket of chilled wine, and the place settings set perfectly. *The guy has his stuff together* she thought to herself. She sat in the far seat and he came out with his invention.

"It smells wonderful and has my stomach growling…wow, it looks great. What is it?"

He looked at her and said, "It's my cordon bleu crescent ring, and you're gonna love it. That's fresh corn off the cob with red and green peppers in the middle. My mouth's watering, too. Let's eat."

After setting the platter down, he sat down and bowed his head and they prayed together for a few moments. After the Amen, he picked up his glass of wine, held it out to her, and said, "Here's to a nice relaxing evening."

She quickly picked up her glass clinked his, and said, "Here-here. Now serve 'cause I'm starving."

Bish cut a healthy slab of the chicken dish, and a spoonful of the corn and another of the green beans, setting them on her plate, and then set the steaming plate in front of Anita. She quickly dug in cutting a healthy forkful of the delicious-looking morsel, lifting it up to her nose and inhaling the aroma, and then putting it into her mouth.

Bish beamed at the look on her face, as she tasted that first bite. "I guess you like this?" he timidly asked her.

Her head bobbed up and down as she placed another bite into her mouth, giving him a muffled umm-hum.

✶✶✶✶✶

Bish picked up his glass and refilled it and hers. He sat back in his seat and watched as she finished her second portion of the cordon bleu dish. She wiped her face with her napkin, picked up her glass, and sat back herself.

"Where did you learn to fix that?" she asked him with a satisfied smile.

"I saw something once and designed my own dish from what I saw. It turned out real good the first time I made it so I put the recipe in my computer and saved it thinking I would make it again someday. So, you really liked it?" he asked.

"Are you kidding…I could eat the rest of it but wouldn't get to sleep tonight," she exclaimed. "Bish, that was wonderful. I can't wait to see and eat what's next."

"Oh, I'll do usual stuff a lot, and once in a while, do something unexpected for you, like tonight. I'm really glad you liked it."

"Pour me another glass of the Zinfandel, please."

"Yes, ma-lady," Bish said with a smile.

"Next I'll come home and you'll be in armor and cutting a slab of meat off a hind-quarter with a sword or something just as fearful," she commented with a chuckle.

"Careful what you wish for, there darlin'."

She gave him a look that more than anything said 'I dare you.' She held her glass out and together they tinked wine glasses again in a silent toast. She looked to the southwest, as they had a more or less clear view from the back patio in that direction and wondered what he really would have in-store next.

"How was work today?" he asked her.

"That murder on the northeast side – drug related – one to the back of the head..."

"Yeah, I remember."

"Nothing new…absolutely nothing. I'm afraid this one will go cold fast. A shame."

"No kidding – a cold case in Cheyenne?"

"Yeah, looks like a professional hit on a local dealer/distributor. Victim knew his killer as the killer was in close enough to tap him in the back of the head. Left powder burns in the hair and little or no blood splatter. Guy hit face first, fracturing the nose and no blood spill so he was dead before he hit the floor."

"Cut the medulla."

"That's what we figured. There was a hysterical woman in an ambulance when I got there. She was strung-out on heaven knows what. She probably saw the whole thing but was too disturbed to talk. They took her to the ER under guard and handcuffed to the bed until they got her sober enough to give us some answers. Lost cause there.

"Funny thing about the site, the place was a mess – trash and dirty dishes and clothes everywhere – and we didn't find any brass. So we figure a revolver or the shooter policed his or her brass. You meet the photag named Malcolm?"

"Yeah Malcolm Arceneaux, from Louisiana if I remember, why do you ask?"

"Nice kid. We should have him over for dinner sometime. I talked with him a bit while he was shooting the scene and he left Louisiana because of the humidity, snakes, and bugs. He said Wyoming had a few snakes and bugs, but was much better. He really likes the Medicine Bow. I told him we did, too. Told him to go climb the Snowies over near Mirror Lake and he's going to – he likes climbing."

"Huh, didn't know that. He'll probably have some good stories then. So let's invite him over. Let me know when and I'll fix something special, like gumbo or something."

Anita broke out into a hearty laugh and said, "Just what the kid from Louisiana would want in Wyoming. How about a nice steak or a roast or something with a Wyoming, western flair…"

"I suppose something like steak, Texas toast, and beans, real trail fare," he answered, grinning.

"You're incorrigible," she told him giving him a sideward glance.

He chuckled and followed up saying, "I suppose I could pick up some buffalo steaks. I bet he'd get a kick outta that."

"Now you're talking, cowboy," Anita said with a smile. "What would you have with it?"

"Why beans and taters of course," he quickly answered with a chuckle.

She laughed heartily again and shook her head, reiterating, "You are incorrigible."

"Tomorrow you're getting a cold *Happy Meal*," he said with a disgusted look.

"Oh, don't be so mean. Remember what we were talking about, inviting a new acquaintance to dinner. Concentrate on that and not being a lousy husband."

"A lousy husband, huh…for that, you get the rest of the dishes. I've already cleaned the tough stuff – you get the rest," and with that, he stood and cleared the dishes from the bistro table and set them in the kitchen sink. "I'll be upstairs."

Anita emptied the remainder of the wine into her glass, stood and went into the kitchen. She threw the bottle into the recycle bin and turned for the sink. It only took her a few minutes and sips of her wine to clean, dry, and put away the remainder of the dirty dishes.

Chapter 4

The aspens were indeed changing, the golden-yellow leaves showing starkly against the greens and browns on the side of the mountain. Fall in the Medicine Bow National Forest was a sight to see and drew thousands into areas of Wyoming to view the golden panoramas of the picturesque mountains and valleys. This particular Saturday was no different from others this time of year, with hundreds of sightseers driving across the Snowy Range mountain pass, stopping here and there to photograph the golden aspens.

Wyoming Highway 130 was the one to take for an aspen viewing adventure. Running from Laramie, Wyoming, to a point about midway between Saratoga and Riverside, Wyoming, it was one of the most beautiful sights to see in the fall in Wyoming. On the right day, one could stop at the Libby Flats Observation Area and get a rare photograph of the sea of green, browns, and gold of the aspens all the way to the Rocky Mountains in northern Colorado.

Libby Shaw, the young woman found at the murder scene in Cheyenne, was taking another hit off a combination meth dust and marijuana pipe. She was sitting in the passenger's seat of Marcus Davis' blue and rust, 1964 Ford Fairlane 500. They were heading west over the pass as Marcus had business to take care of in Saratoga. He was to meet the contact at a bistro in the middle of town. He would leave Libby in the car, as she probably wouldn't be able to walk anyway.

Marcus turned north at the juncture of Wyoming Highways 130 and 230, remaining on 130. Saratoga was about seven miles to the north and it would be a short drive. He pulled into the bistro parking lot. Libby was out like a light. He gave a disgusted look her way and turned for the entrance.

Inside, several tables had customers. Only one had one customer and Marcus assumed that was his contact. He moved over to the table and a young Hispanic-looking male looked up and said, "Ah, you must be Marcus. Please have a seat."

Marcus sat and said, "What's on your mind? It was a long drive over here. We could've met in Cheyenne," he said almost in an offending manner.

"Where I meet people is my affair," the young man answered. "You do not want my business; I will talk with someone else," giving Marcus a stern look.

"Yeah, right," Marcus said. "So, what do I call you?"

"Not that names matter, but you may call me Roberto," the man answered.

"Okay, Roberto, what are we discussing tonight?"

"The recent change in Cheyenne was quite disturbing. Please, tell me about it."

"He was skimming, stealing off the top - several thousand a week. When I verified my suspicions were correct, I fixed the problem. We can tell Mister Salinas there should be no more issues with shortages."

"Ah. Why did you take care of the problem yourself?"

"It was quieter that way I figure. I didn't really need to bring in anyone from out of town since I had the capability to handle the matter myself. I didn't feel I needed to bother you since it didn't really seem that big of a deal."

"What of the police investigation?"

"They're stymied. They have very little to go on, I policed my brass so they don't have that. All they have is a body, a hysterical woman strung out on drugs, and a few items I placed - at my expense, I might add - around the house to make them think it was a drug operation. They have nothing. We can tell Mister Salinas there will be no more problems in Cheyenne."

"Mister Salinas is dead. That is why I am here. I am the person you will be dealing with from now on. I came so that I might meet you and get the real story on Cheyenne."

"He's dead…h…how…when?" Marcus asked disbelievingly.

"No matter, it is done, and now I run the Salinas operation. Contact will still be the same and deliveries should not be hindered by recent events, no?"

"Definitely no, just a little house cleaning is all that was - nothing to worry about. I'm sorry about Mister Salinas," Marcus remorsefully stated, unsuspecting the man sitting in front of him was another Mister Salinas.

"Yes, his death is sad, but we go on, do we not?"

"I suppose so."

"So, you are satisfied with the arrangements we will continue to have?"

"Oh, yeah; you betcha, and if any other loose ends raise their ugly heads, I'll take care of those on my end. You won't need to worry about that. And the good thing about that…it won't cost you a cent."

"That is very reassuring, Marcus. Thank you for your concern and thank you for your regret for Mister Salinas, it is touching."

"No problem, Roberto. I liked Mister Salinas. He was a mentor to me. I'll miss him."

"I believe that concludes what we have to discuss today. If you need to contact me, you may use the same method you used with Mister Salinas. I will get back to you as soon as I can after receiving the message. Thank you for coming."

"Roberto, it was nice meeting you," Marcus stood, extending his hand to shake. Roberto shook it and Marcus ended the conversation with, "I'll see you again some time; take care," and he turned for the entrance to the bistro.

Roberto watched as Marcus left the bistro. He looked at his coffee cup for a moment and turned and looked at three men sitting at a table towards the rear of the establishment. He nodded once and the threesome rose and departed. Outside, they climbed into a rust-bucket Land Cruiser, an old one, which the biggest of the three started the beast and pulled out behind Marcus in his Ford.

At the 230/130 juncture, Marcus turned left to head eastward over the pass once again. The three in the Land Cruiser followed now two cars back. About ten miles later, the Cruiser made its move and passed the first of the two cars. The *Ten Mile Inn* went by in a blur. Just after passing Ryan Park, they passed the next vehicle and moved closer to the blue Fairlane. They followed, watching the rearview mirror for approaching vehicles as the other two they had passed stopped at the Ralph Heston viewing platform – tourists.

The three men knew just where to make their move on the Fairlane. At the perfect moment, the Cruiser sped up to pass the blue Ford and as they pulled next to it, the driver turned into the Ford.

Marcus saw the Cruiser out of the corner of his vision and knew he was about to be hit. He jerked his wheel to the right trying to avoid the collision. His right-front wheel broke traction on the dirt shoulder and slid to the right.

The Cruiser turned into the Ford once again, this time striking the vintage automobile on the left-front quarter panel. It was enough to force the right-front tire to break over the lip of the shoulder.

Marcus knew he was in trouble. He saw the sky as the Ford rolled over the lip and down the cliff face. He heard Libby scream and reaching for her saw her fly out of the passenger door window, vanishing from his view, flying through the air tumbling head over heels. The first impact on the Ford was on its top, crushing Marcus between the top and the steering wheel.

The three men in the Cruiser saw Libby cartwheel almost thirty feet into the air and disappear into a stand of trees. They watched as the Fairlane tore itself apart, cascading down the steep embankment and landing on its top in French Creek. The three men watched for movement from the car and seeing none, slowly pulled back onto Highway 130 and headed for Centennial.

The man in the backseat pulled a cell phone out and dialed a number, waited for an answer, and said, "It is done." He hung up, tore the phone into two pieces, and threw one to the left, the other to the right.

Roberto Salinas let out a sigh and motioned for the waiter for a refill on his iced tea. He picked up the book he had been reading and continued.

✳✳✳✳✳

"Hey, Anita, did you hear?" Detective Michael Hicks asked as Anita entered the office.

"What now?" she asked.

"That woman from the shooting, the hysterical one…the Albany County Sheriff's office found her and her boyfriend, one Marcus Davis, dead in the Snowies. They went over a cliff in the car they were in. She was thrown out of the vehicle and the Marcus guy was crushed when it landed in French Creek."

"Really," she shot back. "Call the Albany County folks and ask for a copy of the formal report and the autopsy reports if they do one."

"Will do, boss," Mike answered and picked up his phone.

"Albany County Sheriff's Office, Deputy Malone speaking, may I help you?" the officer on desk duty said, answering the phone.

"Hey over there, this is Detective Michael Hicks, Cheyenne Police…how's it going?" Mike asked.

"Doing well, what can we do for you?" Malone asked.

"You know those two killed in the car crash on Highway 130, the one that went over that cliff…?" Mike asked.

"Yep, I was on it and it was a mess…didn't even know about the girl until the crows and Magpies began arguing over the leftovers. It was bad. What do you need?"

"The girl is part of an ongoing murder investigation we have. Our chief detective, Anita Bishop, wants copies of everything and the autopsy reports if you do one on them."

"Say, she's the one on the little girl rescue a while back isn't she?"

"She's the one."

"Whoa, I'll send everything we get, putting the alert in the computer now. Give me your email and I'll make sure everything comes your way." The two officers exchanged emails and duty phone numbers and Mike said he'd be over that way in a few days to eat at *Born in a Barn,* and have lunch together. Malone asked if he could bring his lady along and always ready to meet a new lady, Mike agreed. They said their goodbyes and hung up.

"Hey boss," Mike yelled out.

"Yeah," Anita answered.

"Spoke with an Officer David Malone – gave him your contact info and mine and he said we'll get everything they do."

"Okay, Mike, thanks. Hey, David Malone…where have I heard that name before?" Anita wondered aloud.

"He was on that Crash Wagon Canyon case up in Wapiti County a while back. Remember all that gold and the fire-fight in that canyon?"

"Yeah, yeah, yeah, I remember. Thanks again." Mike waived and went back to his computer.

Anita wondered if the two were stoned when they went over the cliff – probably. She went back to her reading of reports on her computer.

✶✶✶✶✶

Officer Nathaniel (Nate) Adams, SWAT Team One, ended his week with a near perfect shooting score. He'd put one in the nine-ring instead of the bull's eye. After all the slaps on his back from his fellow SWAT team members, he was ready for a long, quiet weekend camping in the Medicine Bow National Forest with his girlfriend Trudy Gleason. They would be leaving as soon as he got to his apartment. Her Ford Bronco was already loaded for the three-day weekend they would be spending on a mountain on the north side of Happy Jack Road, a stretch of road between Cheyenne and Laramie, Wyoming.

Nate pulled his blue VW Beatle next to her bronc, honked once, and got out, locking the bug behind him. She met him at the screen door to the kitchen. They embraced and kissed deeply.

"This is going to be a great weekend for relaxation," she said as they pulled apart.

"Yes, indeed, it will be," Nate, agreed. "All packed?"

"Yep, everything's in there but us, so get in there and change so we can get outta here before your phone goes off," she directed.

He practically flew into the apartment to his bedroom, changed into his junky jeans, a long-sleeved flannel shirt, his hiking boots, and finally yet importantly, his favorite boonie rat hat - black of course.

He locked the kitchen door and running, climbed into the passenger seat of the Bronco, which was already running leaned over, and gave Trudy a peck on the cheek and said, "Let's roll, babe."

Trudy backed out of the driveway and turned to the west, heading for Happy Jack Road, otherwise known as Wyoming Highway 210. Both were smiling and thrilled to be on their way. Neither noticed a rust-bucket Land Cruiser pull in behind them and follow along.

✱✱✱✱✱

Thirty-seven miles later, Trudy turned right onto National Forest Trail 701 and headed north for almost four miles, then turned east onto Trail 712. Two miles later, they turned north once again onto Trail 714, and branched onto Trail 713 for their next to last leg of the trip. Three-quarters of a mile later they turned due west onto Trail 713D, now some ten miles from where they turned off Happy Jack. They drove for another three miles and pulled into a heavily forested area with deep grass and several areas for tent camping. No one else was in the area. The two smiled at each other and jumped out, dragging equipment out to set camp.

The Land Cruiser stopped in an area about a mile from where they knew from the topo map they were reading was the spot the two in the Bronco would be camping in. The three men sat smoking in their vehicle and waited.

*****

Tuesday morning, Officer Nate Adams did not show for muster. The captain was not at all happy, and called in a replacement officer that was on call, and then reported a missing officer to the Chief. A statewide be-on-the-look-out (BOLO) for the missing officer was made by the chief at noon after exhausting all avenues of contact for Officer Adams. Every police and emergency agency in Wyoming now knew about the missing officer.

Adams had never missed a day of work, had never called in sick or had to leave work for illness. He was very reliable, and the SWAT Captain was concerned, knowing Adams was going camping for a three-day weekend with his lady, he flipped through his contact listing and called a friend in the National Forest Rangers and asked that they be looking for Trudy's Bronco. The friend notified all the rangers patrolling that day of the request.

Chief of Police Jonathan Webster sat back in his chair and wondered about the missing officer, Adams. He certainly hoped the young man was uninjured, and hoped and prayed that he and his girlfriend were stranded in the woods somewhere because their car broke down or was stuck in the mud. Something stupid like that…yeah, that was what he was thinking. They're stuck in the mud somewhere.

"Ranger base…ranger base, this is Ranger Four…" Ranger Joshua Akins radioed in a shaky voice.

"Go Ranger Four, this is base, Ranger One speaking," Ranger Chief Judson Thomas answered.

"Ranger One, I'm on Trail seven-one-three-echo and…and…"

"Go ahead Ranger Four, I'm here…"

"Oh God, I need help…I found that Bronco…they're dead…you gotta send help…I'm sick."

Thomas heard the young ranger vomiting over the net, then silence. Thomas waited a moment to let the youngster settle down and said, "Ranger Four, do you copy?"

"Copy base, go ahead," Akins responded, again shakily.

"What's your status, son?" Thomas asked.

"I'll be okay, chief, just wasn't prepared for what I found, over," Akins quietly said.

"It's okay, son, go ahead and tell me," Thomas directed.

"Not over the net, sir…please come out here and bring the sheriff's office guys with you…please, sir, I really need help here," Akins pleaded.

"Alright, son, you hang in there and I'll have help on the way in just a few minutes, base out," Thomas answered. He radioed two other rangers and told them to go to Akins' position.

He picked up the phone and called the Albany County Sheriff's Office, and got Deputy Malone, who immediately radioed two units to head for the area in question, and meet the Chief Ranger at the intersection of Trails 712 and 713.

The first sheriff's deputy to arrive was Deputy Thomas J. Gerill, who saw as he pulled up the young ranger bending over and vomiting profusely, the older ranger patting the kid on the back Gerill supposed to support and comfort.

The Chief Ranger motioned for Gerill to remain in his vehicle and follow him. Both rangers jumped into the chief's truck and headed west on Trail 713. When they got to a spot that was surrounded by huge boulders, aspen trees and a few Ponderosa pines, they stopped. The chief ranger got out of his vehicle and motioned for Gerill. Tom (TJ to his friends), radioed his position and directed the second deputy to drive in until finding the vehicles. Gerill got out of his vehicle, putting his Stetson on, and moved to the man standing next to the trail.

"Howdy, I'm Ranger Chief Judson Thomas," the chief introduced himself, shaking Gerill's hand.

"Deputy Sheriff Thomas Gerill," Tom said in introduction. "I told the other unit to come on in here. What do we have?"

For an answer, the chief pointed to the north and said, "About fifty meters in. Get a hold of yourself – it's not a pretty scene."

Gerill gave the chief a pensive look and turned, stepping into the trees and slowly moving to the north. He smelled them first and heard the birds. He broke into a small clearing and the sight that met his eyes made him understand why the young ranger was puking up his guts.

Trudy Gleason and Nate Adams were tied, spread-eagle, between trees. Someone had tortured them to death. Gerill could see the fear and terror set in their frozen faces. The scene was too grisly to look at any longer, so he turned and went back to the vehicles, giving the chief ranger a look as he opened his driver's door and pulled his radio mike.

"Unit five to Albany County base," he said into the mike.

"Go five, this is Malone," Deputy Dave Malone answered.

"We need the coroner at my position, photo team, and forensics team," Gerill said. "Tell the coroner we have two. Tell the photo team to bring lots of film. Dave, this is a bad one, over."

An extended moment of silence met Gerill over the net, then, with a sadness Gerill recognized from his friend heard, "Roger, five, they'll be on their way soonest, out."

Gerill and Malone had been rookies together with the sheriff's office. Both had been with the county for just over two years, and both had already seen enough action to last a lifetime. Both had been on the *Crashed Wagon Canyon* fiasco, and had both been injured in that running gun battle. Neither was prepared for what confronted them.

Gerill keyed his mike once again and said, "Base, you might want to ask the Sheriff to head out this way. He'll want to see this for himself."

"Already advised him, over," Malone answered.

"Dave, call my landline," TJ asked. His phone almost immediately rang. "Dave?"

"Yeah, buddy, what's up?" Malone asked.

"It's really bad man," Gerill said dolefully. "Email your prayer chain will ya? We're all gonna need His support out here, especially the coroner and the forensics folks."

"That'll be my next thing, brother," Dave said to his friend. "You okay?"

"Don't know. I can't unsee what I saw. It's really bad…really bad."

Silence.

"TJ, hang in there, brother. Give it to Him, man, remember Matthew chapter six. I'm praying for you and everyone else out there. TJ, you get a hold of yourself, ya hear? You're in charge out there until the sheriff gets there. Be the leader I know you are and rely on His strength to get through this. Remember too, what Paul says in Philippians, 4:13, "I can do everything through him who gives me strength." So rely on Him to strengthen you, brother. You can do this."

"Why are you so smart?" Gerill asked.

"'Cause I like having the big-head, ya know…"

Gerill shook his head and knew that his friend and fellow Christian was doing his best to lift his spirits. "Okay, I get it and I'll take a deep breath and carry on. Good enough?"

"Yes," Dave Malone said and hung up.

Al Tomlinson, Sheriff, Albany County, Wyoming, arrived on scene and saw his deputy, Gerill, leaning against the coroner's wagon. When he opened his driver's door and stepped out, Gerill immediately walked towards the sheriff with his hands held out, palms out, towards Tomlinson. Al stopped.

"Sheriff, it's really bad in there," Gerill said as he walked up to the sheriff. "You need to take a couple of deep breaths before going in and prepare yourself. I've never seen or heard of anything like what I saw in there…and hope I never see anything like it again. Cheyenne CPD Chief and another officer are on their way. We've confirmed it's their SWAT team member."

"You gonna be okay, TJ?" the sheriff asked.

"Yes, sir, I'll be fine. I've been praying a bunch and have the prayer teams already praying for all of us."

"Glad for the prayer support and let 'em know I said thanks. Concerned for you youngster – you look a little pale."

"It'll make a maggot puke, sheriff," TJ said with his head hung low.

"Lead on, TJ," the sheriff quietly directed.

Once at the scene, Tomlinson took his Stetson off and hung his head. He, too, was praying. "This is a real mess," he said looking up after a few moments of silence. "Okay, get the forensics folks and coroner in here and let 'em do their thing. Lord God, help us, please."

The Albany County Sheriff's Forensics team and the County Coroner eased into the scene area. Two photographers filmed everything, one with video, the other with stills. Between the two departments, it took over five hours for them to complete their work. The sheriff gave them permission to leave the scene.

The Cheyenne Chief of Police, Jonathan Webster, and his driver, Officer Andrew Nelson, a rookie, and Chief of Detectives Anita Bishop, had seen everything they wanted. The rookie was violently ill after seeing what had happened to the two tied and hanging between trees. Anita had him by the chief's SUV, holding a cold compress on the kid's forehead, while he continued his dry heaves.

"I've never seen anything like that," Chief Webster said to Sheriff Tomlinson and Deputy Gerill.

"Neither have we, Jon," Al Tomlinson agreed. "Nor do we ever want to see anything like that again."

"You think your folks got all that brass in there?" Webster asked.

"Probably, they used metal detectors and went over the whole area with a fine-toothed comb. I'm sure they did," Tomlinson assured him.

"How many rounds do you figure?" Webster asked.

"Looked to be more than five-hundred or so, that was quite a pile of it there," Tomlinson answered.

"Why did they shoot 'em up like that?" Gerill asked in wonder.

"We may never know," Webster, answered him. He looked up at the sheriff and asked, "Al, would you ask your forensics folks to take another round of photos in there now that everything's been removed?"

"They already did - both stills and video. They did a three-sixty around the area shooting from all angels. I think they got everything we'll need. I'm not sure I'll ever want to come back up to this area again. I used to enjoy fly fishing for bookies in the beaver ponds to the west of here."

"Too many bad memories now," Webster stated.

"Yep. Come on guys, let's get outta here," Sheriff Al Tomlinson said with finality.

Chapter 5

"Gentlemen, we're investigating the murder of one of our own…and his lady," Chief of Detectives Anita Bishop said to her team. "Okay, what do we have so far?"

Detective Pete Donaldson spoke right up saying, "Based on the evidence at the scene there were at least three culprits. We can only assume at this point they were all male. The poor woman was repeatedly raped before and after she died – coroner in Albany County is running the DNA."

Detective Mike Hicks spoke up next and said, "They were both tortured. Nate's injuries were many. The coroner believes his hands and forearms, along with his feet and lower legs, were shot off - not cut off - shot off, while he hung between the trees – he was tied at the shoulders and the groin and above the knees. The killing injury was gunfire across his mid-section. They were using fully automatic .556 firearms by the looks of all the brass found at the scene."

He continued saying, "Trudy was killed in almost the same manner except that she was shot once in the chest. I'm not going to say everything else with her, if you want to know you can read it for yourselves in the system," he softly said with both sadness and anger in his voice.

The room remained quiet for several long moments while the entire team reeled in their emotions. Anita broke the silence saying, "Let's focus on the Albany County Coroner and the DNA results. If they need any help, we'll get it for them. What about other physical evidence?" she asked.

Pete spoke up for a second time saying, "They collected a lot of bullets from the trees behind the pair, more than enough to get rifling samples from at least three weapons. Again, it was all .556 or .223 ammo. The casings were all from a US ammunition manufacturer, one that allows multiple round purchases up to ten thousand rounds per order. The Albany boys and girls traced it to an online bulk ammo carrier and they're working with the Feds on getting a warrant to trace it further. The ammo dealer is giving them a headache over the Second Amendment, saying that the company's sales are privileged information. The Feds'll get it."

Anita asked, "Motive suppositions?"

"Unknown at this point," Mike Hicks interjected. "There is no reason for Nate and Trudy to be targeted other than Nate being a cop. Albany is wondering if this was just an off-the-wall happening – the two of them were in the wrong place at the wrong time. It could have been a sex angle since Trudy was a rather good-looking young lady and she was horribly violated. Right now Albany, the Feds, and for that matter us, can only speculate on motive. It was not robbery as Albany found money, credit cards, watches, some other jewelry, and all their camping equipment and vehicle untouched. At this point…it's a real head scratcher, boss," he said hanging his head.

Peter followed up then, saying, "It looks like they were rendered unconscious at their camp in some manner. Coroner said they had head injuries consistent with blunt trauma – could have been knocked out or stunned. They were dragged from the campsite to the spot where they were…tied up. They were stripped of their clothing at the site. Nate's wallet was still in his jeans back pocket, again adding credence to it not being a robbery."

"There were no tire tracks to speak of. The ones we did find were off Nate's rig. Albany figures the killers had tree limbs dragging behind their vehicle to sweep their tracks – smart. They did find one boot track in a muddy spot near their camp, which Albany made a cast of. It was not from the boots of the victims. If nothing else, these guys were smart. Albany said all the brass they've dusted had no prints. That's unusual for sure and makes me wonder why they made the effort to not leave prints or tracks, but left their DNA like they did - doesn't make sense to me."

"What else sticks out?" Anita asked.

"The rope they used to tie them to the trees," Mike blurted out. "It was grass rope, not nylon. Nylon would have stretched. The grass rope does not. I researched the rope and the vast majority of them used in crime are nylon of some sort, rarely grass. The rope they used here was a half-inch, what is called three-strand manila rope and is mainly used for rigging or tying down. Truckers use it a lot. I looked and one can get a three-hundred foot spool for about sixty bucks or so. Both were gagged with thin cotton towels with knots tied, which were put in their mouths to prevent screaming, and tied off behind their heads. The cloth can be picked up in any department store or a place like Hobby Lobby."

"Does anything else pop up as unusual or whacky with this thing?" Anita queried.

"They really abused Trudy," Peter offered. "Albany says she was raped repeatedly. They think Nate was conscious and alive through the entire time, making him suffer as she was abused. Albany is sure Trudy was conscious through most of it also."

The room became deathly quiet after that announcement. No one looked at one another, heads down. It was a long, silent moment before anyone moved or spoke.

It was Anita, proselytizing "These guys won't make it to jail if they're caught."

"Amen," Mike agreed.

"Amen," Peter seconded, then a chorus of Amen's from the rest of the team.

Anita looked around the room and all the detectives were looking at her. She slowly nodded her head and said, "No holds barred from today on. Turn every leaf. If need be go to the site and look around. Let Albany know your actions if you do go out there. Look into every aspect. Research everything. Back each other up – what I mean is, when you are finished doing research on something, give it to your partner and let them start from the beginning for a different viewpoint. We need a break on this one, folks. Think outta the box. Get into these guy's heads and think dirty…mean. We gotta find these guys and soon. If Albany calls, go outta your way to help them and I'll expect the same from them. That Malone guy and that other guy…Gerill…they'll help I'm sure. If I hear otherwise that one of you hesitates to help them out…"

She left that in silence. Her team knew she would skin someone alive that didn't go all out on this one. Anita turned to her computer and that was the signal the office meeting was over. All of the detectives got busy, several picking up their phones and making calls.

Mike got up with his mug and strolled over to the coffee pot, one of those thirty-cup jobs, or as Bish would've said, an all-day sucker. Pete got up and followed with his mug.

When Pete got to the coffee pot, he almost whispered, "She wants blood on this one, huh."

"Yep, I reckon so…I do, too," Mike answered just as quietly, spooning in two teaspoons of sugar and another of creamer.

"How can you ruin a good cup a joe with that mess?" Pete said disgustedly.

"Get a grip; you've seen me do this a million times, even when we were on patrol, so lay off," Mike said.

"What's the plan?" Pete asked.

"I'm going to keep at the evidence, play with it, move it around, and look at everything from a different angle, you know. I'm gonna call the Feds and see if they have a match on the bullets Albany pulled…and the brass. Maybe they have something we can use," Mike told him.

"I'm going to pull Nate's cases and see what he was working on or had worked on," Pete said quietly. "Might be something there, but I think I'm stretching the rubber band in the wrong direction - gonna look anyway."

"Not a bad idea actually," Mike agreed. "You even get a smell, let me know and we'll snap that rubber band together."

"Will do," Pete said with a wince and turned for his desk. Mike followed and turned for his desk.

Anita had been watching the pair and wondered what the two had been discussing. She gave a half-smile and shook it off thinking they would tell her if the time came. Her computer beeped and she looked at the screen. It was a spreadsheet with everything Patrolman Nate Adams had been involved in while on the force. She had had the same idea as Pete. She began slowly reading everything. If it had no way of applying to Nate's murder, she highlighted it in yellow. If it seemed to be plausible, she highlighted it in green, and if it seemed to be a real possibility - red.

"Howdy, this is Detective Michael Hicks with the Cheyenne Police Department, how are you this morning?" Mike asked the federal agent that picked up the transferred call.

"Doing well, I'm Special Agent Flores, what can I do for you?" Special Agent Daniel Flores responded.

"I'm working an angle on the murder of Officer Nathaniel Adams and his girlfriend Trudy Gleason and wondering if you could help me with something."

"Oh, man, that was a bad one for sure," Agent Flores, replied. "What do you need?"

"The murders took place in our neighbor county, Albany County. They collected evidence and said they sent the brass and bullets to you for possible identification with weapons. We're wondering if you've had any luck with that." Mike asked.

"Uh, let me see here," Mike could hear keypad keys clacking, "…nothing in the system as yet. Give me your contact info and I'll go check with our lab guys. They might have something but not put it in the system yet. I'll give you a call as soon as I find out something. Good enough?"

"Above and beyond, partner, and much appreciated," Mike said, thanking the guy and giving him his contact information. They ended the call with pleasantries and hung up. Mike sat back in his chair and wondered how long that might take.

"Mike," Anita almost yelled.

"Yeah, boss," he answered.

"What are you doing right now?" she asked.

"Waiting on a call from the Feds on the bullets and brass tracking…what's up?" he asked.

"What's Pete doing?" she asked.

"He's looking at Nate's cases and activities," Mike answered. He got up and went over to her desk and asked, "What's up, boss?"

"Nothing really, just wondering I guess. I had the same idea as Pete and have Nate's cases coming in now. I'm just stymied and my brain doesn't seem to want to work. Figured I'd see what you two were up to and try to get a thought or two going. That's all."

"The Fed I talked to, a Special Agent Flores seemed like a nice guy and is going out of his way to get us the information on the bullets and brass if they have it. It's not in the system yet, and he volunteered to go to the lab and ask. Said he'd call me either way with an answer. Yeah, I was surprised. He said he'd heard about the case and thought it was a bad one and related sympathies to all of us for the loss. He sounded genuine."

Usually, Anita would have said something funny about a Fed that was sincere, but said, "That was nice of him. I hope they have some good information on those bullets and shells for us. Okay, Mike, that'll do. Keep at it, man."

"We're on it, boss," Mike answered, turning for his desk. As he sat down, his phone rang, "Detective Hicks."

"Hey, this is Special Agent Flores," was the answer.

"Oh, man, thanks for getting back so fast," Mike thanked him. "What did you find out?"

"The lab guys and gals are positive the rounds all came out of Ruger *M&P 15's*, a carbine version of the *AR-15* rifle. They're still running the rifling, but I'm not optimistic on that, as they weren't. If they do, you'll be my second call, I promise."

"Wow, great work. I'll let the boss know and please do keep us posted on anything new you hear or see about this case. There are three agencies working the issues and we hope we get a break soon. Thanks a million for this Special Agent Flores," Mike related.

"Call me Dan when we're talking like this and you're welcome. I know how you guys feel…we lost an agent a little over a year ago. I promise I'll keep you up to date on anything we get. I gotta run, and you guys make sure you're careful out there," Dan said.

"Okay, thanks again, Dan," Mike thanked him. After he hung up, he said, "Hey, boss, that was my contact with the Feds and the rifles used were Ruger *M&P 15's*. No word on the rifling as yet, but he promised he'd keep us informed."

Anita gave him a thumb up and went back to reading whatever she was looking at on her computer screen. She was reading Nate's report on his part he had in the Ladies of Cheyenne operation, the one where the abducted children had been rescued, and Bish had been severely wounded. Nate had been the one who had shot and killed Salinas, the abduction ring honcho.

"Donaldson!" she roared.

Pete almost jumped out of his skin as he stood up and said, "Yes, ma'am!"

"Pull up the autopsy report on Enrique Salinas, right now, and print it," Anita practically yelled, but continued staring at her screen, her mouth agape after talking 'at' Donaldson.

Before he left the office to get the report, he stared at Anita for a moment, knowing for sure she'd found something as she was wide-eyed staring at her computer screen, hands flat on her desk and arms extended. The look was one of amazed wonder, and at the same time familiar realization. He turned and left the office.

It took him almost twenty minutes to get the file on Salinas. He annotated the sign-out card and slid the box back into its spot afterwards. He left the records department and sprinted for the elevator, and sprinting just as fast for the office door when he arrived on their floor.

"Here ya go, boss," Pete said, placing the folder on her desk.

"Thanks, Pete," she said. "Mike told me you were looking at Nate's cases…that right?"

"Yes 'um, I got the list just a bit ago but haven't started on it yet," Pete answered.

"I ran the same list and look what I found…pull up a chair," she told him.

He pulled his chair over and sat down to look at what she had. She pointed to a line on the spreadsheet and said, "Nate was on the Ladies of Cheyenne rescue. He was the one, according to his report, that shot and killed Salinas, almost cutting him in half. He says in the report that Salinas had an AK-47 and was bringing it around when Nate cut loose on him with his carbine on full auto. Open up the report and read what it says about Salinas' condition when they picked him up."

Pete opened the folder and scanned several pages before coming to the correct one and read, "Says he was chewed up badly just across his lower midsection, just above the hips. Also says his left arm was severed by the gunfire, just above the wrist. Nate must have raked him from left to right on full auto to do that much damage."

"Nate was injured in the same manner tied between those trees," Anita told him.

Pete's head snapped up when she said that, looking at her with an incredulous look, not believing what she was saying. "You think this was a revenge hit from someone that knew Salinas? How did they know Nate was the one who shot him? That's always privileged information and not for public dissemination."

"Someone must have leaked it," Anita mused.

"Who in God's name would do such a thing," Pete said with revulsion.

Anita looked at him and said, "Get Mike in here, now. Tell him to move it."

Pete jumped up and picking up his phone, he made the page, summoning Detective Hicks to the office. When Mike arrived, panting, Pete waved him over to Anita's desk. She stood, pulled a thumb-drive from her computer, grabbed the autopsy report, and motioned for the two of them to follow her. The three took the elevator down to the garage level, where Anita threw Pete the keys to her SUV. They climbed in and Pete pulled up to 19th Street and asked, "Where to, boss?"

"My place," she answered.

Pete drove to her and Bish's place and parked in the driveway. The three got out and went inside, Anita yelled out, "Bish, get out here, darlin'."

He'd been upstairs writing when she called. At the top of the stairs, he paused, seeing Pete and Mike with Anita. She waved him down and said, "Bring up the computer, will ya."

Bish sat at their little desk and brought up their other computer. It took a moment for it to come up, and once up, she handed him the drive. He inserted it into a USB port, and clicked on the Libraries icon, then looked up at Anita. She and the two Detectives had dragged chairs in to sit with Bish.

Anita looked at Bish, sat down, and said, "Open the one that says, Nate Adams Cases," which he did.

The spreadsheet came up almost immediately and she pointed to the one about the rescue. Bish clicked on it and the report came up.

"See here," Anita, said, pointing.

"Yeah," Bish answered questioningly.

"Read that, then look at this," she said, proffering the autopsy report.

Bish gave her an odd look, looked at the other two men, then did as told and read the information on the computer screen, then the autopsy report on Nate Adams.

After several minutes of quiet contemplation, Bish looked at Anita and said matter-of-factly, "This is not a coincidence."

"No, it isn't," Anita said. "Mike, read it please," she told him since he was still in the dark as to what was going on.

"No, that is not a coincidence," Mike agreed. "What're we gonna do?"

"It doesn't leave this group," Anita said. "I wanted Bish to see it as he may be a target also. I'm going to speak with the Captain and the Chief, then, if they agree, the Sheriff and the Chief of the Wyoming Highway Patrol. They need to know their officers may be targets, too."

"I agree," Mike said.

"Me, too," Pete agreed.

"Yep, me, too," Bish agreed as well.

"Bish, you need to be armed all the time until we sort this out. All of us need to keep on our toes and watch our surroundings. As much as we can, we need to be with people and not alone. That could be the opportunity whoever this is needs. We have a leak somewhere and I'm going to talk to the chiefs to see what they'll allow me to do to find out who it is. I'm sure WHP and the Sheriff's office has copies of this autopsy report and Nate's report on the rescue along with all the other reports. The leak could be in any of the three agencies. I'm gonna have to be careful handling this. But, I want to keep it as quiet as possible, understand," she ended looking at the three.

Mike said, "About what?"

"Yeah, what? Bish asked.

"Good enough," she said to the three. "Bish, you keep on your toes you hear me?"

"Yes, ma'am, I do," he said with a smile then leaned over and gave her a peck on the cheek.

"Wow, we don't get to do that," Pete said with a grin.

"And I better not see you do it either," Bish said with a grin of his own.

"Now boys, settle down," Anita said. "Bish, keep all this under your hat. I'll probably get in trouble showing this stuff to you, a civilian now. But I figure you're just as much a target as the rest of us if it is someone going for revenge. I thought we'd pretty much cleaned out all of Salinas' people. Might be someone out there taking over the operation and wants to get back at us for some reason."

"That Salinas guy have any kids?" Pete asked.

"None that we knew of," Mike answered.

"No indication of that from all the pre-action investigating," Bish said. "I'd remember that."

"I never saw anything indicating that he did," Anita offered, then, "doesn't mean there isn't one around somewhere. That may be reason to investigate further. Maybe the Feds have something we don't," she said, looking at Mike, since he had the contact. "I'll ask the other chiefs if they know anything. In the meantime, you two look into the aspect, and Mike, you keep up with your friend with the Feds." She looked at Bish and said, "And you, stay outta trouble."

"Yes 'um," Bish said with a grin. He pulled out her drive and handed it to her, got up and went into their living room and opening a small, decorative chest on the mantel, pulled out a Gen4 Glock 19, with three magazines. He insured the firearm was loaded, and then stuck it in the small of his back in his waistband. The additional three magazines he put in his pockets.

He looked at Anita and asked, "Satisfied?"

"Yes, keep it with you all the time if you would," she directed.

"I intend to," he answered. "I'm gonna tune up our two ARs as well, one up in my office and one down here, both with extra mags, too."

"That'll do," she said. She moved over to him, gave him a hug and a kiss, and said, "We need to get back, I'll see you tonight."

"Yes, boss," Bish, said.

Mike and Pete both chuckled at that and turned for the door. Anita gave Bish another kiss, then let him go and turned for the door.

Just as she reached the door, Bish said, "Hey," and as she turned to look at him, he added, "I got this, okay?"

She nodded agreement and left, closing the door. He moved over to it and threw the dead bolt and locked the knob. He didn't bother with the chain, as he knew they really didn't do any good if someone wanted in. He went to the kitchen and locked that door, looking through the windows at the surrounding area and not seeing anything out of the ordinary, went upstairs and opened his gun case with the pair of Stag Arms *AR-15's*, and fourteen, twenty-round magazines. He and Anita both preferred the twenty-round magazines over the thirty because they made the rifle a more comfortable platform for the two of them.

Bish pulled an ammo can out of the closet that held boxes of .556 ammunition, with fifty-five grain bullets. These he used to fill the fourteen magazines. He loaded a single round into each rifle, and then inserted a magazine into both. He took one rifle and six additional mags to his library/office, and leaned the rifle next to his desk and placed the mags on a bookshelf.

He took the second rifle and the remaining six mags downstairs, setting the rifle against the fireplace and the mags on the mantle. Satisfied, he went into the kitchen, poured himself a glass of iced tea, and went back to what he was doing in the library.

Chapter 6

Roberto Salinas was a sneaky kind of fellow. He learned from his father early on, that one needed to be cunning in the businesses of drugs and smuggling. One thing he remembered his father saying was to keep one's friends happy, and one of Roberto's friends was the son of Dante Black Cloud, the late leader of the mercenary unit hired by Enrique Salinas to protect the Wyoming complex holding the captive women and children. He, actually, was the first to die in the police action that claimed Roberto's father.

Dante's son, Chogan Black Cloud - Chogan means 'Blackbird' in his native language - was a trained mercenary like his father, who started the boy in the hard life of the mercenary business. The youngster had been on his first foray as such when he was seventeen years old, was wounded, and after the action, he was paid one-hundred thousand dollars for his part. The wound was superficial, a bullet leaving a wide groove in his upper left arm. Nothing serious, but it did bleed profusely and worried him for several weeks afterwards.

Roberto and Chogan met when they were children, being cared for by Isabella the nursemaid and teacher for the abducted children of Enrique Salinas. Their fathers were out on a business trip so they were under her care until their fathers' return. She was currently serving life in the women's max in Canon City, Colorado. The boys had been together for almost a month on that occasion and became fast friends, bonding in a friendship that would last a lifetime.

"Chogan, my friend, how are you this fine day?" Roberto asked when Chogan answered the call with a crisp enunciation of his name.

"Ah, Roberto, all is well on my end; how are you my friend?" Chogan answered.

"I'm good. I'm calling to let you know the first of our tasks has been completed," Roberto began.

"How so?" Chogan asked.

"Tied between two trees and after long hours of suffering, ended with a flourish," Roberto explained.

"That is good to hear," Chogan said. He was smiling. "When do we begin the second adventure?"

"First things first, Chogan," Roberto told him. "I need to see you and make a few plans. I'll send the usual transportation for you and we'll be meeting at the same place our father's met for business conversations. It will all be on me my friend. You do not have any pressing activities pending do you?"

"No, no, nothing upcoming…I'm free and will enjoy time with you," Chogan said, smiling.

"Very good. Be at the pickup point at six tomorrow morning and I will see you tomorrow afternoon. We will have a fine dinner and some excellent scotch together tomorrow evening. How does that sound, my friend?"

"Excellent, Roberto, excellent as always. I'll see you tomorrow then," Chogan ended.

"Excellent indeed, see you tomorrow afternoon," Roberto said ending the call and hanging up. Both would be on their way to Barbados tomorrow for a week or so of business meetings to discuss the futures of several people, namely those that had any involvement with their fathers' deaths in Wyoming.

*****

"Ah, my friend," Roberto Salinas said, standing to embrace Chogan as he arrived at the resort. The two embraced and slapped each other on the back, saying greetings as they embraced. Once apart, Roberto told the concierge to bring Chogan anything he wanted, which was promptly done.

Roberto asked Chogan to have a seat and the two sat together and leaned back in their beach recliners to enjoy the setting sun.

Later, at dinner, the two enjoyed surf-n-turf and talked of insignificant things, their homes, their acquaintances, their cars… When the meal was complete, they drank eighteen-year-old Macallan scotch, smoked Cuban cigars, and continued the small talk. It was well past midnight when the two shakily rose and went to their separate private bungalows to sleep.

The following morning, the two enjoyed a light breakfast of English muffins with strawberry jam, fresh cut orange and apple slices, and apple juice. This they enjoyed on the beach, watching the tide come in while eating.

"That sound is so soothing," Roberto, said.

"Which sound is that…there are so many this fine morning." Chogan asked.

"The surf, of course," Salinas answered. "I could almost lie back and go to sleep again listening to that soothing, rhythmic sound."

"Yes, I suppose I could also," Chogan agreed. The two became quiet after that and Chogan knew his friend was about to broach the subject for which he was brought to the island nation of Barbados to hear. He patiently waited for Roberto Salinas to begin the conversation. It would be business, of course.

"So," Roberto began, "the first is out of the way. I have a contact that provided the list of names of those that had the major leadership positions for the attack that killed our fathers. The first was the man that shot and killed my father," Salinas explained, morosely.

"Do you know who killed my father?" Chogan probed.

"Not absolutely, however it was one of two on the list. They were snipers. My contact told me your father was first to die in the attack. I'm sorry to say that my friend."

"Then let me have their names and I will take care of them in my own fashion," Chogan menacingly said.

"Easy, Chogan, easy…I will give you the entire list and let you have your way with them all. My interest in the list is over.

This is why I invited you down for this meeting. And, to see you and enjoy your company for a while, my friend," Salinas said, smiling.

"You spoil me Roberto, but, I do indeed appreciate it. Coming here always brings me pleasure. My father and I visited here several times in the past, I believe at the advice of your father if I am not mistaken."

"Yes, father loved coming here. It is a very relaxing atmosphere is it not?"

"It is indeed, my brother. A grand setting for sure…and the sunsets are magnificent. Surely you agree with that."

"I do…yes, I do," Salinas said, reaching for a pitcher on the small bistro table and pouring more apple juice for both. "I do have some suggestions for the list, but we can discuss that later, maybe in a day or two. For now, I believe the two of us need to relax and enjoy the music of the sea," he said ending the conversation as he leaned back in his beach Adirondack.

Chogan did the same, sipping his apple juice and watching the seagulls soaring just above the waves, dodging each other like enemy aircraft in dogfights. He smiled, closed his eyes, and listened to the ocean swells coming in and receding. The sound was soothing indeed.

✱✱✱✱✱

An hour later, the resort captain gently touched Roberto Salinas on the shoulder. Salinas woke with a slight start and asked, "Yes, what is it?"

"Sir, the two of you have been asleep for an hour in the sun, please forgive me for waking you, but you will be burned to a crisp if you stay out here longer," the captain explained.

Salinas smiled and said, "Yes, thank you very much. You have saved my friend and me some misery. Thank you very much," Salinas said again as he got up to wake Chogan.

The two went to their suites, showered and changed clothes, and a Rolls-Royce Phantom picked them up at the front entrance. They were on their way to Diamond Valley, to have lunch at The Grove Beach Bar and Grill, one that served an array of foods. They were seated in the Carriage House poolside restaurant, with both a view of the pool with the lovely bikini-clad ladies, and the ocean with its waves crashing against the volcanic rock.

Salinas ordered the grilled Mahi-Mahi, and Chogan had the shrimp kebabs with mango lime chili sauce. Both ordered Long Island iced tea with their fares. The breeze coming in off the ocean kept the pair cooled in the noonday heat, and the iced teas helped.

Salinas had asked the Maître d to seat them in a secluded area, one that still had a view. Once their meal was complete and a second round of iced tea was served, Salinas began the reason for the meeting saying, "The two main characters I want to see taken care of are the Bishops. She was the designer of the action against our fathers, and he was her partner throughout the investigation. He was very nearly killed in the action, receiving a crippling wound to his liver. He is now medically retired. She has been promoted to Chief of Detectives of the Cheyenne Police Department. These two were the originators of our fathers' deaths and I want them to suffer all the more for it."

"Then I suggest they be taken care of lastly, as they will suffer through the loss of the others first," Chogan recommended.

Salinas looked at his friend in thoughtful contemplation before speaking. "Yes, I agree. The Bishops should be made to suffer a great deal and suffering includes the loss of friends and coworkers. Yes, I do agree with you," Salinas said, casting a cruel looking smile towards his friend. "See to it. Whatever you need…money is no object. You need men, get them. You need guns, get them. Whatever you need, get it. Understand?"

"Yes, Roberto, I understand," Chogan said with an evil grin of his own.

"When I get back to the states, I will begin the planning process. I'll be at my cabin in Colorado, so I'll take my sat-phone with me. I suggest you acquire a few burner phones and give me the numbers. After we talk, you can destroy the phones leaving nothing to chance for the authorities. They will not be able to track my sat-phone."

"We can do that at the airport when we return to the states," Chogan said. "I will pick up a half-dozen and give you the numbers. That will solve the communication issue. Six phones should be enough."

"That should be more than enough. I will have reconnaissance begun and planning upon my arrival at the cabin. I have two trusted supporters that will do the recon for us. They are almost invisible and will pose no threat to the overall operation."

"Then I will trust your judgement, Roberto," Chogan said.

"You want to borrow my three men when the time comes?" Roberto asked. "They can do amazing things. You must see the pictures of Adams and his woman, and then you will know what they are capable of."

"If I do, I'll call you and let you know where I want them. Do you want to know any of the operational aspects of the task?"

Salinas mulled that over in his head for a moment and said, "No, but do inform me when you have finalized one of the contracts; that I will want to know. The satisfaction of seeing Adams and his woman in those photos was…most gratifying."

Chogan looked at his friend with an almost disgusted look not believing Roberto could find enjoyment from the grisly death of another human being. Certainly, Chogan had killed his share of men and women in his time, but he never enjoyed it, rather feeling that the act of killing was a necessity. He quickly changed his thinking and the expression on his face.

Roberto Salinas had a faraway look and became quiet. Chogan knew his friend was thinking about the future and how those that would soon die would look. He wondered, too, about his friend's sanity, and thoughtfully stayed quiet.

Their lunch meeting soon ended on a silent note of understanding between the two. Both stood, Roberto nodding to the Maître d, meaning to have his car brought around, and they left together in the Rolls, going back to the resort. Roberto went to his suite for the rest of the afternoon, and Chogan, made a bee-line to the Rum Shack, which happened to be just around the corner from his suite, ordered a Honeydew Mojito, took a sip, thanked and tipped the bartender, then continued to his suite.

He quickly changed into his swim trunks, a tank top, and slip-on water shoes, donned a forest green boonie-rat hat, got a towel and his drink, and then went out to his beach Adirondack chair. He sat, took a sip of his drink, and then sat back to enjoy watching the water activities going on in his viewing range.

A catamaran under power, the sails not up as yet, slowly made its way from south to north across his vision. It was a sleek vessel, on which he wished he were aboard as there were several bikini-clad ladies lounging in several places on the deck. He saw one look his direction and he waived. She waived back and threw a smile. He lay back, got comfortable, readjusted his hat to shade his eyes, took another sip of his drink, and then gave a great sigh. He was content.

Roberto was not so easy going. The first thing he did was pour himself a tumbler of scotch, picked up the sat-phone and called one of his employees, Mister Allister Stevens, telling his butler to go and prepare the Colorado cabin for an extended stay. He would be returning in less than a week and wanted the house to be ready. Stevens assured Mister Salinas the home would be ready, and knowing Roberto's menu, drink, and clothing choices would have everything at the ready for the boss when he arrived. Stevens made several calls after hanging up from speaking with Roberto, and got the ball rolling on preparing the house for an extended stay.

The refrigerator and freezers would be stocked. The bar would be restocked with Roberto's preferred drink menu items. His closet would be filled with clothing and shoe choices. The master suite bathroom would be stocked with all the necessities and cleaned to sparkling perfection. The whole house would be swept, vacuumed, mopped, and dusted before the arrival of Mister Salinas. Every light would have a new bulb installed; the television and stereo in the den would be tested and replaced if necessary. Salinas enjoyed his classical music and Stevens would have the necessary music selections waiting. Stevens would have everything just so for his employer. The last thing Stevens did was to call and make travel arrangements for himself to Colorado. He would have Mister Salinas' Bentley taken out of storage and have the vehicle completely gone over from a maintenance standpoint and then detailed to a high luster.

Allister Stevens, a forty-eight-year old, five feet, nine inch tall man, weighing in at one-hundred sixty-nine pounds, raven-black hair, and chocolate brown eyes, was a trained man servant, training in the famous *London Etiquette School for Service*. The training included defensive driving techniques from the prestigious London Metropolitan Police Academy. He had also undergone intensive training in Martial Arts for most of his life, and had taken defensive shooting techniques training with a retired Special Air Service (SAS) trainer. He was a master shooter, with his weapon of choice being a Gen 4, Glock 19 nine millimeter. When he drove Mister Salinas around, he carried the Heckler & Koch MP5 nine millimeter, and the Benelli M4 Tactical shotgun, model 11703, in twelve gauge in addition to his sidearm. When it came to protecting his charge, Stevens was a complete no nonsense protection expert.

✱✱✱✱✱

Six days later, Salinas' private jet landed at Denver International Airport and taxied to a private hanger. Stevens, along with the sparkling Bentley, patiently waited for Mister Salinas. As Roberto exited the aircraft, he turned at the bottom of the steps and told Chogan to take the plane to wherever he needed to go, giving the pilot a thumb up in the process. Salinas turned and made his way towards the Bentley. Stevens opened the door for Salinas and closed it after the boss was comfortable within. Stevens moved around to the driver's door and got in himself.

"Home, Allister, I'm tired," he directed.

"Yes, sir," Stevens said with his slight British accent, something Salinas loved, but Stevens attempted to hide. He actually loathed the accent and wanted to sound more *American* with his speech. He started the Bentley and pulled out of the hanger area taking great care not to hit the aircraft sitting next to the car.

The drive from the airport to Salinas' Colorado home took almost ninety minutes. Stevens pulled up to the front door, where a house servant waited. Stevens got out and opened the door for Salinas who went straight to his bedroom. Stevens had the servant take the luggage and went to put the Bentley into the garage, wiping the vehicle down after parking it. Satisfied, he closed the garage and went into the home through the back kitchen entrance. He pulled a bottle of eighteen-year-old Macallan scotch, unseating the cork, taking a quick and satisfying sniff to ensure it was as advertised. Pleased, he re-set the cork, filled a tumbler with ice and the bottle of scotch onto a tray, and took it to Mister Salinas.

Entering the bedroom, Stevens said, "I took the liberty of opening a fresh bottle of scotch for you sir. Shall I pour for you?"

"Yes, go ahead, Allister," Salinas said, sitting at a small desk in the spacious room. "Allister, may I ask you a question?"

"Certainly, sir," Stevens said stopping what he was doing and paying strict attention to Salinas.

"Why are you so formal with me all the time?" Roberto asked.

"It is my training, sir," was the answer.

"Can we just be friends and you can call me Roberto? You do not have to be so formal with me all the time, you know."

"Again, it is my training, sir," was the same answer. "I am your paid subject – your employee – and it is my duty to be such that I am when in your presence."

"Well, personally I wish we could be friendlier towards one another. I know what I hired you to be, but I think I would prefer having a pal around rather than a prim and proper man servant."

Stevens gave a slight smile and said, "I suppose, if it is your wish, that I could be a bit less…formal in personal settings such as this. I believe you Americans call it being *laid back.*"

"Yes, you can be laid back when we are in settings where it is just the two of us for the most part, even around the home when there are other servants about, I will not mind at all. We should talk more and get to know one another better instead of this formal quietness you normally have when I am around."

"Actually sir, being friendly with you would be quite unusual in my line of work. I dare say the school where I trained would not approve. But, I am willing if you wish it."

"Great! So, tell me about yourself…where are you from? What are your desires? What do you want for your future?" Salinas asked rapid fire.

"I was born in Liverpool, England, actually in the small hamlet of Everton on the northeast side of Liverpool. We had a flat near the cemetery, which I hated, as the crematorium would send the foulest smelling odor our way on occasion. I was so thankful when father sent me to school in London, where I began my training as a manservant."

"I suppose that would have been foul-smelling," Salinas commented. "I would have been thankful to leave that area myself. So, what are your desires…what do you want to do in the future?"

"I love the outdoors and working for you in the places you live, have given me ample opportunity to sample the great American outdoors," Stevens answered. "I thank you for that, sir. The National Monuments and National Forests you live near fit my wants and needs greatly. I do appreciate working for you in that regard. As for my future, I should like to retire with a small home near or next to a National Forest in Wyoming. I do love Wyoming."

Salinas looked down at his desktop and brought to mind his father's demise in Wyoming. He sadly looked up at Stevens and said, "My father died in Wyoming. He loved it, too. Are you saving for your small home?"

"Yes, sir, I put away fifteen to twenty-five percent of my earnings each pay period, both for my retirement and for a home."

"That is a good saving plan for your future. What would you do with your time as a retiree?"

"I would hike, fish, climb mountains, and sketch scenery when I saw something worth the time. I might even write a fictional book or some poetry. I think I should like to try hunting also. I believe I would enjoy my time as a retiree," Stevens said, smiling. "How about you, sir, what are your plans for retirement?"

"I would most likely stay in Barbados, reading good books, most likely written by you, and sip Mai Tai's or scotch on the beach. I do indeed love that island paradise."

"Too much sand for my tastes, sir," Stevens said with a grin and both erupted in laughter. It was a humorous moment, as Salinas already knew of Stevens' distaste for sand.

After a moment of laughter, Salinas said, "You hate sand and I hate Wyoming, two completely different peas in this pod." Both gave another chuckle.

"Still, sir, you would be most welcomed in my home anytime you wished to visit. I would always have a bottle of Macallan eighteen lying in wait."

"Ah, my friend, that would be perfect, and I suppose it would be on the front deck overlooking a wilderness vista of some sort or another."

"That would be my wish, yes. My dream would be a two-bedroom home with two baths all on the main floor so that I might have one-level living if I wanted. A full basement also, which would be my man cave. The second story would be my library and writing studio. I would have gables on all four sides, with large windows for viewing the countryside while writing. I would be able to move my writing desk to whichever window I so chose to view from while creating stories or poetry...” Stevens let the sentence fade as he got a faraway look in his mind's eye.

Salinas noted the pause and looked at Stevens, seeing the look on the man's face. He gave a small grin and let his servant have his moment in a faraway place, choosing instead to sip his scotch in the welcomed silence.

Chapter 7

The unusual storm came out of the southeast, a very rare occurrence in Wyoming, and in every case, abysmal. Folks in southeast Wyoming first noted the darkening skies to the south and east, and that the wind was flowing in, albeit lightly, from the southeast. Everyone in Laramie County, Wyoming, knew when the wind came from that direction and with a cloud cover forming as it was the weather would be wicked.

With the ever-darkening skies, the first flash of lightening came and the thunder startled many. Soon, it resembled an artillery barrage dueling to the east and south of Cheyenne. Flashes due east, quickly followed by flashes to the south, and then body trembling rumbles following the light show. The wind picked up and soon the flags flew straight out to the northwest, proudly whipping in the torrent.

The cloud cover was the proverbial thundercloud gray color and rolled with the wind currents. It was as if God had a huge wooden spoon mixing the clouds in a great bowl. Lightening was almost continuous as the storm moved to the northwest. The rain now came in torrents, unusual for Wyoming for sure, and heavy, with water cascading down the furrows in the neighborhood streets, some gathering enough to become small streams down the paved ways.

By the time the storm reached the Medicine Bow, it was at its zenith. Those camping in the forest had done what they could to protect themselves from the tempest. Those tent camping got wet. Those in hard-side campers were tossed back and forth by the winds.

Kevin Lindsey and his wife Barbara had just settled in to watch a movie while waiting out the storm. He had started their generator just before the storm hit, and Barb had put some water on to boil. Now, the two were getting comfortable under their mink blanket to watch the movie. Kevin reached for the two cups of steaming breakfast black tea with honey. Both loved that flavor, and with the hint of sweetness the honey gave, were very enjoyable to the couple.

Kevin was with the Cheyenne Police Department, SWAT Division. Now a lieutenant, he had been recently promoted following the rescue of the girls from the Salinas compound. His team had suffered one dead and two wounded during the action. He had come through unscathed even though at the forefront of the action.

He and his wife had bought the camper as a gift to each other after his promotion and loved it. She laughingly joked they had paid their dues, sleeping on the ground for so many years in tents, that they now deserved a camper such as the one they were enjoying, and the electric fireplace that came with it.

✳✳✳✳✳

The shooter hated rain. It fogged the scope and made movement miserable for him even though the heavy rain masked his movement towards the camper. The thunder helped also. He had low-crawled to within four-hundred yards of the camper, and had watched his target prepare and start a generator just before the storm hit. He had smiled at that, knowing the sound from the generator would also create enough noise to mask his movements.

Once the storm hit where he was waiting, he rose into a kneeling position and waited. The rain cascaded down his ghillie suit, one he designed to be a ghillie blanket when he stopped. It blended well with the surrounding prairie grasses and trees, a mixture of tans, browns, greens, and black threads and cloth strips. Soaked as it was now in this storm, the weight increase was telling on his stamina and he knew he would have to rest before his shot. He was now knee walking towards his target, and coming to a small boulder in the path he had chosen, he paused, pulled out his Bushnell *Bone Collector* range finder, and took a reading on his target, the camper window where he could see the two heads as they watched the television. Once he had the device steady, he depressed the sighting button and the readout posted four-hundred twenty-one yards, twelve-hundred sixty-three feet. He was shooting a Remington Model 700 SPS-X, in caliber .308. He was using a one-hundred forty-seven grain, full metal-jacketed bullet and knew with his loads, the bullet would hit in just over a half-second.

He put away the ranger finder and pulled a lanyard attached to his drag bag. Once it was within reach, he untied a flap, untied a suppressor, setting it aside, and then untied the rifle, pulling it forward.

He had made modifications to the rifle, one of which was threading the barrel end to receive the suppressor he'd made for it. It would mask most of the sound, but to someone close, the shot from the rifle would seem much farther away than it actually was. He screwed the suppressor onto the rifle and then brought the rifle up and took aim towards the camper.

With the *Vortex Diamondback Tactical* six by twenty-four, with a fifty-millimeter objective lens diameter scope on top, the camper looked just feet away. He knew with the rain and the winds, he would have to aim a bit high and to the right, or eastward, to ensure a proper hit. He changed his magnification from the maximum to eighteen. Now he could see both heads in the scope. He looked at each for a moment, and then loaded three shells into the rifle. He chambered the first and aimed at the head on the right.

He made a slight windage adjustment and one click of elevation. He looked again at the surrounding trees and grasses, gauging the winds. The rain was still falling heavily. He looked at the head on the right once again, gave a slight nod of his head in satisfaction, then took in several deep breaths. He looked at the grass near the camper one final time, brought the scope onto the head on the right, slipped the safety off to fire, took a deep breath and slowly let some of the air out. He gently squeezed the trigger.

The recoil didn't surprise him as he was expecting it just when he knew it would come. He quickly ejected the spent round, letting if fall from his hand onto the drag-bag, and chambered the second round in one fluid motion. He quickly moved the cross hair to the second head and watched as it lifted some, he knew in surprise, because of what happened to the one on the right. When the head hit what he thought was the apex, he gently pulled the trigger once again. This time, he watched as the head bobbed as the bullet went through.

He waited for several minutes, ejected the spent cartridge, and then ejected the third, unneeded bullet, which he placed back into its holder, securely. He made sure both spent rounds were in the drag-bag, pulled the rifle down, and unscrewed the suppressor, placing it into its protective sleeve in the drag-bag. Next, he retied the rifle into the bag and closed it, and turned to begin his long trek back to his truck. He knew he didn't need to go check on the two bodies in the camper, as he knew they were both done for.

✱✱✱✱✱

The first bullet hit Kevin just to the right of the external occipital crest just above the inferior nuchal line, which caused a blowout of the pons, the portion of the brain stem just above the medulla oblongata. It traveled through his lower frontal lobe and exited through his right eye. Kevin died instantly, without pain, never knowing that he was dead.

Barbara on-the-other-hand, knew what happened to her husband after seeing the explosion of brain tissue, blood and skull parts hitting the refrigerator/freezer unit across from them. Even so, she died instantly as well, without pain. Some might debate that she knew all too well, what killed her since she knew how her husband died.

The shooter, however, didn't care at all. His job was done. As soon as he got to his truck, he would make a call on a burner phone he had, saying one word when the answer came. He knew the second half of his one million dollars would be deposited in his Cayman Island account. He would drive out, clean the truck thoroughly at a local car wash, drive it to the Little America resort in Cheyenne, and wait for his ride to the Denver International Airport, where he would board his flight to the islands while awaiting his next contract.

When he reached his truck, he stowed his drag-bag and ghillie suit in a hidden compartment made for the task. He was smiling as he pulled the burner phone from the glove-box, pressed the speed dial button he needed and waited for the answer. When it came, in the form of a male voice saying, "Go ahead," the shooter said, "Completion." He heard the phone hang up on the opposite end, so he hung up himself and destroyed the phone. As he drove along trail 701J in the Medicine Bow National Forest, he pitched pieces of the phone out the window. He was smiling the whole way.

As he reached the trail head of 701, his turning point, he stopped and pulled his own phone out bringing up the internet and his bank, checking his account and seeing the full amount had been deposited. This made him smile all the more. He continued on.

When he reached his next turn onto trail 712, his smile was broad indeed. He was having a grand time slipping and sliding in the mud on the National Forest dirt tracks. He was to take 712 all the way back to Happy Jack Road, turning left to head back to Cheyenne.

He had just topped a rise, the highest point on Trail 712 when his last thought was what he would have for dinner at Little America that evening. His truck slowly came to a halt, the dead driver no longer feeling anything, and sat there at idle with the rear tires slowly churning in the muck.

After several minutes, three men in another truck drove up to the shooter. One got out and moved around to the driver's side of the shooter's truck, reached in and put the truck into park and turned the ignition off. The other two men in the truck got out, and reaching into the back of their truck, brought out three six-gallon cans of gasoline. One of the men doused the shooter's truck from front to back and inside with the volatile fluid. Another set the other cans inside with the shooter's body, one on either side.

One opened the secret compartment and pulled out the rifle and ghillie suit the shooter had hidden, then another placed a timed charge in the truck. The three got back into their truck and headed out of the Medicine Bow.

Fifteen minutes later they saw a glow behind them, knowing the device they'd set had just gone off. The shooter and his truck would be incinerated by the gasoline. Not much more than ashes and charred metal would remain for investigators.

The larger and older-looking of the three men pulled a burner phone out of the truck's glove box, hit a speed dial number, and waited. When the answer came, the man said, "Mission complete."

"Very good…very good indeed," Roberto Salinas said. "Take the next three days off and enjoy yourselves somewhere. I've loaded more than enough money into your account. Call me the morning of the fourth day."

"As you say, jefe," the man said, closing the phone and throwing it as hard as he could against some boulders, shattering the thing into many small pieces.

The man in the back seat, the smallest of the threesome, asked, "Denver for fun?"

Chapter 8

Pete Donaldson practically flew into the detective squad room. He looked around the room frantically until his sight rested on Anita at the coffee pot filling her mug. "Anita!" he yelled.

Her head whipped around to where he was and when she saw the look on his face, asked, "What is it…what's happened?"

"The Albany County folks found Kevin and Barbara Lindsey shot to death up in the Medicine Bow," he answered morosely. Once he'd said it, his shoulders slumped, as he was friends with pair. Too, they attended the same church together. Kevin had been a deacon.

Anita looked at Pete and after a few moments of contemplation asked, "What's the story, Pete?"

"Unknown, boss…just got the word," and that's when her phone rang.

Anita moved over to her phone and answered saying, "Bishop." She listened for several minutes, slowly hanging up the receiver and looking at Pete. Her gaze was steady and intense. After a few more minutes thinking, the silence in the room hanging like a heavy fog, she quietly said, "Pete, recall everyone…get 'em in here now, please."

"Yes, ma'am," he just as quietly answered, sitting down and began making calls to his teammate's cell phones. All of them had questions, but Pete told them all to hustle in, that Anita would brief the team when everyone was accounted for and in the squad room.

"Boss, they're all on their way in," Pete told Anita.

"Good. Now call in Andrew Nelson, Constance Dominguez, Clint James, and Thomas Alton. Tell 'em to report in field-dress uniforms with full load-outs. Once the rest of the team gets here, you and they need to change and draw weapons. We're going to war with someone," she paused, then said, "and we will be ready."

"Yes, ma'am," Pete said, then picked up the phone and called the armory to relay the order for the team to arm up.

Mike Hicks was next to show up. He looked at Pete, who slowly nodded his head negatively, gave a slight nod of understanding, and sat at his desk. He activated his computer, looking more at Anita than the screen.

The four rookies showed up together, decked out in their field uniforms and sporting M-4 rifles and extra magazines and ammo. As they entered, Pete pointed to desks in the back and gave a 'move-that-way' motion with his head. They quietly moved over to the desks and sat down to wait. These four rookies were on Anita's team when the Ladies of Cheyenne Rescue took place, and had been instrumental in collecting evidence that led to the rescue. They knew computers and modern communication devices like no others.

Antonio (Tony) Lanclos and Stephen (Steve) Wren, both detectives from the DCI, were last to arrive. They were both in field uniforms and also sported M-4 rifles, magazines, and extra ammo. Again, Pete pointed to their desks and nodded. They sat down and began loading magazines. The four rookies seeing this also began loading mags.

Pete got up and motioned for Mike to follow. They went to change uniforms and draw their weapons. Anita went to her locker in the ladies shower and changed there, afterwards going to the armory and drawing her M-4, magazines, and ammo.

Back in the squad room, they all loaded magazines, giving each other nervous looks. When Anita had her seventh magazine fully loaded, she put one in her M-4, without loading a round, and the other six she placed into the sleeves of her chest rig with armor plating front and rear. She was just about done with this when her phone rang. She answered with, "Bishop."

It was several minutes and what looked to be a page and a half of notes in her field book. After what seemed a long time, she said, "Got it," and hung up. She looked at her notes for a moment, shook her head, and stood up. She looked at each person in the room and they all knew her look, a mixture of sadness and anger.

She took a deep breath and said, "You remember the storm a few days ago…?" Everyone nodded. "It looks like Lieutenant Lindsey and his wife, Barbara, were shot and killed during that storm. They were in their camper, both shot from long range. Both were shot through the head, back to front. Bullets were found lodged in the refrigerator across from where the pair was sitting. Another camper camped down the trail from the Lindsey's, became suspicious before they packed up and went home, noting the Lindsey's truck had not moved all weekend. And, the lights were on inside and outside the camper. Very unusual, so the campers went down to check on their neighbor and found the pair." She hung her head again, pausing.

She followed with, "Albany County Sheriff's office is spearheading the investigation since the murders took place in their county. We'll assist as needed, no questions asked. We've now had two of our own murdered in Albany County, along with their ladies. Both were on the team that took out Salinas in the rescue.

"I don't believe in coincidences and neither does the Chief and our division commander, Captain Carlisle. We three agree our people that were on the mission to Salinas' compound, are now being targeted for some reason, most likely revenge. That means every person in this room save you two," she said and pointing at Lanclos and Wren. "If that is the case, we're all in danger. The Chief wants us with someone at all times – no exceptions. We all need to be…aware…of our surroundings at all times now. Weapons go home with you. Keep them handy, it just may save your life."

She looked at Mike who instantly became attentive to her and she said, "Mike, please give the safety briefing and annotate such on each person's record. I have a call to make."

She sat back down and dialed Bish's phone. He answered on the first ring, "Hey, babe, what's up?"

"Bish, we have a problem," she began.

"What…what's happened?" he queried suddenly alert.

"Kevin Lindsey and his wife Barbara were murdered while camping in the Medicine Bow. They were over in Albany County, so the sheriff's office over there is doing the investigation. Bish, you have your AR-15 and your Ruger nine out and loaded?"

"Of course," he answered.

"The chief and the captain and I all agree on this - we really think someone is going after folks that were on the Ladies of Cheyenne Rescue. That means you and I are targets also. I mean Nate and Kevin had integral parts in the rescue, Nate being the one who shot Salinas, and Kevin the leader of the assault team. We're not positive on this, but it would pay to be prudent and keep a good watch out – you need to keep the doors locked while you're up in your library writing. I know we've already talked about being ready, but now, I really want you ready."

"Oh, Lord in Heaven, I can't believe it, honey," Bish said to her. "You really think it could be a revenge thing?"

"Bish, we're acting on conjecture right now, but better prepared than not," she said.

"Kevin was a deacon with his church…I wonder if they know yet?" he said into the phone.

"Don't know, babe, but I'm sure they'll know before long. That's not my worry right now, you are. If you're not, you need to get prepared for…anything. I don't know what, but I think if whoever this is, and they're obviously out for revenge, we may be high up on their hit list for our part in the operation."

"I see your point," Bish said. "Okay, I already loaded your rifle and it's by the banister and you know mine is with me and my nine is always loaded. I'll get both and have 'em with me all the time – good enough?"

"I'll be okay with that. You keep them handy alright?" she requested again.

"I promise I'll have both with me everywhere I go…promise," he reiterated.

"I gotta go Bish; I don't know what time I'll get home so dinner is a whatever thing tonight. Bish…I love you," Anita said in earnest.

"I know you do, and I love you, too. Be careful and check six! See you later," and he rang off. Bish stood, went downstairs, got her rifle from where he left it by the fireplace, maxing out his pockets with the additional six magazines, and then went back upstairs. He already knew the doors were locked. He leaned his rifle next to his desk and put the magazines in two stacks on the desk so they would be handy if needed. He went into their bedroom and retrieved his Ruger *SR-9E* and the additional magazines for it. These too, he placed on his desk.

✶✶✶✶✶

Anita hung up the phone and looked on as Mike was ending his safety briefing to the team. Once he was done, he looked at her and gave her a thumb up.

She looked around the room, and every eye was upon her. She stood and said, "Everyone ready?" She saw nods from everyone on the team. "Good. Again, I don't want anyone alone. Connie…you can bunk with Bish and I in our guest bedroom if you wish. I can go with you when we leave and you can pack a bag – sound good?"

"Yes, ma'am," Patrolman Constance Dominguez said.

"Good. Now, everyone, I'm serious about this and I'm sure the Chief will back me up, but don't be alone," she said, looking directly at the rookies. "Keep a close watch over each other out there and please be aware of your surroundings. Don't stay still in one spot for too long. Move around…don't sit next to windows when you can get away with it. Check your highs and lows. Watch for snipers on rooftops. Don't take anything for granted. Please. I don't want to lose any of you, you hear."

Several "yes ma'am's" were heard and every head was nodding.

"Pete…" she called out.

"Yes, ma'am…" Pete answered.

"Call Albany County, please and see if they need any assistance. Let them know we're all loaded for bear and will not be pulling any punches. We have been authorized and directed to use lethal force as necessary."

"Mike…"

"Yes 'um…"

"Make a list from everyone of what they may need. I'll see if I can make it happen. You four," she said pointing at the rookies, "get together and start doing an internet scan on Salinas. Specifically, look to see if he had any children or other close relatives. Get every shred of information you can. I'll expect a briefing right after lunch. Move it."

The four rookies quickly brought up their computers and began running search engines on Salinas.

Detectives Lanclos and Wren sat quietly, waiting for who knew what kind of orders from Chief of Detectives Anita Bishop. They kept their eyes on her and waited.

Anita stood behind her desk, hands on her hips, and lips twisting, she deep in thought. What else could they be doing to prepare. What else could they be looking at while waiting for who knew what? What else is there…?

Detectives Lanclos and Wren both saw her as she lit up with thought…a revelation. She looked at them still in thought then said, "Tony…Steve, I want you two to run phone reports on everyone on the department." The two looked at each other, surprise written on their faces as that would be a major undertaking. "For starters, concentrate on secretarial and support staff. Check financials, too - one on the phones and one on the financials. Anything out of the ordinary, I want to know about it straight away. And do not, and I mean do not, speak to anyone about what you're doing. Got it? (nods) Go." The two quickly pulled their chairs together to talk strategy.

Anita, satisfied, sat at her desk, and continued her thinking process. She felt she was forgetting something. She picked up her phone again and redialed Bish. When he answered, she said, "Hey, kid, you have your thinking cap on?"

"For you, I'll put it on right now," he jokingly said. "What's up, babe?"

"Bring that detective mind back up and think about Salinas and the rescue," she asked. "Write down anything you come up with. If we haven't already come up with the same thoughts, we'll be ahead of the game with your mind on board. No matter how trivial, write it down. Can you do that for me?"

"Sure thing, boss; I'd love to help. I sorta feel like that fifth wheel, you know, lying around and not doing anything, so I'd love to wake the brain up. What are you doing so far?" he asked.

"Have the rookies doing the internet thing on Salinas; Pete's talking with Albany County investigators asking if they need anything; Mike is making a list of what we may need; Tony and Steve are running phone and financial records of department personnel. The chief, captain and I all feel we have a leak and I want to know who it is. Once I find out, I'm arresting them for being an accessory to murder in the first. They'll never see free daylight again."

"Okay, got it. I'll fire up a brainstorm of my own and let you know what I come up with tonight."

"Speaking of tonight, I'm bringing Connie home to stay with us in the guest bedroom until this thing is over. You okay with that?"

"You're making everyone stay with someone for safety, huh."

"Yep; figure that's the prudent thing to do. The three rookie males are bunking together at James' place. Everyone else has someone so we're covered. I've directed everyone to take their M-4s home for added firepower. Just in case, you know."

"Yes, ma'am, I do. My AR is right here at my side, yours is leaning on a bookshelf to my right, and the nine is on my hip. It'll be nice having Connie here. I'll call out for Pizza tonight. Want wings, too?"

"That'll be good," Anita told him. "Make it two extra-large pizzas and a triple order of wings. I think I'll bring all four of the rookie's home tonight for dinner."

"That'll be neat; I'll put a few extra beers in the fridge so if they want they can have a cold one."

"I'm sure that'll help," she said, laughing.

"Okay, kid, I got my brain fired up. I'll have everything ready for when you and the gang get here. Check six, darlin', I love you."

"Will do, lover, I'll see you later," and with that, she hung up.

Chapter 9

One week later, the three men were back in Cheyenne, eating breakfast at the R&B Breakfast Club, a mom-n-pop diner on Lincolnway. Two were having the chicken fried steak with eggs over easy, home fries, and wheat toast. The third was having two eggs over easy, sausage patties, home fries, and an English muffin with strawberry jam. Both entries were worth the time and effort. Good food while enjoying the Elvis Presley memorabilia plastered on the walls and beneath the table coverings.

Between bites, the three smiled at each other. They'd had a nice week off, staying in a nicer hotel in Denver. They had even taken in a Colorado Rockies game. They spent some time in Cabela's, and hit several nightclubs with live entertainment, a memorable one having an impromptu comedy night, which they enjoyed very much.

On their seventh day off, Salinas called them and told them to return to Cheyenne, rent the presidential suite in Little America for him and another suite for them. He would join them in a day or two. They would wait for his call. In the meantime, they would put their well-earned money to good use, eating at all the good restaurants in town.

Salinas called the morning of the third day while they were at the R&B having breakfast. They told him they would be along shortly, after they finished their meal.

Back at Little America, the three made their way to the presidential suite, knocked quietly on the door and entered when told to do so. Inside, they waited in the living room, looking around at the plush surroundings. Nothing too good for the president it seemed.

"Gentlemen, good morning," Salinas said eloquently as he entered the room. "I hope your breakfast was to your liking?"

"Yes, sir, very much so," the thickset of the three answered.

"Good, very good; I want my men to take care of themselves you know," Salinas said while sitting in a comfortable chair. "Gentlemen, I have another assignment for you. So far, the three of you have done very well. I was most impressed by the way you handled the first assignment."

"Thank you, Mister Salinas," one said.

Salinas opened a leather portfolio he brought into the room and withdrew several papers. The men could hear the pages rustling together as Salinas looked for the page he wanted. After a moment, he found the one he was looking for and motioned for the largest of the three men to come get it, which he promptly did, then returned to his seat.

Salinas drew in a deep breath and said, "The second and third names on that list. I want them taken care of. I want it messy – a statement – understand?"

"Yes, sir," came from the three simultaneously and no smiles, all business.

"Where is no matter to me, but, I do want it to be shocking, somewhat like those two camping in the tent. That was impressive to me, thank you for your efforts." The three gave small, evil smiles knowingly. "These two will be dangerous. These are two of the detectives that went after my father and destroyed his empire, one that I now am rebuilding. I want no blunders. No mistakes, understand?"

"Yes, sir," came the replies.

"Take as much time as you need as I am in no real hurry. Your reconnaissance needs to be complete for these two. Make no mistakes, gentlemen, they will be two of your most difficult assignments of your entire lives. Be as thorough as you can be on this one, gentlemen. It will take great effort and finesse."

The heavyset man said, "It will be done Mister Salinas, with no problems, sir. We will begin reconnoitering, immediately, sir."

"I'll deposit the usual amount into your account," Salinas said. "If you need more money for specialized equipment, just let me know in the usual way. Clear?"

"Yes, sir," the man said.

"I will be staying here for another week or so," Salinas told them. "Do not act until I've left the area. I am planning to go on another trip. While I'm gone, you may act."

"Yes, sir," the man said again. "Sir, if I may?"

"Yes."

"The other names on this list...are they to be taken care of also?" the robust man asked.

"Yes, why do you ask?" Salinas returned.

"If an opportunity presents itself, may we act...?"

Salinas smiled, thoughtfully, and after a moment looked up at the man and said, "As you wish."

"Thank you, jefe," the big man said with a smile.

Salinas stood, a clear indication the meeting was at an end. The three men got up and left the presidential suite and went to their own to begin planning. They knew their business - that is, taking lives - and knew they had to have as much information on the two targets as they could accumulate. That would be their first priority.

When the three got back to their suite, the big man, obviously the leader of the trio told the two to gather paper and pens or pencils and they would prepare. The items needed to do the recon would be many; weapons and ammo, explosives if needed, vehicles, surveillance equipment, listening devices, etc.

After several hours of discussing and writing, the big man gave the two their missions and he told them what he would be doing and where he would be going. The first man would go to the Verizon office and pick up a dozen or so burner phones. The second would go to Sportsman's Warehouse to look at their weapon selections, and to pick up several range finders, binoculars, listening devices, and equipment bags for carrying the material. The big man would take an Uber to several local used car dealerships and purchase vehicles suitable for their plans.

Another thing the big man would purchase at a shop in the mall was a selection of drones for their observation use. Drones could also be fitted with explosives and used as bombers. This the three relished. They had used drones on several of their previous hits, and the three enjoyed the way cars disintegrated when hit from above with one of their bomber drones. The three would almost go out of their way to use the devious devices.

When they felt they had everything they needed listed, they cleaned up their materials, packed their belongings, and checked out of the hotel. They got into their van and drove to a trailer park just off Interstate 80, renting a trailer for six months, paying cash, which the park owner appreciated. They moved their stuff into the trailer and ordered pizza and wings to be delivered. They would stay inside for the remainder of the day.

*****

Bish had just woken from a nap when his cellphone rang. Blinking his eyes several times rapidly to clear the cobwebs, he looked at the display and saw it was Anita. "Hey, babe, what's up?"

"What are you doing right now?" she asked.

"You want a normal call or an obscene one?" he jokingly responded.

"Get your pants on, cowboy, this is a business call," she said, heavily laced with sarcasm.

He sat up and seriously asked, "What's the matter, Anita?"

"Nothing, just wondering if you want to go out for dinner with Connie and me," she explained. "We're going to the *Two Doors Down* for dinner. We're both in the mood for one of their burgers and a heap of fries," she told him.

"I'll throw on some jeans and sneakers right quick and be ready at the door for you to pick me up," he quickly said.

"See you in ten," she said and hung up. "We gotta go get Bish, he wants a burger, too," Anita told Connie.

"Three's better…more conversation," Connie said laughing.

"Bish has never been accused of being a conversationalist," Anita responded. "I guess we'll see when we get there."

The two police officers climbed into Anita's SUV, and headed for the Bishop's place. It took eight minutes and Bish was waiting on the porch as she pulled up. He raced down the steps and sidewalk and hopped into the back of the rig since Connie had shotgun.

"Howdy ladies! How's the world treating ya?" Bish yelled as he buckled up.

"We're fine," Anita answered as she pulled out. They drove to and parked in front of the restaurant, jumped out of the SUV and went inside. Bish moved forward and ordered first, ordering a *Teriyaki Burger,* fries, and sweet tea with lime.

Anita was next, ordering a *Bacon Cheese Burger*, with fries and sweet tea with lemon. Connie stepped up and ordered a *Classic Burger*, with fries, and an appetizer of *Jalapeno Bottle Caps.* Bish stepped up and said, "Add some cheese sticks and onion rings to the order, please and pulled his wallet out to pay for the meals.

Drinks poured, the three sat in a booth with Anita and Bish facing the street. It took about ten minutes for their appetizers to arrive and they dug in like hungry animals. Bish asked for a bottle of ketchup as he liked it on both the cheese sticks and onion rings.

Anita began the small talk asking Bish, "So, what all did you do today?"

"I finished up cleaning the garage, then went upstairs to the library and did some writing," he answered.

"What did you write?" Connie asked.

"I'm beginning with short stories and have even written some poetry," he told them. "I figure start small and build my writing skills before I take on a book project. I have begun a few book projects, but they're mostly just notes and some research, you know, ideas in a file in the computer. I haven't really begun writing anything from a book standpoint as yet, just some ideas."

"Sounds you're on the right track, I think," Connie said between bites.

"I hope so," he told her.

"I think you are, too," Anita said. She looked at Connie and said, "You should see him on weekends, he almost locks himself in his library and does research or writes away. I've watched him a few times and he doesn't even know I'm standing there. He's so cute that way."

Bish quaffed and said, "Now I am going to lock the door."

Connie and Anita both began to laugh as their burgers arrived. They got their hands out of the way as the server set their meals down with a huge smile on her face, wondering what was so funny with this table. The laughter subsided as they began eating their dinner.

Bish, of course, drowned his fries in ketchup, and smiled broadly, as he hefted a forkful of the beauties into his mouth. The table became quiet as the three enjoyed their meals.

Bish was first to stop eating, smacking his abdomen and uttering a hearty, "Ahh that was great. Thanks for the suggestion ladies; you sure know how to treat a guy."

"Wait a minute," Connie said, "didn't you pay for this meal?"

"Yes, but it was your idea, correct?" he asked. Both nodded their heads.

Anita was next to give up and said, "I'm full," as she pushed her burger basket away. Connie did the same and they all sat back, sipping their tea.

"Now I'm in the mood for a nap," Bish said.

"No, you'll ruin your sleep tonight if you nap this late," Anita shot back.

"Naw, I'll just call it a pre-sleep nap…anyway, I'll take some of the good meds and sleep all night anyway," Bish told her.

"You still have problems?" Connie asked sympathetically.

Bish looked at her and responded, "Yeah, a few. It is getting much better though. I don't take the meds very often anymore, but they do help me sleep. Even if I roll over onto my right side, where all the damage is, I still sleep. Used to, if I did that I'd be up all night long hurting."

"I'm really sorry that happened to you. We prayed and prayed while you were in surgery and then during your recovery. Our church had a major turnout for a prayer service for you and Anita. It was so touching to be there."

"I really appreciate all the prayers," Bish said sincerely. "I'm still writing thank you cards. I don't know if I'll ever be done, especially with all the LEO's that showed up for the wedding. I'm sure I'll miss a million or so," he ended with a chuckle.

Connie and Anita both laughed and Anita said, "Yeah, I'm still having writer's cramp with all the cards we're doing. I agree with Bish and don't feel we'll ever be finished. So many people came to the wedding…and those that came during his time in hospital. I bet Wyoming will never need blood again."

"The whole team gave blood," Connie said looking down, reminiscing. "It was almost funny as we all had the right blood type for you Bish. The lab people thought it unusual to say the least. We still laugh about it."

"Enough reminiscing," Bish said, "let's get outta here and head home. I'm ready for some scotch out on the back porch."

"You and your scotch," Anita said sliding out behind him, then adding, "I'll have rum, and coke with lime, bartender."

"Oh, me, too, please," Connie said, pouting.

"I suppose I can be persuaded," Bish said, "but we need to stop by the Class Six on the way home."

"Class Six?" Connie asked not comprehending what that was.

"Oh, sorry, it's an old military idiom that meant the local liquor store," Bish explained. "Some liquor stores on military installations were named that, usually attached to the non-commissioned officer's club."

"Okay, I get it," she said.

They pulled into the *Outlaw Liquors* on the east side of town, his favorite, and bought another bottle of rum, one of bourbon, and another of bottle of eighteen-year-old McCallan scotch for himself.

The clerk knew him and she said, "Hey, Bish, how's it goin'?"

"Wonderful, Janie, I have two beautiful women in the truck I'm taking home tonight, so with this, I'm set," he said with an evil grin.

"I'm tellin' Anita, you moron," Janie said.

"Cool it kid, one of 'em is Anita," Bish said, signing the slip and picking up his package. Back in the truck, he handed the bag to Anita.

"What did you buy?" she asked questioningly while opening the bag.

"Just the usual is all," he answered.

"Bish, you need to lay off the scotch…the doc said," she scolded him.

"You know I only have one shot a night if I drink any at all, so give me a break," Bish shot back. "He did give me permission for one drink a night and I don't even do that."

She shook her head and looked back at Connie who gave her a sheepish look, not wanting to get into the argument. "Is this me being persuaded?"

He looked at her right quick then eyes back to the road and said, "Yep."

She sighed deeply, looked back at the road saying a kind of long and drawn out, "Okay," and drove on to their place.

✱✱✱✱✱

"Do you see them, my friend?" one of the men said to the bigger man in heavily accented Hispanic English.

"Yes," answered the big man.

"See…now you can see their faces as they are walking into that home," the man said again.

"Yes, yes, I see," the big man said in a condescending manner. "Can you get closer? Enough so that you can see that address?"

"Yes, senior, just a moment, I have to let them get inside so they don't hear the machine," he said, piloting the drone. Once the people entered the home and they saw the door close, the man flew the drone downward until they were able to verify the address.

"Yes, that is the one," the big man said, smiling. "Go up so we can see all around the home. "Oh, that is perfect. Can you stop right there and let us look for a while?"

"Certainly," the man said and put the drone into a hover. After a few minutes, he checked his battery life and knew he had plenty of time left, so he flew to the four cardinal compass headings out a way from the home and let the big man see for himself. After hovering on the east side for a few minutes, his last compass heading, he landed the craft near their truck and let it cool down.

Twenty minutes later the three were headed back to the place they'd rented to watch the video and take notes. They would discuss options well into the night, arguing through most of the evening over whose idea was the best to make a real statement.

The biggest of the three interjected saying, "This is Wyoming. We must make a statement that will hit at their hearts. El Jefe wants a statement made and we need to make one that will strike the hearts of every person in Wyoming." The room became quiet after that.

One of the two said, "Then I think we should go to bed and sleep on this. We can begin again tomorrow." The other two nodded and got up.

Officers Timothy Dalton and his partner, Officer Willie J. Smith, just returned home from eating out. Tim turned and locked their front door and then went to the sitting room to enjoy a game show. Neither he nor his friend had any idea they were under surveillance.

Chapter 10

The following week, el Jefe flew out of the Cheyenne airport in his private jet to parts unknown and the threesome had a greenlight from the boss to proceed at their leisure. El Jefe had provided another large sum of money for the trio as he would be incommunicado for some time after he left. The three would have no trouble fulfilling their mission with the funds they had on hand.

The three had taken a trip to Wheatland, Wyoming, and had rented a small home on the northeast side of town, off East Oak Road. They moved most of their meager possessions into the place, and then headed back to Cheyenne for their work. They would hole up in Wheatland for a time after the job was completed.

They had picked up another vehicle and between the three, had ensured it was in perfect condition for their getaway. Plates were current, all lights checked and rechecked to ensure none would be inoperable when driving, a full tank of gas, and a fresh oil change. They would travel at seventy-seven miles an hour just to fit in on the interstate highway. And to test everything, they made the trip back and forth to Wheatland several times. They saw State Troopers several times and were not even looked towards so they figured they didn't need to change anything on the car.

On the last trip, they stopped on Dell Range Boulevard back in Cheyenne and ate at Applebee's restaurant. "This will be our last meal out, boys," the large man told the other two. "We will be acting soon. El Jefe is gone and we are free to act when we wish. I believe this Friday should be the day, giving us two days of final preparation. We have everything we need, all will be prepared, and all we will need to do is act. The two will not suspect anything when we hit them with the drone," he ended with a smile, the other two smiling along with their leader.

After their meal, they left and went back to the trailer they'd rented. They packed their gear and their personal items. The gear, they packed in the first car they bought - their personal items in the new car. Both would be driven to the area of the job, the first to be left behind. They had already wiped it down with bleach and then wiped it dry with cotton cloths to reduce the amount of DNA left behind and to completely erase all fingerprints. They would wipe it down once again Friday morning before they left on the mission.

✱✱✱✱✱

Monday morning, Anita entered the office, early as usual, and began a thirty-cup pot of her favorite coffee. She was happy. She, Connie, and Bish, had had a nice weekend. The two ladies had made a terrific dinner Saturday night, and Bish had cooked three wonderful porterhouse steaks on the grill Sunday afternoon after church. They had watched football both days, college on Saturday and professional on Sunday afternoon into the evening.

She poured herself a mug of coffee when enough had perked, and sat at her desk, bringing up her computer and began to read the 'daily-dailies', those daily reports that alerted all officers to policy changes, upcoming meetings, possible additional duties or assignments, and other important information an officer needed to know.

Anita had just finished reading the reports when Mike came in, "Coffee's ready, Mike," she said.

"Good, I feel like I'm gonna need it," Mike replied.

"Have you seen Pete yet?" Anita asked.

"Yeah, he's downstairs…be up in a minute," and poured Pete a cup of joe also. Mike went over to his desk, brought up his computer and began reading the daily-dailies. He was about half way through when he heard someone at the door. He looked up and saw Pete standing there, and his friend looked very pale, just standing there staring.

"Pete, you okay man?" Mike asked.

Anita looked up at that and saw Pete in the doorway, and immediately stood, seeing he was very pale. As she stepped up to him she quietly asked, "Pete, are you okay?"

He looked down at her and looked afraid. He slowly shook his head and said, "They found Willie and Tim. They're…they're dead…murdered. They found them in Willie's house; had to go look for them since they didn't report for work at shift change. They've been tortured to death. The captain said to tell you and for Mike and I to head over to Willis's place over on Thirteenth Street." He remained standing in the doorway, now looking at the floor.

The rest of the team either stood or sat there staring at him. Anita took the initiative, as the leader was supposed to do, and walked over to Pete and, after putting her hand on his shoulder, said, "Pete, you want to stay here and get a cup of coffee? Mike and I can handle this."

"N…No, the captain said for the three of us to go…I'm good," he stuttered and moved over to the rack and got his coat. Mike did the same. Anita looked at the two, gave a shrug of her shoulders, and went to get her rifle, coat, and bag. "Let's go," she said quietly and moved towards the door.

✳✳✳✳✳

Willie and Tim had gone together and rented a small two-bedroom cottage on Thirteenth. It had a small shed in the back, no garage, and not much of a yard to speak of, some would call it a postage stamp yard. They parked in the street. It was surrounded by a privacy fence and had gates on three sides.

As the three detectives pulled up, there were several other police vehicles, lights ablaze, parked haphazardly in the street.

The crime scene van was there also. She saw the captain's vehicle pull up behind hers as she stopped. The three got out and waited for the captain.

"You three better suit up before you go in," Captain Daryl Carlisle told them as he exited his vehicle. "They told me it is quiet a mess in there."

Anita popped her trunk and the three suited up with knee-high pullover crime scene booties, and put on elbow length gloves. Each donned a knee-length plastic apron, a mask, and a surgical cap topping off the ensemble. Anita closed the trunk and looked at the captain.

"Norman in there?" she asked the captain.

"Yeah, and Arceneaux is with him," the captain said sadly. "They're doing it all, stills, video, and some of that close-up stuff with the micro lenses. Norman's team is collecting everything they find…hang on," he said as his radio beeped. He listened for a minute then said, "Anita, you and your men are cleared in." He stood by his vehicle, shoulders drooping in sorrow.

As Anita, Mike, and Pete headed for the front door, she told her fellow detectives, "Guys, keep this professional. Look at everything. Use a pencil or a stick to move things, but only after they're photographed and videoed. Get a crime scene guy to bag anything of interest to you and we'll look at it closely after they process it. Remember, we're looking into the murder of two more of our own so do it right," she ended. She stopped at the front door, took a few deep breaths, as did her partners, and she opened the door.

The smell was the first thing to hit them as they entered. The scent of blood and excrement stung their nostrils as they moved into the front room. It held two couches, a rack of TV trays, two end tables, a coffee table, and a wall-mounted flat screen TV. Nothing looked amiss in the front room.

Through an archway, they could see a small dining area with a round table and four chairs. The kitchen was behind it. Both looked perfectly normal for a couple of bachelors living together. They saw thrown away TV dinner trays and empty beer and soda cans in the trash. A few dirty dishes in the sink. They peeked out the back door and saw a pair of crime scene guys out there searching for evidence. They saw nothing out of the ordinary.

The entrance to a small hallway that led to the bedrooms was just off the dining area. Mike motioned for Anita to go first, ladies first after all, and he and Pete followed. They met Arceneaux coming out of the first bedroom. The eyes behind his face shield said it all. He lifted the shield and said, "Nothing like I've ever seen or want to see again. Watch your step in there," and he moved towards the dining area.

Anita stuck her head in the bedroom doorway and looked. The site the met her gaze froze her where she stood. Mike Norman was taking stills of what looked like Willie, spread-eagle on the bed. He looked up at her, straightened up, and moved her way. He stopped in front of her and blocked her vision and that broke the trance she was in.

Once her eyes were on him, he said, "Be careful in there and watch your step. You gonna be okay, Anita?" he asked her sincerely.

She looked at him, took a deep breath, and said, "Yeah, Mike, I'll make it; you and Malcom done in there?"

"For now, yes. We've shot a ton of stills and video and taken a few micro shots in there, and we're done with the other room also. I think that is Tim Dalton over there," he said pointing, "and Willie's in here," he said pointing to the room he was leaving. "Watch the bathroom as we haven't processed it yet. We've done all the photos, but no processing yet."

"We'll just look and not go in then," Anita said, and then stepped around him and entered the room with Willie. She almost lost breakfast. She stood eyeing at the scene before her. She took a deep breath and began professionally scanning everything from where she stood. First thing she noted was the sheets, blankets, and pillows had all been pulled from the bed and piled in a corner. The only thing on the mattress was what was left of Willie.

She looked at his body and saw that death was long in coming. He had suffered greatly. Much more than any human should have. As she gazed at the body of the patrolman on the bed, her anger rose. Her hands began to shake.

She jumped and shot a look at Pete as he placed a hand on her shoulder, "You okay, boss?" he timidly asked.

"Anger…pure anger is building; Nate first, then Kevin, and now Willie and Tim," she said. "They're our family, Pete, our brothers. This ain't right you know…it just isn't right."

"Yes, ma'am, you're correct," he told her, scooching a little so Mike could enter.

Mike looked around for a few minutes and said, "Willie's been dead for at least twenty-four hours, maybe longer. That means he died Friday night or sometime Saturday. We'll see about Tim in a minute." He moved closer to the bed, watching his step as he moved. "He's been gutted."

Pete meekly said, "What?"

"Willie's been gutted. His internal organs are gone. This is just his shell," Mike observed. "Heart, lungs, pancreas, liver, spleen, intestines -all gone - he's been cleaned out."

"Why in God's name would someone do this?" Anita said, rhetorically.

"Whoever did this is sick…just plain sick…and evil beyond measure," Pete uttered quietly.

Mike pointed and said, "Look at his nose. I bet his brain is gone."

"What makes you think that?" Anita asked, stunned.

"There's swelling around his nostrils, not much blood, so I'm guessing like the Egyptians did to mummify someone, they pulled his brain out of his nose. I'm just guessing, though. Autopsy will tell."

Pete turned and left the room and stood in the hall. Anita and Mike finished giving the room the once-over and moved out into the hall also. The three made their way to the second bedroom and found Tim much the same as Willie. No sheets, blankets, or pillows on the bed, just Tim, tied spread-eagled and with the same injuries as Willie.

Each took a glance in the bathroom as they passed on their way out of the house. Once outside, they gathered out in the yard and helped each other take their personal protective equipment clothing off and place it in an evidence bag. Then the three stood together with their hands on each other's shoulders and prayed. The captain broke in with them and prayed. Two patrolmen standing watch did as well. The group prayed together for nearly twenty minutes and when they did finally break apart, there wasn't a dry eye in the bunch.

Anita was first to speak, "You going in, captain?"

"No, I got enough from the description Norman gave me," he said, sadly. "That's four of our guys and two of our ladies. Someone's gunning for cops and their families and we gotta nip this in the bud quickly. Who would do such a thing? We gotta pull records and see if anyone's got this big of a beef with our department."

Pete entered the conversation by saying, "All four of them were in on the Ladies of Cheyenne Rescue. You think it might have something to do with Salinas? He have any kids that we know of?"

"That's something we'll have to check on," the captain said. "I don't recall seeing anything in the reports about a family member. No siblings, no mother, or father; unsure about children. He could have had one or a dozen for all we know and they're in another country or somewhere. We'll have to check."

Suddenly, a patrolman came running and yelling, "BOMB, we have a bomb, don't use your radios and leave to the east, the Bomb Squad is on the way!"

"Where is it, son?" Captain Carlisle asked.

"Looks like it was flown in a drone and hit Willie's car, sir," the patrolman answered and followed with, "It cracked the windshield but didn't blow up. If it had, we'd really have a mess here."

"Okay, son, we're leaving," the captain told him. They all moved to the east, walking and gathering civilians along the way. They turned as the Bomb Squad arrived and took over the scene. It would be a while before they would be able to leave.

"Captain, we'll take care of checking on Salinas and any family he may have had," Anita said, looking at Mike, who gave her a nod.

"That'll do, Anita, and let me know if you find anything new," Captain Carlisle said.

Just then, the Bomb Squad lieutenant came out and gave the green light, so Anita said, "Pete, let's ride," and turned for her SUV. Pete got in to drive and Mike got in behind Anita. She always rode shotgun when out with the guys. It was a quiet trip back to the CPD. Not one of the three said a word the entire ride, their minds, albeit reluctantly, processing what they had seen.

When they got back into their office, everyone was waiting, her entire team, along with the junior patrolmen they had adopted, Andy Nelson, Connie Dominguez, Tom Alton, and Clint James. Tony and Steve were there also. Anita called everyone together for a quick prayer session. It was hard once again as they all felt a need to not be godly, but to go out and get some evil payback of their own.

Anita felt this and said, "Everyone get a cup of joe or whatever and have a seat." She stood watching as the other eight police officers got coffee, tea, or a soda out of the fridge.

Once everyone was seated, Anita looked at them all and said, "I know all of us want some payback. Nate, Kevin, Willie, and Tim were not only our brothers, but our friends and family. Lady and gentlemen, we need to get this emotion reigned in and under control. No screwing around. No more being alone. And since Willie and Tim were together, that means we MUST!" she yelled, "be ever diligent to our surroundings. You MUST be watchful and not be alone. Connie, you'll stay with Bish and I since you've already moved in. All of you get together and make arrangements to stay together at all times.

"You've already drawn weapons and ammo…carry 'em at all times – I don't care what anyone else says, stay armed to the teeth. Take no chances. Someone with a real axe to grind is hunting US! That someone is a professional. They know what they're doing."

She paused to think after she said that, and said, "Pete, you and Mike, Tom, and Clint…I want you on the Salinas thing. Check everything. See if he had a kid or two out there we don't know about and they want revenge. That, boys and girl, is what we're probably dealing with – a revenge affair. If it is, we ARE all in danger – everyone who was in on the rescue of those little girls is in danger. And, I want you to check with Albany County and see if they've learned anything new on the other two cases. This looks a lot like what they found up in the Medicine Bow with Nate.

"Tony, Steve, Connie, and Andy, you check with Norman's team and see if they've pulled anything useful. If so, run it to the fullest. If they don't have anything yet, I want you four to interview everyone on Thirteenth Street to see if they saw or heard anything out of the ordinary." She stopped talking again, standing there looking into all the expectant faces.

After several minutes of this, she said, "Okay, team, get to it."

It was like someone had poked a wasp nest as every person in the room moved to do Anita's bidding. Pete, Mike, Tom, and Clint headed for the records room. They would collect every piece of physical evidence from the rescue and bring it back to the squad room. Tony and Steve headed for the crime scene lab to see if anything useful had been found. On his way out, Tony told Connie and Andy to get on the computer and start collecting names of people that lived on Thirteenth Street. They would be interviewing all of them.

Anita sat at her desk, satisfied with what she'd told the team. She picked up the phone, dialed the captain's office, and when Tabitha, his new secretary, came on, asked to speak him.

"Anita, what's up," Captain Carlisle answered.

She told him what her crew was up to and he approved. She told him they were armed to the teeth and he also approved that. She told him about having them all stay together, that no one was to be alone, and again, he agreed, even telling her the department would pick up the tab if anyone on the rescue thought they needed to move into a hotel to feel safer. She appreciated that.

"Cap, they have itchy trigger fingers…I can read it in their eyes," she told him. "They want payback and I can't blame them."

"Anita, you and I feel the same way, don't we," the captain probed. "If you catch these guys and they resist even a little, I give you and your team the green light to shoot. Get my drift?"

"Yes, Cap, I got it," she answered, her eyes gleaming, head slightly bowed, and giving a mischievous grin.

He snickered then said, "What about the Albany County Sheriff's Office, have you heard anything new from them?"

"I have Pete and Mike checking with them, we'll know soon if they do," she responded. "I cannot get over how similar Nate's death was with Willie's and Tim's."

"How so?" the captain asked her.

"First of all, same kind of rope, tied in the same type of knots," she began. "Then, the wounds…they seemed similar also, not the same, just felt alike…similar…does that make sense?"

"Yeah, what else?"

"The gags they used were the same type also. Did you see the photos from the gags used on Nate and Trudy?"

"Yeah."

"I bet when the coroner gets those out of Willie and Tim, they'll be almost exactly the same. I think we're dealing with the same killers here. I don't believe Kevin and his wife were killed by these guys, a professional hitman did that. These guys are sadistic the way they have done these homicides."

"Why do you say 'guys'?"

"On two occasions they've captured, tied up, and tortured two people. There's gotta be more than one; at least two. If there are more than two, then this is a real scary group and we have to be on our toes from now on until we get 'em."

"That I agree with," the captain said and at the same moment, his computer dinged with an incoming message. He looked and said, "Message from Norm." Anita perked up at that and wondered what Norm had sent. The captain opened a file attached to the message and said, "Anita, come down here and look at these."

She hung up, got up, and went as fast as she could to his office. Once there, together they looked at his fourteen by twenty-four inch touch screen. He was slowly clicking through photos and as he moved to the next one, Anita said, "No - move back - go back to the last view."

The captain made the click and the photo on the screen changed to the previous view. She was concentrating on the photo, the captain moving his eyes from her to the image and back again. Finally, "What…what do you see?"

"Hang on…what is it? There's something out of place here…odd."

"What?" the captain asked moving his head closer to the screen.

"Got it! Here," she said pointing, "it looks like something was on the floor, here…here…and here, while they were in the act. See how the blood splatter is around these areas. Something was there and moved after they were done."

What Anita had seen were three distinct blood-free areas on the rug. "Can you call Norm and ask him if they measured these?"

The captain grabbed his phone and dialed Norm's number, "Norm, Captain Carlisle, hey, these photos you sent, take a look at number seventeen-delta. Yeah, that's the one…you see those three areas on the rug that don't have blood? Yeah, did you measure those by chance?" The captain grabbed a pencil and a pad of paper and began writing.

"Yeah, got it, thanks, Norm," the captain said then hung up. "One is twelve by fourteen inches and the other two are eight by twelve. What do you think?"

"They took their organs – to sell…to eat?" she commented. "I don't know, but I bet they had coolers sitting there waiting to put the organs into. They probably had dry ice in them to keep the organs viable."

The captain looked at her, wide-eyed, and picked up his phone. He called the chief and briefed him on their thoughts. At the chief's request, Carlisle sent him the file with the photos and cc'd Anita. The chief told Carlisle he would put the word out about the organ harvest, and alert everyone to be watchful for anyone wanting to sell organs on the market.

"Chief Webster is gonna put the word out," Carlisle told Anita when he hung up. "He thinks they'll want to sell 'em."

"That's gross," Anita morosely commented. "It's morbid, but their deaths just might save someone else's life."

The captain looked up at her and said, "That's not the way I want our guys saving lives."

The silence in the room suddenly felt heavy. Anita said, "I guess I'll get back upstairs, captain, let me know if you need anything." she said and turned for the door.

"Anita," the captain said, stopping her in her tracks, "Don't take any chances out there and tell your team to do the same, okay…"

"Will do, boss," she answered.

*****

Back in the squad room, she called everyone that was still in the office together, opened the photo file the captain had sent and immediately went to photo seventeen-delta.

"Take a look at those blood-free spots on the carpet," she told her team. She gave the measurements and said, "What do you think?"

Mike and Clint were back from the records room with their load of evidence and Clint chimed in first, saying, "Coolers…they must have drunk a load of beer while killing Willie and Tim."

Mike said, "No…organs…they harvested the organs to sell. There are some major dollars for fresh organs on the black market. I bet that's what they did."

The room became quiet. Anita almost smiled with Mike's equally surprising revelation that she had had with the captain.

"Mike, the captain and I came to that conclusion a little while ago…good call," she said to Mike and the team. "This is the kind of thinking and investigating we need on this. Think outta the box. I'll send this file to all of you and I want you to look these over with a fine-toothed comb. Look at every detail and ask about everything you see that might help us bust these guys."

"Bust…? Let's just kill 'em," Clint said.

"Clint," Anita said almost condescendingly, then in a lesser tone, "The captain has given us the greenlight to use deadly force with these guys…IF necessary." That comment made the room go silent again.

Pete and Tom came in right then with their load of evidence, and stopped cold when they saw the looks on their teammate's faces.

"Come on in, guys, drop that load and come look at this," Anita told them, which they hurriedly did.

The two men leaned in close to the screen and looked at it for a few minutes, and then Tom said, "Looks like they had some coolers or something sitting on the floor…see the carpet in these three spots with no blood? About the same size as coolers I'd say."

Pete agreed saying, "I agree with him, but for what reason? Did they enjoy a cold one while murdering our friends or what?"

Anita chimed in with, "The captain and I, and Mike agree with our thought on those spots. Yes, they were coolers, but for harvesting organs to sell on the black market, not beer."

Pete and Tom stood straight up at that and stared at Anita, who continued saying, "I'm sending this photo file to all of you and I want you all to go through them with a fine-toothed comb. Anything looks weird or out of place, speak up."

Chapter 11

"They must have been dressed in huge condoms," Mike Hicks said drawing a few chuckles from the team. The murderers had left nothing behind, no DNA, no fibers, nothing. The entire team had gone over every shred of evidence from the Smith/Dalton murders and the Ladies of Cheyenne rescue and had come up with nothing save the imprints on the carpet.

The room seemed ice-cold for a while. Everyone sat looking at each other, not sure where to go next with this case.

"Okay, go over it all again," Anita ordered. "Details – look at all the little things. Do both cases again." Moans from the room, but they bent to the task, especially going over the photos again, and again. They were putting the photos up on the big screen, and it resembled a movie theater with everyone sitting in a half-moon around the screen, drinking something and munching on snack foods.

Anita sat and stared at the photos on her screen, scanning each one. She silently prayed *Lord please let me see something, or even one of the team. Father in Heaven, we need to get these evil men before they murder someone else, thank you, Father, in Jesus' name, Amen.* Her eyes feeling the strain, she pulled out a bottle of eye drops and put two in each eye, catching the overflow with a tissue. She blinked rapidly for a moment and then went back to staring at her screen.

"Yo! Everybody come look at this," Tony yelled out. Everyone turned and looked at him. He was pointing at his screen.

Anita was the first to move, getting up and going over to Tony's desk. "Whatda you have Tony?" she asked.

"Look here," he said pointing at his screen. It was a photo of the room that Tim Dalton was in. Tony was pointing at the bedpost where Tim's hand was tied.

"What?" Anita asked.

"Look at the fingers, several are bent abnormally," Tony answered. "They must have been trying to get them to answer questions first, you know, before they killed him. Maybe they did the same to Willie…"

"Put it up on the big screen," Anita ordered. "Mike, call the coroner's office and see if they've finished up the autopsies." Mike scooted back to his desk to make the call.

The photo popped up on the big screen and the entire crew appeared to get closer, looking at Tim's hand. Sure enough, on the big screen it was obvious his fingers were misshapen. Subtle as it was, it was now plainly visible.

"Mike, ask about the fingers of both of their hands," Anita said looking and pointing at Mike. "Tony, what number photo is that?"

Tony gave her the number and she called the captain from her phone, told him what Tony had found and told him they were working the issue right then. She told him she had a call into the coroner's office for results if there was any as yet. The captain said he would call and ask for a quick turn around on the autopsies. Anita thanked him and hung up.

"Tony, great job," Anita told him. "That's what I mean by looking at the little things so keep looking everyone. She looked at Tony again and had a smile on her face. She gave him a subtle shake of her head. He acknowledged with a slight shake of his own.

✳✳✳✳✳

The three men were enjoying themselves in Cocoa Beach, Florida. They were having a nice holiday after the work they'd done in Cheyenne. The beach was great, the weather was perfect, and the Mai Tai's were flowing freely for the three.

El Jefe had not called as yet, but they were not worried. He would call when he called and that was that. They would not call him unless it was an absolute emergency situation. When he did call, they had some interesting news for their boss, Roberto Salinas, and most likely Chogan Black Cloud in the background.

Renaldo del Monte, the larger of the three men and leader of the small group, stood up and said, "Amigos, let's go inside and have a nice steak. My treat; come on, let's go."

The other two got up and followed their leader into the resort's restaurant, where they all ordered Porter House steaks with the trimmings. Renaldo had scotch, and the other two a beer. They talked while they ate, mostly about the bikinis they had seen on the beach earlier that day. They never discussed business in public.

Renaldo's phone chirped and looking at the screen, he said, "It's him," and answered, saying, "Good evening, el Jefe."

"How did it go?" Salinas asked.

"Very well, senior, very well."

"I hear background noise, where are you?"

"We are having dinner together."

"Please go outside…I will call you in five minutes."

"Yes, el Jefe." He hung up the phone, told his compatriots, and went outside to await the call, which came exactly five minutes later.

"Tell me about it," Salinas told him.

Renaldo detailed what all they had done and Salinas was delighted to hear all the sordid details. After that discussion, Renaldo said, "And senior, we did something extra I believe you will like."

"Yes, what is that?" Salinas asked.

"We harvested their organs and sold them on the black market. You have an extra one point two million dollars in our joint account now."

Laughing uproariously, Salinas said, "Renaldo, you have outdone yourself. That is the best thing ever. I am sure their fellow police are stymied and horrified by this. You have done something most excellent. Thank you my friend. Please, use some of the money to pay for your vacation, but not too long, I have more for you to do. We will meet in the north place to discuss what I want next, say in two weeks."

"It will be as you say, el Jefe," Renaldo answered.

"Good. I will see you then. You and your men enjoy yourselves, I must go," Salinas said and hung up.

Although most unusual, Renaldo accepted the assumed kindness of his master. He would pay the bill with the money garnered from the sale of the organs they had taken from the two men. Renaldo even chuckled as he went back inside the restaurant to finish his meal and have another two fingers of scotch. It would be a nice vacation indeed.

✳✳✳✳✳

Mister and Missus Smith were first to arrive to pick up their son and take him home. They were escorted to the detective squad room by the chief and introduced first to the captain and then Anita and the rest. They asked numerous questions, most of which could not be answered as the investigation was on going. Too, the staff did not want to share details of the murders. Parents did not need to have that in their minds eye for eternity. The couple did understand and asked that when the murderers were captured, that they be notified. They would return for the trial. Captain Carlisle assured them he would personally take care of that, and he explained he would call if it came to pass that if the person or persons that did the deed were killed when attempting capture, he would inform them of that as well.

The couple said their good byes and left with the chief, the sorrow of the moment clearly written on their faces. The crew stood or sat, quietly after they left, not wanting to be the first to break the silence. All were saddened by the event, which was much unexpected and for that matter, a shock.

Anita broke the silence, "Everyone," when they had all turned her way, "take the rest of the day off. Go home and watch cartoons or something happy. But, remember to stay frosty and watch your sixes. I don't want to do this again. Take appropriate precautions, but let your hair down some. After this, I need some of Bish's scotch."

"Here-here," from Mike, knocking twice on the desktop.

"Connie, let's get outta here," Anita said, picking up her coat and bag. She watched as the others, after donning their jackets, also picked up M-4s and extra ammo to go with them. She pitied the poor person who might try to lock horns with any of her people. She put her coat on and, looking up, saw Connie standing next to the door, her M-4 held at the ready position. She nodded to the youngster and said, "Let's go home…I wonder what Bish will cook up for us tonight?"

✱✱✱✱✱

Bish had outdone himself…again. He'd prepared a stew pot full of chicken and sausage gumbo, with shrimp, which he served on hot rice. He'd even prepared what he called his homemade cornmeal spikes, cornbread sticks about six inches long and deep-fried for crispiness.

When the ladies walked into the house and smelled the aroma, they about melted. They both threw off their coats, dropped purses, and weapons and practically ran to the dining room. Bish seated both and after he sat down, said the blessing and served the meal in large soup bowls as the gumbo was a fluid mixture of roux and savory morsels.

"Oh, my, I've never had anything this delicious," Connie said between mouthfuls.

"Thanks, Connie, I appreciate that," Bish said, smiling.

Anita, nodding her head gave a mumbled mouthful agreeing with Connie. Once she swallowed, she asked, "Bish, where did you get the recipe for these cornbread sticks?"

He pointed to his head and said, "My own invention. There's a secret ingredient that comes from Louisiana that I add to the mixture. Helps to keep the bread together better and adds to the crispiness when cooked. You like 'em?"

"Oh, yes," Anita said, smiling and taking another bite of her dinner.

"Connie, you like the dinner?" Bish asked her.

"I feel like I'm in a five-star restaurant," she answered with a big smile. "It's great."

"The wine isn't that good," Bish said, grinning. "How'd work go today you two?"

That froze the two ladies, who glanced at each other, Connie's eyes big as saucers, wondering if Anita would tell him. Anita took a deep breath, gave a small understanding smile to Connie, turned and looked at Bish and sullenly said, "Willie Smith and Tim Dalton were murdered this past weekend at Willie's place."

Bish sat up, sat his fork down, and closed his eyes. He'd known both patrolmen for over a year and they had both stood by him and Anita during his stay in hospital and recovery time at home, including driving him to physical therapy sessions and such.

Anita and Connie watched the redness rise in Bish's cheeks, as he took a breath and asked, "Any clue who killed them?"

"No, the killer or killers left nothing behind – no DNA, fibers – anything," Anita answered him.

"Do I wanna know particulars?" he timidly asked, opening his eyes and looking towards Anita.

"No," was her one syllable answer.

Bish eyed her for another moment then shrugged and took another bite of his dinner. From that moment on, dinner was a quiet affair. Afterwards, when everything had been cleaned up and the dishes washed, Bish went up to his library and closed the door. Anita and Connie stayed downstairs in the living room.

The following morning breakfast was just as morose. The three barely said a thing to each other after Anita's blessing. She and Connie were already dressed and ready for work, promptly leaving right after they ate.

Bish locked up the house, grabbed his weapons and ammo, and went to his library to read and write. He sat his ammo on a shelf next to his desk, and leaned his *M&P-15* against the desk on his right side. He pulled his sidearm, a Ruger nine millimeter, eased the slide back just a hair to ensure a round was in the chamber, then ejected the magazine, checking to ensure he had a full load. He even pulled his two spare magazines and ensured they were ready.

Satisfied, he brought up his computer and clicked on the file with his book. The file dropped into another line of file boxes, and he clicked on 'Research', and the file opened with more than twenty *Word* and *Excel* programs. He double-clicked on a file named 'Lands' and the document opened up on the screen. It was his notes and research information he'd gathered on the land where his fictional tale would take place.

Bish studied his notes for a few minutes, and not quite satisfied, started his second computer, the first not being hooked up to the internet, and brought a map program once the system was up. He sat quietly viewing the map, from time-to-time tracing a line or a creek with the cursor. He would enlarge the view to see details. This map review lasted close to an hour.

He shut down the map program, then got up and moved around some to get the circulation moving in his legs. He knew from talking to other writers that sitting too long without moving around might create circulation problems in one's legs. This he did not want.

After he moved around for a while, he moved back to the first computer, opened up a blank document, and began typing. Bish was an adept, self-taught keyboard operator, and could type out sixty to sixty-five words per minute. An hour later, he had nearly thirty-five hundred words of material written. He sat back, did a quick review of what he'd written, and saved the document. He got a thumb-drive, his backup for his book, and saved the same document to it, thus backing up the material. He pulled the drive out and went downstairs to get a cup of coffee.

He smiled at what he'd accomplished that morning, satisfied with his writing. The story he was concocting was an adventure that took place in a fictitious land with green grass and flowing rivers, certainly not Wyoming, but a complete product of his imagination.

Chapter 12

The dawn brought high winds, nothing unusual for Wyoming, especially Cheyenne, and after the ladies had left for work, Bish cleaned the kitchen and put a pork roast in the crockpot to cook all day. With the winds, the trees in front of his place creaked and groaned in the tempest. He wondered if one would lose a great limb, one that might come crashing into the house.

He went over to the front window in the living room and peered out. But, it wasn't the trees that caught his attention, rather the black SUV that just parked across the street from his place. Bish's eyes narrowed as he saw the driver place the vehicle's transmission into park. There were three people inside.

Bish went back to the kitchen and snatched his rifle and extra loaded magazines and his cell phone, and went back to the front room. He looked over and saw the deadbolt was thrown, knowing the heavy oak door would hold to a lot of pounding once locked. He made sure he had a chambered a round in his AR, ensured the safety was on, and then went back to peering out the front window.

The three men had not moved. They were still sitting in the SUV. Several questions came to Bish's mind as he watched them. Foremost was why were they just sitting there? He moved back from the window, went into Anita's little office, and got a pad of paper and a pen. Next, he went to the garage and got a pair of binoculars, then back to the front window.

He used the binoculars to look closer at the SUV, took down the plates, obviously a rental from the number, and he could see a rental agency sticker on the driver's side bumper. He would call the plate in to Anita in just a bit, but he wanted to keep an eye on these guys for a while. All three were now turned in their seats and looking at his place.

Bish wondered if these guys were the ones taking out cops and their families. His anger wanted to unload the M&P-15 into the SUV and take these guys out, but his logical mind said he wasn't sure who these guys were or what their intent was. So he waited. His right hand held the binoculars to his eyes and his left fingered the barrel of the rifle.

He watched as the man sitting in the passenger side of the SUV raised a camera and took photos of his home. A moment later, the driver started the vehicle and pulled out leaving towards the west. Bish just watched.

After he was sure, the SUV was not returning he called Anita, "Hey Bish, what's up, darlin?"

"Darlin...I like that," Mike said with a snicker, garnering other snickers from around the room.

"Tell him he's just jealous," Bish said into the phone.

"Maybe later, what do you need?" Anita asked him.

"Had a strange thing happen after you guys left this morning," he began.

"What's that?" she asked.

He told her about the SUV, the three guys in it, and the one guy taking the photos. She asked if he'd gotten the plate, and he gave it to her to run. She said she'd call him back in just a bit, and to keep his weapons handy and hung up.

He turned for the kitchen, made himself another cup of coffee, and waited for her call. It came five minutes later, and when he answered, he said, "This better be an obscene phone call or I'm hanging up."

Anita laughed and told him about the SUV, verifying it was a rental from the Denver International Airport. She asked him, "What do you suppose it's doing in Cheyenne?"

"Other than taking a look at our house...I don't have a clue," he answered.

"I think I'll go to the captain and see if he'll let us bust these guys for something," Anita told him.

"I bet he'd let you, too, after all the murders that have been going on," Bish said. "Let me know what he says. Maybe I'll get in the Jeep and go run 'em down for you."

"No, you won't, or I'll bust you," she told him.

Mike chimed in again saying, "Can I watch?"

She pointed at him, but when Bish said, "You still have those fuzzy handcuffs, don't you?" she blushed and turned from the other detectives in the room.

"Bish…," she said in a scolding tone. "You stay in the house and keep an eye out for that SUV again, you hear?"

"Yes, mommy," he answered in his little boy voice. "I promise and I'll have my weapons handy at all times. Good enough?"

"Yes. I'll have my guys do a BOLO for that SUV. If we see it, we'll keep an eye on it. You be careful. I'm gonna go see the captain. See you tonight," she ended.

"Okay, see you later," and he hung up.

Anita told the rest of the team what had happened and that she was going to see the captain with the information. She left the room going to the captain's office and once inside, explained what had happened, about the BOLO, and asked for his advice.

"If we get a hit on the BOLO we'll just watch 'em," he began. "I don't want to pick 'em up yet, especially since they haven't broken any laws yet that we know of. Parking on the street and taking a picture of who knows what isn't a crime, but, with all that has happened, it is very suspicious. Did you tell Bish to weapon up?"

"Are you kidding…he's always got a full load," she answered dryly. "He did load up his M&P and all his extra mags, so I feel he's prepared."

"Good, and tell him to wait until they're in the house…I don't want to have to arrest him and go through the process to exculpate him for manslaughter. Now, sit down, I have something to discuss with you. I was just about to call you down when you came in. I have a preliminary blood screening on Willie and Tim - looks like they were drugged with a sedative. During the call with the coroner, she said she found a small puncture wound on the back of Willie's thigh, and one on Dalton's back, up high on his shoulder. I don't think either one of them would have let someone get that close to use a syringe, so after mulling it around in this old brain I got, I think they were darted…you know, with an air gun of some kind, like a veterinarian or a game warden might use darting animals."

Anita was staring at the captain and said, "That makes sense. I'll get a message out to everyone on the daily-dailies and warn 'em."

"Already have it drafted up confidential," he told her. A confidential message meant not to share the information with anyone outside police agencies. "I'll put it out in just a bit with an alert to be read right away. Make sure your people wear their vests – might prevent a stick. I do want you to tell Bish. He may not be active, but he's still one of us…family. You tell the big lug I said to keep his head on a swivel. If these guys are going for people on the rescue, we all gotta be careful."

"I gotcha captain, and I'll tell Bish," she said. "He'll appreciate it."

"Now get outta here and go catch bad guys," the captain said pointing to the door. "But be careful, girl, don't want anybody else getting hurt or worse."

She got up and left the office, a knowing grin on her face – the captain really cared for everyone even though he was rough and gruff.

Back in the squad room, she briefed everyone on what the captain said and told them the urgent daily daily was about to hit. She wanted everyone to read and sign off on it as soon as it came in.

"Does everyone have their vests on?" she asked her crew.

Nods all around the room and a few "yes ma'am's" came across. She reached behind her desk, retrieved her vest, and headed for the ladies room to put it on.

As she reentered the squad room, she yelled, "Mike!"

He jumped like he was scalded and said, "Yo!"

She wiggled a finger at him to come to her desk and he jumped. "I want you to call all the veterinarian's offices in town and see if they've sold a dart gun and horse tranquilizers to anyone in the last six months. Check and see if they loan 'em out, too. If no luck here in Cheyenne, move on to Fort Collins, Colorado, and if no luck there, start checking them in Denver. Take Connie, Andy, Clint, and Tom to help you on this."

"Got it," and he turned to the task.

Anita emailed the captain and told him what she had Mike and the young ones doing. She received a quick reply acknowledging the report. She turned in her chair and gazed out the window, trying to think of other ways to work on this case.

She was chewing a hangnail when Clint James yelled out, "Got one!"

She jumped up and went to his desk as did Mike and Connie. "Whatcha you got?" Anita asked.

"Vet over on Pershing sold a gun with two CO2 cartridges, two vials of horse tranquilizer, and six darts to a guy a week before Nate and Trudy's murders," Clint answered. "He said the guy was Hispanic looking, but maybe from South America somewhere. He said he had an accent that he couldn't place. I asked him what kind of credentials the guy had to buy the stuff and the vet said the guy knew horses, er, could talk horses very good. Knew his stuff he said and told the doc that he had two unruly horses that needed to be settled down to shoe 'em. The doc was very cooperative and gave us the guy's name, address, and phone number. None check out. The address is a fictitious ranch that's supposed to be out east of town near Pine Bluff, the phone number is bogus, and no hits on the name in Laramie County."

"Good work, Clint, great job," Anita told him while giving him a pat on the back. "Work up a quick paper and I'll send it to the captain - he'll flip. I wonder why six darts?" she mused.

"Oh, the doc said they come in a six pack," Clint told her.

"Ah, that makes sense then," Anita said. She looked at Mike and said, "So, it looks like it's pretty easy to get that kind of stuff. I wonder if this is our murderer?" said rhetorically.

"Ten-to-one it is," Mike answered. "Shoot, I'd go twenty-to-one on this one. I wonder if the coroner can match the drug in Willie and Tim with the meds the Vet has."

Anita looked up at him and said, "Go to the Vet, get a bottle – use petty cash - and take it to the coroner and find out. Take Clint with you, he deserves to get out." She grabbed Mike by the shirtsleeve as he turned, stopping him, and looking in his eyes earnestly said, "Watch each other and your own six out there."

He gave her a pat on the shoulder and said, "Will do boss."

On the way out the door, she watched Clint rack a round into his M-4 and check the safety. She smiled and thought they would be fine.

*****

Bish felt out of sorts. He was nervous. He felt like he was just sitting around the house doing nothing, even though he was writing and doing research. He knew it was because he used to be a cop and when he felt like this, he would go out and investigate something. But now, Anita, his wife, had him thinking better on matters like that. Other than continuing his research on topics for his book, he didn't know what else to do. The house was clean, so to the kitchen and the garage, the laundry done, bed made…he was going stir crazy.

Just to move around, he got up, went downstairs, and looked through the front window…no SUV. He decided to go check out back. Cradling his rifle in his left arm, he headed for the kitchen and the backdoor.

His cell phone rang and he nearly jumped out of his skin. He looked on the display and saw it was Anita…, "Howdy darlin, what's up?"

"If you go outside make sure you have your vest on, they're using dart guns with horse tranquilizer," she began. "That's how they're subduing everyone. We wondered how they got Willie and Tim down without a fight."

"Yes, I'm doing fine also, how about you?" Bish said, rather sarcastically.

"Sorry, hi Bish, how's it going?" she answered just as sarcastically.

"I wondered about that myself, how it was that Willie and Tim went down without a fight," he said. "Who figured that out?"

"The coroner's preliminary report on fluid and toxicology screens said they were drugged. She called the captain and told him about both having small puncture wounds resembling needle marks, Willie's on the back of his thigh and Tim's up high on his back." She went on to explain her conversation with the captain, the Vet idea and how Clint James had found the Vet in town that had sold the materials they believed to our murders. I sent Mike and Clint to the Vet's office to buy a bottle of the tranquilizer so the coroner can compare drugs. We'll see. If they match, then we have our guy or guys."

"Did the Vet have security cameras?" Bish asked.

It got quiet on the phone for a moment while Anita thought that one over and she said, "Hang on Bish, I gotta make a radio call." She was back in a moment and added, "I called Mike and told him to check on the camera angle. Thanks for the suggestion. I can only hope they have the video from that far back."

"You know, I'm going stir crazy here, sitting around thinking I'm accomplishing something at my desk upstairs," Bish complained. "Any suggestions…and don't say clean the house as it's pristine."

"Let me think on that for a bit, darlin'," she said. "I'll get back to you."

"I'll be careful and I promise I'll put my vest on if I go out. You need anything at the store?" he asked.

"Not that I can think of right off…if I think of something I'll let you know. Gotta go, see you later."

"Love you, babe," he said and hung up. He went to the front closet and took his vest off a hanger and put it on, and then a light jacket over that. He closed the closet and turned for the back door, first opening his AR's action and activating the bolt assist device (BAD). A BAD allowed the shooter to have the action on a semi-automatic rifle open and ready to go, with the safety off. The switch was inside the trigger guard so the shooter only had to tap that switch and immediately have their finger on the trigger with a rifle ready to shoot – it was an action that took only a half-second.

Outside, he first took in a deep breath of fresh air then moved to the back fence, opened the gate and looked both ways in the alley. Nothing appeared out of the ordinary. He went back inside to the front door and went out front, again taking in a great gulp of fresh air and looking both ways on their street. Nothing appeared out of the ordinary there either. The sun was shining on that side of the house so he sat down on the front steps and relished being outside. He closed his eyes and turned his face towards the sun, letting the heat bath him.

Getting a shot of vitamin D, he thought to himself, *and a little suntan with it.* He sat there for close to fifteen minutes basking in the sun. Taking one last look both ways, he went back inside and made for the kitchen. It was almost lunchtime and he wanted some chicken tenders and tater tots for his. He threw two tenders and a dozen tots into the air fryer and set it for the proper temperature and time. He got out a paper plate, pulled a paper towel off the spool, folded it for his napkin, got out a fork, and set it all on the dining table. He pulled a bottle of ketchup out of the fridge and set it on the table also.

He was sitting at the table staring off into nothingness when the dinger went off on the air fryer. He got up, rolled everything onto his paper plate, sat back down, said the blessing, and ate his lunch. He was enjoying it when his cell phone rang…Anita again.

"Yes, oh mighty leader," he said, smiling.

"Yeah, right," she shot back, then, "You still bored?"

"I suppose I will be when I finish lunch…just sitting around again, why?" he asked.

"You said the word research earlier and that got me thinking," she told him. "I called the captain and he's all for it – want a non-paying research job for a few days, maybe longer?"

"That's right up my alley - sure, what do you have in mind?"

"You can come here to the squad room and we'll have a desk and a computer set up for you. Cap said he would give you access codes so you could assist with what research and information gathering we needed for our investigation. He said he agreed with my idea because he knew I would be telling you everything anyway, no sense in keeping you outta the loop. So, what do you say?"

"When do I start?" Bish asked.

"Tomorrow morning soon enough?" Anita asked him.

"That'll work. I'll even wear my vest."

"Good enough. I'll let everybody know you're coming in. See you tonight."

"Great, see you in a bit," and Bish hung up. He stood up, pumped his fist, and hollered, "Yes!" He cleaned up his dish, the fork, threw the rest away, and went back upstairs and continued writing with a renewed vigor. Tomorrow would be a much better day.

Chapter 13

Promptly at 0700 hours the following morning, Anita, Connie, and Bish walked into the squad room to the resounding yells and clapping from the others present. They all hopped up and went to the door to welcome Bish back into the fold. The first hour of his day was sipping hot joe from a donated I♥CPD mug and chatting to the team about the case and anything else they wanted to talk about.

At 0810, Anita stopped the festivities, saying she needed to get Bish down to the captain's office so he could be issued codes for the computer. She told the crew to get to their daily-dailies and reports.

At the captain's office, he popped up from behind his desk, "Bish! So good to see you my boy, how are you feeling?"

"Not too bad, cap, a little sore some and I get an ache every now and then, but I'm really doing very well," Bish told him, shaking his hand vigorously.

Captain Carlisle sat on the corner of his desk and motioned for Anita and Bish to sit in the visitor chairs. "You look a hundred percent better than when I last saw you. You have color back in your face and you've filled out some. She feeding you well enough?" the captain asked, sending a sideways glance at Anita, but with a smile.

"Yes, she throws something in the trough every now and then," Bish began, and got smacked for the comment. "Yes, Cap, we eat well."

"Good, good, you need to put back on more of that weight you lost. Seriously, though, you look much better I'm happy to say."

"Thanks, Cap," Bish said. "Glad to be back…sort of."

"Yes, this is a good idea Anita came up with…gets you outta the house and us some valuable work done," the captain responded.

"It's a good fit for everyone," Anita said.

"I agree," the captain said. "Bish, here's your codes," he said, handing a sealed envelope to Bish. "You come in any time Anita is here and help out our team as much as you can, but not as an officer. I consider you a technical expert. If you want, I'll pay you out of my petty cash fund."

"No, that won't be necessary," Bish quickly said. "I'm just happy to be outta the house for a while."

"Well, on the days you're here, I'll buy lunch," Cap said.

"Now that I will take you up on," Bish said with a chuckle.

"Alright, you two…we both have work to do, Cap, so we'll be leaving," Anita said commandingly.

"Guess that's my marching orders, Cap," Bish said to the captain and standing up. They shook hands again and the pair left.

They took the stairs instead of the elevator, and after the second step, Anita turned around and latched onto Bish, giving him a passionate kiss.

"I'm going to like the fringe benefits around here," he said with a huge smile.

"Too, bad we can't lock all the doors to this stairway, I'd do more than just kiss you, you big lug. You sure you're okay with this?"

"Yes…yes indeed I am," he said with a huge grin. She kissed him again, turned and headed up the stairs.

In the office, Bish was pointed to a desk by Clint, who said, "You need anything, just let me know. I'll beg, borrow, or steal it for you."

"Thanks, kid, I appreciate it," Bish told him, shaking his hand. "So, what am I looking for today?" Bish asked him.

"I'm still checking veterinarian offices in the area and even into Fort Collins. I may even go into northern Denver and ask around there. We're looking for any Vet that may have sold, or had stolen, a dart gun and all the stuff to go with it. We're pretty sure that's what this guy, or guys, used to subdue Willie and Tim."

"I thought you found the vet here in town," Bish said.

"Yeah, I did, but there may be others. If so, that'll help with our investigation. The vet here in town is looking at his security system cameras to see if they kept the videos from that far back. He should be calling me this afternoon."

"Okay, where would you like me to start?"

"How about you start with the vet offices in northern Denver and work your way north…I'll continue from here and we'll meet in the middle kind of."

"Sounds great," Bish said and sat down after getting another cup of joe.

$$*****$$

Three days later, Clint and Bish had contacted every veterinarian's office between norther Denver and Cheyenne. Two other offices had had similar experiences with an individual fitting the same description. Those offices would be sending video to Clint as soon as available. The Cheyenne vet had indeed found the video from the day of service and had sent a copy to Clint via email.

"Bish, would you load it so we can play it on the big screen?" Clint asked.

"Sure," Bish answered.

Sure enough, the video showed a clear shot of the man in question. They were able to print a few still shots of his face from the front and one side. Anita immediately requested from the captain that a BOLO be put out to observe only. It went out within an hour.

The next morning, one of the other vets sent their video to Clint and when viewed, they found out it was the same guy. The third video showed the same person also. Now they were getting somewhere.   The guy in the videos had enough tranquilizers to drop an entire herd of horses, and eighteen darts to use in the process.

"Detective Bishop," Anita said answering the phone.

"Anita, Captain Carlisle here."

"Hey, Cap, what's up?"

"The Chief's made our suspect the number one on our Ten Most Wanted List for Cheyenne and Laramie County. It's still an "observe only" order, but everyone in Laramie County is watching for this guy. If someone finds him, who do you want to send out first?"

"Mike and Clint," she said, noting both of their heads popped up when they heard their names. She motioned for them to come over. Bish got up and went over to her desk also.

"They'll do nicely," the captain said. "Make sure they have extra ammo."

"Will do, Cap."

"I'll let you know. Tell them they're on standby will ya?"

"They're standing right here already, Cap…I'll let 'em know."

"Okay, talk to you later."

"Yes, sir," she said and hung up. She briefed the trio and told Mike and Clint to go home and get ready, that they would in all likelihood be out for quite a while once the contact was made. They headed out right then, taking their weapons and ammo along.

Bish went back to his desk and continued trying to contact the person authorized to release the surveillance video from the rental agency at DIA. If they could match the same guy with that video, then they would certainly have a huge lead.

He was getting very upset with what he felt was the royal runaround, when he decided to call an old friend with the Denver Police and call in a favor. The conversation lasted almost a half hour and mostly dealt with how Bish was doing after his ordeal. The favor was done and his Denver contact said she'd have the video that evening or else. Bish thanked her profusely and hung up.

He briefed Anita and said he was heading home and asked her what she and Connie wanted for dinner.

"Mexican," was the answer from both.

That meant Bish was heading for The Tortilla Factory and ordering a Mexican hamburger platter for Connie, the Steak Tacos platter for Anita, and he would have a full order of Super Burritos and a side order of a quart of their hot green chili sauce. Of course, they had to have the homemade tortilla chips and salsa.

At home, Bish put everything in the oven, set on low temperature to keep it warm, and poured himself a glass of iced tea. He sat at the dining room table and relaxed. He knew the ladies would be home in a half hour or so. He was thinking about the Denver fiasco when his phone rang…Anita.

"Yes, my dear," Bish said.

"Food ready since you have a couple of starving ladies heading your way?" she asked.

"Yep, in the oven staying warm; if you're on your way, I'll take it out, put it on plates and warm it up right," he told her.

"You do that 'cause we're on our way."

"Okay, babe, it'll be ready when you get here…rum n coke, too?"

"Did the sun come up this morning?"

He laughed and said they'd be ready also. She said bye and hung up. He got up and went into the kitchen to prepare, first putting the hot green chili sauce into a pan and then on top of the stove to heat.

He was preparing Connie's plate when he heard a knock at the front door. Every muscle in his body tensed. The knocking came again, so he got his rifle and eased towards the front door.

"Who is it?" he asked through the door.

"Fed-Ex…I have a rush package from the Denver Police Department for a Mister Samuel Bishop…I have to have a signature for it please," came the reply.

Bish moved the curtain on the door just enough to see out, and saw the Fed-Ex truck and the young man in uniform with a package and a clipboard waiting on the porch. Bish opened the door and the guy handed him the clipboard and a pen.

"Wow, this is the first rush delivery for a police department for me. What'd you do?" the youngster asked.

"I got shot and this is the money they owe me," Bish deadpanned.

The kid's eyes got big and he handed Bish the package and said, "Have a good evening."

"Will do, kid, thanks," Bish replied.

He set the package down on the parson's table and went back to preparing dinner. He did breathe a great sigh of relief as he went back to the kitchen.

Anita and Connie showed up ten minutes later and the house smelled wonderful. Bish began setting the table and pouring drinks as the ladies shed their accouterments in the front room. By the time they'd put everything down, he was just setting their drinks down on the table.

"Come on, ladies, have a seat and let's eat," he directed. He gave Anita a smooch as she passed and hugged Connie. He seated the ladies then sat himself, said the blessing and they ate.

"What's the package?" Anita asked between bites.

"It's the video from the DIA car rental agency," he told her. "My friend on the force down there owed me one and since I was getting so frustrated with the runaround, I gave her a call. I figured she'd just email it to me, but she sent it by Fed-Ex instead. We'll run it in the morning."

"Wow, must have been some favor, dude," Connie said smiling. Bish just grinned.

"That'll be one to see," Anita said. "If it's the same guy as the one from the three vet's offices, I think we'll have our suspect firmly identified. All we'll have left to do is locate him."

"That will indeed be the task…Mike and Clint out hunting?" Bish asked.

"Yeah, along with every sheriff's deputy and state patrol trooper, too. Hopefully the guy will want to go out for dinner or something and someone will see him. That'll be the ticket," Anita said, taking another bite.

"What do you think, Connie?" Bish asked.

All he got was a nod of her head. She was really putting away the food, and, she'd drowned the burger platter with the green chili sauce. Bish chuckled and continued eating.

That evening they sat in the living room discussing the next day's activities and hoping the guy at the rental place was the same dude.

"Here's to hoping," Bish said, raising his glass. The ladies said here-here and raised their glasses. "I cannot help but wonder if we're not dealing with several murderers."

"What do you mean, Bish?" Connie asked.

"The first case, Nate and Trudy, the murderers left tons of DNA and other physical evidence behind, yes…" The ladies nodded their heads. "The second murder, Kevin and Barbara, nothing save the bullet remnants you found in the camper, right…" Nods from the ladies again. "Then Willie and Tim – a real mess there according to you, but absolutely no DNA or other physical evidence, like Mike said, it looks like the murderer was wearing a body condom…right?"

"Right," Anita agreed. "That does make sense, and with the evidence we do have, and especially the photos and the information from the Vet, I think we're dealing with one or more culprits, and they're the same at all three murder scenes - just my gut feeling."

"I still think we need to broaden our horizons so-to-speak," Bish said. "Look at other people, not just chase this ghost guy. Did Nate and Trudy have needle marks?"

Anita looked at Connie, who shrugged her shoulders. "Good question," Anita said. "I don't recall seeing anything on the autopsy report, but I just scanned it since it was so ugly. I'll have to take a closer look tomorrow morning," she mused and got silent, thinking hard by the looks of her body.

Bish and Connie did likewise and the three sat there thinking. That went on for close to an hour, when Bish got up and went into the kitchen. He came back out and asked the ladies, "Want a refill?"

Both shook their heads and Connie said goodnight and went to her room. Anita said she needed sleep also and got up to leave. Bish collected glasses, placed them in the sink, checked the back door ensuring it was locked, took a quick look around the back yard, then checked the front door. Nothing moving in the front either and no black SUVs parked out front. Satisfied, he gave the door one more look confirming it was locked, turned out the lights and went upstairs. In their room, he leaned his rifle next to Anita's and put on his sleeping shorts, crawled into the bed and was out like a light. He didn't even realize when Anita got into the bed and turned out the lights.

Two blocks to the west, a man sitting in a black SUV, noted the time the lights went out in the Bishop house and wrote it down on a clipboard. He started the car and left the area traveling west. He drove to the Hitching Post Inn and parking in front of his room, got out and went inside to find the other two stretched out on their beds watching an *NCIS* rerun on the television. He sat in the easy chair and watched with them. Not a word was spoken.

Dawn eased in with cloudy, red, yellow, and orange skies. This was no reason to worry in Wyoming as the old Navy adage about 'red sky at morning,' didn't mean a thing in the Equality State. Bish had already started the coffee and was looking out the front window checking out the sky to the east. Their home for the most part, faced west and the back to the east. But, from

150

the front, one could view the eastern sky to the southeast. This morning, it was beautiful.

Connie came out of her guest room, stretching and yawning. "Morning," she said to Bish as she strolled past to the kitchen for a cup of coffee.

"Mornin'," Bish returned. "It's one of those Kodak moments outside. The sky is beautiful this morning."

"A red one?" she asked.

"Yeah, take a look out back," he told her.

After she poured her coffee, she went and gazed out the back door. "Oh, wow, it is beautiful today. We have rain in the forecast?"

"Nah, the usual dry, windy day today," Bish answered.

"Bummer, we could use the moisture," she noted. "My sinuses are going nuts with the dryness."

"I'll fill the humidifier tonight and turn it on for you…should help some," Bish said.

"Thanks, I'll take it," she said with a smile as she sat down across from him. "Coffee's good, thanks."

"You're welcome. Anita's still out like a light, at least she was when I left. The clock'll go off here in…" and they heard it go off, bringing a laugh from each. Bish got up, poured Anita a cup of joe, then sat back down and waited.

When she came down the stairs, she looked at the two sitting at the table and asked, "What have you two been up too?"

"Just sipping coffee and looking at the morning sky's all," Bish said, holding up her cup that she took.

"What's wrong with the sky?" she asked.

Connie answered, "It's beautiful this morning…one of those Kodak mornings."

Anita, in her morning trudge, moved to the back door and looked out. "Nice," she said and trudged back to the table and sat next to Bish. He leaned over and gave her a peck on the cheek.

"I didn't even feel you get into bed last night," Bish told her. "I think I was out before my head hit the pillow."

"Yep, you were breathing deeply when I crawled in," Anita said. "You didn't even flinch when I gave you a kiss on the cheek."

"I was the same way," Connie said. "I don't think my head hit the pillow either. I slept all night."

"All three of us did then," Anita added. "I slept like a rock."

"It's okay for me to stay home and write today, yes?" Bish asked Anita.

"Yeah, I don't think we have anything pressing for you to help with," she answered. "I'll let everyone know. Keep frosty though, you hear."

"Yes, o' Maternal One," he said sarcastically.

Connie busted out in laughter and gave Anita a look, laughing even more.

"That does it…you're walking to work," Anita said sternly, but with a grin.

"I'm glad I'm staying home," Bish said meekly. "You two will be at each other's throats all day now. I'm staying here where it'll be quiet."

"Quiet, right – you and Ozzy with the Black Sabbath music at two-hundred decibels," Anita almost mumbled. "Quiet…"

"The only way to play that music," Bish appealed.

"That's right," Connie agreed. "Gotta be loud or it just isn't…right."

"That's right, girl, you tell her," Bish said backing up Connie.

"You two are incorrigible," Anita said shaking her head and leaving the table. She went upstairs to get ready for work. Connie did the same. Bish cleared the dishes and began cleaning the kitchen. He would be upstairs in his library all day, writing and listening to good music.

*****

No one noticed the black SUV pass from north to south in front of the Bishop residence. The person in the back seat taking photos as fast as they could as they went by. Three sets of eyes watched the home as the SUV passed. Again, the vehicle didn't stop, just continued upon its way southward.

Chapter 14

Anita pulled her CPD SUV into the underground parking garage for officers and official vehicles only, and parked in her space. As she did so, the black SUV moved by the entrance from west to east, doing just under the posted thirty mile per hour speed limit. Again, the passenger in the rear seat was taking pictures as they passed.

They stopped in at the bagel shop just down the street and had a bagel and a cup of coffee. The jovial threesome laughed a great deal as they sipped their coffee and ate. No one else in the small bistro could hear the conversation, but it must have been funny as the three men continued laughing almost the entire time they were there. They paid their bill in cash, and left after the second cup of coffee.

Back in their SUV, they pulled into the northbound lane of I-25, and headed for Wheatland, Wyoming. A little over an hour later, they pulled into their driveway at the house they rented northeast of town. Inside, the man with the camera pulled the card, inserted it into a computer, and began going through the photos, highlighting those that caught his attention.

Renaldo, with a worried look on his face, said, "These will be too much trouble I think. The Bishop home is too close to their neighbors for noise. Since el Jefe wants their deaths to be special (getting a chuckle from the other two), we will need to get them alone somewhere, dart them and take them some place to make another example of them."

"Back to the forest," one of the others suggested.

"Perhaps," Renaldo answered, "but I feel a more memorable scene will be needed for the Bishops. A place, which will be so shocking to the public the memory, will last for many, many decades. The event must paralyze the county."

One of the two men, the one who would become the new boss if something was to happen to his friend, Renaldo, spoke up saying, "Renaldo, I think we should do someone else first…save these two for last. We need to instill fear into their hearts. Make them aware no one is safe. That we can take anyone anytime we want and have…our fun," he ended with a snicker and a sneer.

"I agree with him," the other man said pointing towards the former. "We can have more fun that way. If we kill the Bishops we will need to leave…for good."

Renaldo looked at the two and after a moment of contemplation, said, "Let me think on this," and he went to his room.

*****

The next day, after long thinking hours, Renaldo came into the house. He had been in the back yard - that side of the house faced northward - and had come to a conclusion. "Amigos, we will do as you suggest and wait to take care of the Bishops later. We will focus our efforts on Captain Daryl Carlisle. I want you two to go back to Cheyenne and begin watching him. Remember, ensure you are not seen, and switch out the vehicle. Now move," he directed.

The two jumped up packed some gear in backpacks and headed for the SUV. They would drive to the airport in Cheyenne, change out the big black SUV for another vehicle of some sort, large enough for the three and comfortable enough for Renaldo. He did have his standards.

They picked up a white Cadillac *Escalade*. It was a nice vehicle. They went to Perkins on Dell Range Boulevard and ordered their lunch. When the server delivered their food, one asked if they could borrow the facilities' phone book. She was happy to help and brought a banged up Cheyenne directory to their table. He opened it and found that Carlisle did not have an unlisted phone – the man still had a landline – old fashioned they figured. The directory had his address listed also, making their task that much easier. He wrote the address down on his napkin and when the young server came by again, he handed her the book with his thanks. They finished their meal and departed checking a city map they had picked up at the Southeast Wyoming Welcome Center off I-25, and finding where Carlisle's home was located. They would make their first drive by and photograph the place.

As they drove past Carlisle's home, they shot many photographs. The home was in a fashionable part of town on the northwest side, and had very large yard. The home had a three car attached garage. It would make their tasks much easier with that much room…to play.

When they got to their hotel room, they placed the memory card into their laptop and brought up the photos. Together they sat around the small table and stared at each photo as it appeared. One took notes while the other advanced the photos in the computer. Shot after shot filled the screen.

They had finished all the photos when Renaldo showed up and said to go through them again, except to go through slower. The three gazed at the photos for over an hour. Renaldo called a halt just after noon and the three went to dinner at the Perkin's Restaurant. They discussed fishing in Wheatland Reservoir Three, deliberately staying off their main subject.

On their way home they stopped by a local Wal-Mart just down the street from Perkins and shopped, picking up items they would need while having their fun. Cotton rope, duct tape, mechanics gloves, several fishing knives, and a few lures just to make it look good.

Back at the vehicle, they added the new items to the others in two backpacks. They were ready to play.

"Tomorrow, I want you two to go by the Carlisle place again and take more pictures," Renaldo ordered. "Try to get some views of the back yard if you can…there was an alley behind the home, yes?"

"Yes, Renaldo," the one driving quickly answered.

"Then try to go down the alley and photograph everything you can," he ordered. "Take this vehicle as it looks suitable for that neighborhood. Watch your speed and driving. We cannot afford an encounter with the police now so be careful. And I'm sure our benefactor would be most displeased if we're caught."

The two underlings looked at each other knowing that if they were caught, it would not be good for them.

*****

Morning came and Captain Carlisle got out of his CPD SUV and headed for his office. He turned before he got to the door as he heard a quick honk of a horn. It was Anita and Patrolman Dominguez. He leaned on the passenger door as they pulled up, "Howdy, ladies, what's up?" he asked.

Anita, concerned, looked at him and said, "Did you notice that white Escalade on your six? It was with you most of the way from where we pulled in behind. It followed you here and went by as you pulled in. I think it was a rental."

"Go park and both of you come to my office," Carlisle said and headed for the door. Up at his office, he accepted a cup of coffee from Tabitha, and told her to show Bishop and Dominguez in to his office as soon as they showed up.

That was only a few moments and Tabitha waived the two in without a sound, noting the concerned looks on their faces. Tabitha shook her head and made another pot of coffee, knowing it looked to be a long day. She also wondered what was up, and took a fleeting, nervous glance back into the captain's office.

"Okay, ladies, tell me about this white Escalade," the captain instructed.

Anita spoke – "Cap, we turned in behind it as you and it passed us. I didn't think anything about it until it turned with you every turn you made. And when you turned in here, it slowed and the person sitting in the passenger seat appeared to be taking photos or something as it passed."

"Plates?" Carlisle asked.

"Yep, got 'em, and it's a rental from over at the airport," Anita answered. "I've already called it in and told two of my guys to go get the video of the day it was rented."

"Good…good," the captain said. He sat thinking for a few minutes then said, "I want you (pointing at Connie) and Patrolman Clint James for a protection detail. You go and tell him, then pack your bags and come back here. Weapon and armor up…scoot."

"Yes, sir," Connie said as she got up to leave.

Tabitha smiled at Connie as she passed, then a look of concern crossed her face.

"Anita, I want you to get with Markel and arrange cameras around my place – front, back, and sides – and have another team get my wife outta there and to a safe place. I'd rather not know at this point where you have her, just get her safe."

"I'll have Pete and Mike handle it, Cap," Anita told him.

"Good, they'll do fine." Carlisle sat thinking for a while longer then looked up at Anita and said, "Good catch for you two. You think I'm taking too much of a precaution here with what I've ordered?"

"With what has happened to six of our people in the last year, no, not at all, and I think it's a good plan," Anita told him earnestly. "We'll keep a close watch on your place and you, and maybe we'll get these people. I got the willies when I realized they were following you, broke out in goosebumps all over. Cap, I wanted to light 'em up right then, but they hadn't done anything wrong, really."

"I trust your instincts, Anita, and with what has happened, I want to protect all of us as best we can. Who was Clint staying with?"

"Tom and Andy…they were staying in Tom's apartment."

"Okay, I won't have to worry about someone being alone out there."

"No, sir, we're still covered."

He sat quietly, his chin in his hand, a finger tapping on his cheek thinking through what he'd done. "I promise you I'll have my armor on if I go out. Just get my wife somewhere safe. If these people try anything, I think we'll be ready for them this time," he told her with a deadly look. "Now get and tell Mike and Pete to be gentle with her."

"Will do, Cap," Anita answered and got up to leave.

✶✶✶✶✶

Back in the detective's squad room, Anita quietly called Mike and Pete over and filled them in. Together they donned their body armor, collected their weapons and ammo, nodded to Anita as they headed for the door. They would take Mrs. Carlisle to a hotel somewhere and hunker down. Where they held up would be a closely guarded secret between the three, Mrs. Carlisle, Mike, and Pete.

Anita called the rest of the team together and briefed them on what had transpired, and on what the current plan was. She told them Detective Markel from the Photographic Evidence Lab and his team, were out placing cameras around the captain's home as they spoke. They would be watching twenty-four/seven from then on.

Right then Tony and Andy returned from the rental place near the airport. "Got it," Tony said, referring to the tape. He went over to Anita's desk, handed her the disc, and she loaded it. Across the room on the big screen, they watched as two Hispanic-looking men made the deal for the Escalade. The two were all smiles as they provided driver's licenses, proof of insurance, and the money for the rental. They used cash. The clerk remembered the transaction and gave Tony and Andy copies of the driver's licenses and insurance paperwork. All were bogus.

"At least we'll have nice photos of those two to pass around to our people," Tom Alton said.

Anita printed hard copy photos of both and told Tom to get the BOLO okayed by the captain and then out to everyone with the department, with the alert they were to be kept under surveillance only, not to approach unless they were breaking the law. Same if they find the white Escalade. Tom ran from the office.

"Everyone, we need to be careful," Anita continued. "I want you all to be in your body armor anytime you're outside. Weapon up also and have your extra ammo handy. If these two are the murderers, we need to approach this as a possible deadly encounter. No telling what these people may do. Approach with extreme caution if and when we find them, take no chances. Call for back up before approaching them. The chief has already given the department the greenlight on using deadly force with the murderers, just remember your safety procedures, and watch what is behind any target you may have. I don't want any innocent civilians harmed by friendly-fire."

She paused, looking at each of her teammates. "Ladies and gentlemen, all of us," and she emphasized this by pointing to herself, "must be on our toes. Stay sharp and keep your focus on this one; safety first!" and another long pause. "Steve, you take Tom. I want everyone looking for that Escalade. Go."

Anita watched as those not already out on a task put their body armor on and collected weapons and ammo, and then watched as they left the office. She stood by her desk and she transformed. From a determined leader, her demeanor changed to one of drooping shoulders and a facial change to one of a combination of fear and sadness. She just as suddenly felt covered in goose flesh. Her mind reeled with the abrupt thought of disaster, one that would befall her team.

She began to cry. It only lasted a few moments then she got a tissue and wiped her face and eyes. She blew her nose, threw the tissues in the trash, and sat at her desk, grabbing the phone and calling home. Bish answered on the second ring.

"Hey, babe, what's up?" he asked.

"You need to get over here right now," she told him, deadpanned.

"Something new come up?" he asked. "I'm on my way."

"Bish…wear your armor and weapon up," she warned him.

"Will do, Anita," he said with new concern and hung up.

✵✵✵✵✵

Bish arrived in just under twenty minutes, AR-15 slung over his shoulder and additional ammo bandolier over the opposite shoulder, his nine-millimeter on his right hip. He strode straight to Anita's desk where she was sitting and asked, "What's the deal?"

She explained.

Bish stared into Anita's eyes and finally asked, "So, why have you been crying?"

Her expression changed to surprise and she said, "I've suddenly had unhealthy thoughts…about my team."

"How so," he pressed.

She looked at him, pointed at the guest chair, which he sat in, and said, "I don't know…I just got a bad feeling this was going to go bad for my team. Disaster I'm afraid is what I felt, and the feeling won't go away."

He watched her every move and twitch and knew she was sincere. She really felt great concern for her team and was obviously worried by the feelings she was having. "You know what Matthew chapter six says about worry…?"

"Yes, I've read it a multitude of times," she said to him. "Jesus says '…do not worry about your life' in verse twenty-five. It's not me I'm worried about, it's my team. We've already lost si…"

"I know, I know," Bish interrupted. "I know we've lost six of our own. We cannot afford to lose anyone else. Now we know a possible vehicle so the PD will find that soon. There cannot be that many white Cadillac Escalades running around

Cheyenne. Should be a no brainer finding that needle in this haystack we call home. I assume you've included Sheriff's and State's folks on the BOLO…"

"Of course," she answered curtly.

"Easy there, tootsie, we're still on the same team. With them on the BOLO and all of our folks, the Escalade should be showing up soon. It's gotta be around here somewhere. When you find it, we will probably be able to crack this wide open soon afterwards. You know that, so stop worrying.

"And remember what Jesus says in verse thirty-three, 'But seek first His kingdom and His righteousness, and all these things will be given to you as well.' So give it up to Him, pray, and you'll get results."

"Will you pray with me?" Anita asked him.

"Anytime, anywhere, my lady," he answered and reaching out for her hand. They prayed together for several minutes and when they finished with a joint 'Amen', he held her hand a moment longer giving additional moral support to her.

"You know, I love you," she said quietly.

"I get that impression," he said with a smile. "Want to go add our eyes to the search?"

"Yeah, I wanna get outta here…the walls are closing in on me," she answered, getting up and donning her body armor, collecting her M-4 and extra ammo. She put on her coat and together they left the office.

They stopped by the captain's office on the way out and told Tabitha what they were doing and said that the office was empty for now, that everyone was out looking for the Escalade.

Tabitha watched as the two went to the elevator and entered. As soon as the elevator door was closed, she reached into her purse and brought out a burner phone and hit the speed dial. It rang twice and she said, "They know about the *Escalade*, and have the entire force out looking for it along with the sheriff's office and State Troopers." The phone clicked and she folded it closed, returned it to her purse and went back to what she was doing.

*****

Anita, driving, pulled out of the garage and turned to the west. They would check the hotels near the I-25 and I-80 interchange. Heading down west Lincolnway, they passed a few car dealerships and the Down Home Diner, turning onto Fleischli Parkway as there were several hotels down this road. They checked all three and even made a run through the Home Depot parking lot – no white *Escalades* were seen.

"Where to, cowboy?" Anita asked.

"Take I-25 up to Central and let's check those," he answered.

She pulled out and did just that. They checked the two hotels up on that end of town, took a look in the Ace Hardware parking lot, and then took Manewal Drive to Yellowstone Road, again, no luck on the Cadillac.

"Dell Range…?" she asked.

"I suppose," he answered.

She took a right onto Yellowstone, and then a left onto Dell Range Boulevard. There weren't any hotels on Dell Range, but there were multiple shopping centers and restaurants. They drove through the Lowe's parking lot, then around the mall. They swung around and went down Meadowland Drive from west to east, coming out across Dell Range from Walmart. They went through that huge parking lot and then the Sam's Club lot and still nothing.

"Cross Prairie Avenue and I'll take you to lunch at Perkins," Bish offered.

"I could eat," Anita said and turned to cross-Prairie. When they pulled into the Perkins parking lot – bingo - a white *Escalade* with the right plates sat in a slot. Anita immediately got on the radio and called it in. Both had forgotten about their hunger. Anita pulled around and parked on the far side of the eastern portion of the open lot.

Bish charged his AR-15 using his BAD leaver, and pulled his nine millimeter and ensured a round was in the chamber. He loosened both of his spare magazines for his handgun, and made sure his extra magazines were loose in his shoulder bag. He looked at Anita and said, "I'll be right over there," pointing at a GMC 2500.

"Keep your head down, sugar, I'll be right here," Anita told him. She saw Mike and Pete pull into the lot and she radioed them to cover the south side of the building and lot. As other patrolmen and deputies arrived, she directed them to areas she wanted covered, and within ten minutes of her initial call, the entire establishment was covered by multiple police and sheriff's department personnel. There was little chance whomever drove the *Escalade* could get away.

*****

It was a half-hour wait once everyone was in position. The two concerned Hispanic-looking men stepped out of the front door and turned left to go to the *Escalade*.

"Halt!" Anita yelled. "Do not move! Raise your hands above your heads and do not move and you won't be hurt."

The two men stopped dead still, raised their hands and looked around. They could clearly see many rifle barrels aimed in their direction. Police and deputies quickly ran up to the two and took control of the two prisoners.

"Take them directly to booking, making sure they get DNA samples, and lock 'em up," Anita ordered. Other officers used the yellow police tape to cordon off the Cadillac and waited for the forensics team to get there to process the vehicle. All the two had on them were two wallets with false identification, seven hundred dollars and some change, the keys to the Cadillac, and more key-cards from a local hotel. Anita directed

Mike and Pete, along with two other patrolmen, to go and watch the room.

She and Bish stood by waiting for Detective Michael Norman from the Crime Scene Team and his crew to arrive. He and his assistant and photographer, patrolman Malcolm Arceneaux, arrived almost a half-hour later, and after climbing into their protective biohazard suits, went to work.

Bish snuck into Perkins and came out with two cups of coffee, a chocolate chip cookie for him and a blue berry muffin for Anita, who was very surprised and very appreciative.

"None for us?" Norman asked, smiling.

"You have a gofer," Bish responded, pointing towards Arceneaux.

"He'd probably tell me to go jump in a bayou or something," Norman retorted.

"Then I guess you'll just have to go in yourself," Bish said. But, he did go back inside and get two more cups of coffee and two more cookies.

When he gave the treat to the two forensic team members, Norman said, "Thanks, darlin', you'll make someone a terrific wife someday."

"He already has," Anita, joked, and everyone, including Bish, laughed.

Bish and Anita watched the teams work the area. After a few minutes of this, Bish took a sip of his coffee and said, "Did you notice the look on their faces as they came out of the restaurant?"

"Not really, why?" she responded.

"They looked concerned, nervous…almost as if they were going to the car to run," he explained. "Almost like they knew we were gunning for them."

Anita looked at her husband with a surprised look and very quietly said, "We've been aware we might have a leak in the department somewhere, but I never figured this."

He looked at her and asked, "What do you want to do about it?"

She immediately went into deep thought.

✳✳✳✳✳

Several hours later, Norman and Arceneaux completed their processing of the *Escalade*. Anita had already called a tow company and had a truck standing by to take the car to the impound lot.

Norman walked over to Anita and Bish after taking off his biohazard suit and said, "We have a ton of evidence – DNA, prints, and fibers – to process. Arceneaux even found some blood spots so we'll get DNA from those. I'll get the results to you on most everything in three days; the DNA will take at least a week to process all the samples we recovered."

"Thanks, Mike," Anita thanked him. Then, "You find any phones?"

"Yeah, four – two on the creeps and two in the glove box, unopened burners by the looks, why," he returned.

"Be very careful with the two that you found on the pair and do whatever you need to get them activated so you can see the histories and such," she ordered. "Let me know as soon as you're successful with that – Mike, it's very important."

"You got it," he said, then, "I'll let you know as soon as we get anything worthwhile, how's that?"

"That'll be fine. If you get anything earth shattering, call me any time. Tell Malcolm we said thanks."

"Will do, see you later," a very tired and stressed out Norman said to her. "Bish…"

"See ya, Mike," Bish said with a guy wave.

Anita and Bish waited, watching the *Escalade* being hooked up to tow. When it and a patrol car left the scene, Bish said, "Can I take you to dinner…we're already where I want to go eat," he said sending a thumb over his shoulder towards Perkins. "We were going to eat here earlier, so we may as well go on in and have dinner."

"Yean, I could eat, sugar, lead on," Anita agreed.

After dinner, Anita drove back to the station and went to her office - Bish went home. Anita called Mike and Pete giving them an update on the case. She told them to keep Mrs. Carlisle under wraps until the DNA evidence was processed, and to keep vigilant for the time they would have her under their care. She hung up and looked at the rest of their team and told them all to go home and get some rest. She complimented them on such a great response for the day's event and that they had all done a great job. And then she told them all to stay frosty.

Anita watched as the group slowly filed out of the office. She was sitting at her desk when her phone rang...it was Captain Carlisle and he wanted a full report on the day's investigation. It took her almost forty-five minutes, and along with his questioning, another half-hour. After he hung up, she got up and left for home, a very tired, and worn out detective.

Chapter 15

Bish was sitting on the front porch of his cabin, leaning back on his left arm, sipping a hot cup of coffee out of his right hand. All was quiet on his little piece of paradise. The Jeep was backed into its usual place, completely unseen by any prying eyes or drones. Not that he cared. If someone saw, then they saw. He would live with it.

He tossed what was left of the cold coffee in his mug, set it on the porch, and picked up his Bible. It was his way of owning up to what it said in the first half of Psalm forty-six, verse ten, where it says, "Be still and know that I am God." He enjoyed sitting outdoors and reading the Bible. He did feel closer to God when he did this. He fondly opened his Bible, a New International Version (NIV) and turned to Psalm thirty-seven, verse seven, and read, "Be still before the Lord and wait patiently for Him; do no fret when men succeed in their ways, when they carry out their wicked schemes." Be still. One must be still to read the Bible and then will want to be still just to try to comprehend the magnitude of what is written within.

He always thought the Bible had great advice. He frequently recommended folks read it as even if they had hard hearts, they would at least know how to live their lives since the book had so much good advice. Lessons on manners, law, sex, marriage, sin, investing and money matters, family matters, taking care of children, widows and orphans. It even has advice on how to take care of the earth.

He had come to the cabin for some alone time with God. He needed answers and wanted to have some private conversations with the creator of all. He loved knowing he had a direct line to the most powerful person, Jesus, in the Universe. All he had to do was think it, feel it, or say it aloud and Jesus would receive the message. Answers…well, they came as they did in God's own time and way, which he felt he would never understand. He was even a bit unclear about how the Holy Spirit fit into the picture, having the power to relay to Jesus the proper information even when Bish himself had no idea how to put it – that was a real head scratcher. Together, those three, God the Father, God the Son, and God the Holy Spirit, had a real thing going for their love of mankind – all of mankind, not just Jews or Christians, everybody.

Bish's philosophy was simple – his faith in Jesus produced obedience to God. He learned quickly after becoming a Christian, that some of what his life was, could never be again. He stopped barhopping, gazing at pornography, stopped cursing almost completely (he still fractured that concept now and then), and looked at life and what he did in a completely different light. Before actually becoming a Christian, he'd opened a Bible maybe four or five times. Now, every day brought a Bible reading, even if just a few verses somewhere. He had Bibles all over his house and a few in the cabin. His phone had two Bible apps. He felt a kind of emptiness if he didn't have a Bible within arm's reach.

He enjoyed reading the many Psalms, and every July, he read the book of Proverbs as it has thirty-one chapters, one per day in July. Why July…it was his birth month. And Proverbs was a great book to understand daily life. It was just as up-to-date in the twenty-first century as it was when it was put together sometime between 700 to 650 B.C.. The book had been around almost three thousand years and was still current. Wow.

Sitting on the porch, he remembered the other thing in the Bible that genuinely perplexed him - that being the love that God and Jesus showed for us. Bish was convinced that Jesus was born of the virgin Mary, that the Lord had impregnated her through the Holy Spirit. He believed Joseph forgave her after his encounter with an angel in a dream, and wondered why magi would travel for months to see this child, knowing He was a King of some kind. How did they know that? The other thing that Bish felt sincerely about was the fact that Jesus was treated horribly by His own people, suffered through a scourging, had to carry His own cross, and was then crucified on it and died. And on the third day of His death, Jesus rose from the dead, and there were hundreds of witnesses to that fact.

That a man, sinless - albeit God on earth - went willingly to the cross to atone for our sins, was just about unbelievable for Bish. And he sadly shook his head knowing that millions of people will have hard hearts and not accept who Jesus was, is, and always will be.

When asked, Bish would tell folks that Jesus was his Best Friend, his Mentor, his Savior, and his King. Most would shake their heads and say he was wasting his time with all that religious stuff. Bish would always tell them he would continue to pray for them and ask that God soften their hearts so they would understand. But he knew that literally billions of people would die and go to hell in the end, and that saddened him the most. Billions. He got up, picked up his coffee mug, and with his head down, went inside the cabin to make his dinner.

*****

Anita and Connie had stopped by Kentucky Fried on the way home and picked up a half-bucket of extra crispy and a salad. That was their fare for the evening along with a rum-n-coke. Connie said a prayer and they begin to eat their dinner.

"Connie, tell me your story…how did you become a Christian?" Anita asked between bites.

"My mom and dad," she began. "Dad was a Deacon at our church. We read the Bible every day. I think that's how I learned to read, not with a primer but with the Bible reading Psalms, Proverbs, and the Gospels. Mom would kneel with us at night and say our prayers before we went to bed. I was eight years old and we were at Vacation Bible School that summer when I realized who Jesus really was and what He really meant to me. I remember the moment vividly and how I felt. It was peace and goodness. I went and told my counselor and together we prayed and that's the moment. We walked together to the lakeshore, collecting friends and other camp staff along the way, and clothes and all went into the water and I was baptized. It was a great day.

"When I got home from camp and told mom and dad, they prayed with me, thanking God for my understanding and acceptance of Jesus."

"That's a good story, I like it," Anita said. "What was the most amazing thing for you, about Christianity that is?"

"Oh, that's easy," Connie said. "It's the fact that Jesus always has been, is now, and always will be God the Son. That freaks me out some."

"Why's that?" Anita asked.

"Just think about that – was, is, and always will be! He's forever…forever has been and forever will be. He's alive right now sitting to God's right. It's just incomprehensible to think about sometimes. Sadly, it gives me a headache if I think too long on it."

"I know just what you mean," Anita said earnestly. "I go blank thinking about it sometimes. My mind just seems to go 'blue screen' if you know what I mean. I guess that's part of the faith we have to have in Christ, to think about it and live with it even though we do not understand fully. I feel that's the way God wants it. We're not meant to understand fully, just know, and accept Jesus for who He is, and was, and will be."

"I couldn't have put it any better," Connie said, understanding. "My mind's racing right now. Probably won't get a wink of sleep. I'll blame it on you."

They both laughed.

✶✶✶✶✶

Patrolman Arceneaux almost jumped out of his skin when the cell phone he was processing rang. He actually sprang up out of his chair and looked wide-eyed at the thing as it rang and vibrated on his work area.

Detective Michael Norman yelled, "Malcolm, you know you're not supposed to have a phone in here!"

"Not mine, boss, it's the one we took from those two dudes at Perkins," Malcolm explained still standing and staring at the ringing phone.

Norman came flying over and stood staring also. The two stood there mesmerized by the device. Finally, Malcolm asked, "Should we answer it?"

The two cops looked at each other and both shrugged their shoulders. Malcolm, gloved, picked the device up, and saw on the display 'unknown'. He hit the answer button and said, "Hello."

A moment of silence, then a dial tone came across the speaker. Malcolm held it to Michael's ear for a second then hung up.

"There was a silent pause when I said 'hello'," Malcolm told Michael. "You think our people could trace the call anyway even though it said 'unknown'?"

"No need, this is obviously a burner phone so chances are the other one was also and is already being destroyed," Michael said. "I'm sure whoever that was knows the owner of this phone is not around anymore. I'm going to go see the captain, be back shortly," and with that left their lab.

On the way to the captain's office, Norman called Anita and told her to meet him there. They arrived at the same time and she asked, "What's up, Michael?"

He pointed towards the captain's office and Tabitha waved him on in. "Captain, Anita, we just had an interesting happening down in the lab. Malcolm was processing the cell phone from those two dudes at Perkins, when it rang - scared the poor kid outta his skin almost. Anyway, Malcolm answered it and said 'hello'. He said there was a moment of silence, and then a dial tone popped in. I think the cat's outta the bag on the two we arrested. Whoever that was knows that something has happened to those two."

Anita immediately said, "I agree. Any other news from the lab…DNA or something?"

"No DNA results as yet, but blood types match the blood found at the Dalton/Smith murder scene," Michael explained. "That's not enough for court, but is a great start. We've put a hustle up order on the DNA evidence with the Department of Criminal Investigation (DCI) folks and they're working as fast as they can."

Captain Carlisle chimed in with, "I'll call the chief, and ask that they be granted emergency overtime funds. Maybe they can go to a twenty-four hour shift on it until the results are in. I'm very interested in those findings. If the DNA matches, those two will never see the light of day again, and whatever judge has them, I'll fight for the death penalty. They killed cops after all."

"We're with you on the death penalty, Cap," Anita said agreeing. "So, what are we to assume about the phone?"

Michael answered, "Not much. The display said 'unknown' and the phone we have is a burner phone so I'm betting the other one was too, and is probably already destroyed. The thing I'm happy about is we now know there is at least a third party out there."

Anita and the captain's heads popped up at that realization. At least three, maybe more, was the unsaid though going through their minds.

"What about finger prints lifted from the vehicle?" the captain asked Michael.

"All were from the two, save two, and those were a forefinger and a middle finger from someone else," Michael answered. "I have one of my guys going over to the rental agency to print everyone that might have had contact with that car to rule them out. I'll know for sure by tomorrow afternoon."

"Good," the captain said. "You and Malcolm keep up the good work and send me the photos of the two and the vehicle as soon as you can. I want to go over them with a fine-toothed comb."

"Send 'em to me, too," Anita requested.

"Okay to both of you when I have 'em ready…should be in a couple of hours," Michael said.

"Good work Norman and tell that kid the same from me," the captain said, ending the short meeting.

Anita and Michael left together and nodded to each other as they went their separate ways. Anita, upon returning to the squad room, briefed her team on the short meeting with the captain and Michael. "As soon as those pictures get here, I'll send 'em to all of you and we'll go over them. I want you to go over them with detail in mind like before. Look at the little things. Something may be out of the ordinary and lead us to the third person." She sat at her desk and called Mike and Pete and updated them. Now it was a waiting game for the DNA results.

Chapter 16

Roberto Salinas stepped out of his shower and began to dry off. He was getting ready to go out to eat a nice dinner. As he dried off, he had a feeling he was being watched and turned. There in the doorway stood Chogan Black Cloud.

"I've told you not to do that, sneaking up on me like that," Salinas said with ire. "Someday you just might get shot doing that."

"Forgive me, but we had an issue in Wyoming," Chogan said as a way to defuse the situation.

"What has happened?" Salinas asked.

"Renaldo called…his two assistants have been arrested by the police and are being held for suspicion of murder. The rental car they had has been impounded also."

Salinas stood there, the towel draped around his waist, in deep thought. "They do not know who I am, or you if I am not mistaken."

"That is correct, el Jefe," Chogan assured.

"Call Renaldo and tell him to stay in Wheatland until further notice, that we," he indicated waving his finger between Chogan and himself, "will provide another pair of assistants. Tell him not to worry about the other two…they are a lost cause."

"Right away, el Jefe," Chogan said and turned to do as commanded.

"Chogan…"

"Yes, sir…"

"Make sure the two new men are competent and will comply with orders."

Chogan nodded his head and went to make the call.

Salinas finished drying and went into his bedroom to get dressed for his dinner. When he was dressed, he went into his den and pressed a button on a console near his desk. That sent a signal to the employee area, which said, bring his car around.

Two minutes later, Salinas was helped into the Toyota *Land Cruiser*, buckled himself in while the driver got in, and he gave the signal to go. The driver already knew the place to go and knew the safest route to the establishment, which took twenty minutes to reach. Salinas told him to return in two hours promptly and got out.

The Maître d'hôtel smiled broadly when Salinas entered and said, "Welcome back, sir…please allow me to escort you to your table," while taking Salinas' overcoat. He handed the coat to a server and led Salinas to a corner booth, the one he always sat in for his dining experience. The Maître d' straightened a few things on the table and brushed an imaginary piece of lint from the tablecloth, ensuring the cleanliness of the setting, and ensuring everything was presentable.

"I'll send the head server right away, will you be having a beverage prior to dinner this evening?" the Maître d' asked.

"Yes, I would enjoy several fingers of eighteen year old Dalmore please, neat," Salinas responded with a smile.

"Right away, sir, and if I may be so bold, our pan-seared, butter-roasted, thick-cut steak is splendid tonight," he explained to Salinas.

"I always take your advice Samuel…please tell the chef to make mine a center cut, and medium rare, with those small baked potatoes he prepares and a salad with Italian dressing."

"Right away, sir," Samuel said with a smile and left.

The head server brought Salinas his before dinner cocktail and asked if there would be anything else he might require. Salinas thanked him for the scotch and said nothing else for the moment.

Salinas turned in the booth and looked out over the expanse of the Denver metropolitan district in the distance, the skyline lit up brilliantly. The restaurant was located on the west side of Denver, set on a ridge along the face of the Rocky Mountains, and had a spectacular view of the mile high city. He sat quietly, sipping his scotch and enjoying the view.

His cocktail at an appropriate level, the head server appeared and asked Salinas if he would like a refill.

"Not this evening, but I would like a bottle of the *Caymus Cabernet Sauvignon* from Napa Valley with dinner, please."

"We have an excellent 2002 vintage I recommend."

"That will be fine."

The sever turned and first, told the chef to prepare Salinas' dinner, then left for the wine cellar, returning with the seven-hundred dollar bottle of wine, used an air pressure wine bottle opener to pop the cork, then set the bottle into a bucket of ice since this type needed to be served at or near sixty degrees Fahrenheit. He slowly rotated the bottle in the ice to allow cooling of the bottle. Their cellar was kept at a strict sixty-two degrees Fahrenheit, so it would not take long to reduce the wine's chill to at or near the sixty degrees recommended.

Salinas had finished his scotch, and sipped water from his glass to ease the after taste. He was still watching the Denver skyline and marveled at the number of aircraft lifting off and landing at the Denver International Airport (DIA). From where he sat the airport was some thirty to thirty-five miles distant. A clear sky that evening made for unobstructed observing of the aircraft action at the airport.

He was pleasantly surprised when the server gave a quiet 'ahem' and offered the wine cork to him. Salinas took it, gave it a sniff, and smiled. Napa Valley wines were among his favorites and he knew them well. He smiled and nodded at the server and the man poured less than an ounce into a wine glass and handed it to Salinas, who swirled the wine around the hand-made Riedel wine glass, held it to his nose and with his mouth open, inhaled the aroma.

His smile told the server all he wanted to know and held his hand out for the glass, filling it with almost exactly three ounces of wine. He handed the glass to Salinas, set the bottle in the bucket of ice, and asked, "Shall I serve dinner now, sir?"

"That will be fine, yes," Salinas said with a smile. He picked up the glass and sipped his wine...excellent.

The meal was just to his liking and taste. The chef knew how to make the steak taste like it had only a hint of butter and garlic, and the potatoes were excellently made. The chef had added baked carrot spears, which he knew Salinas enjoyed, and topped it off with a nice house salad.

Salinas enjoyed his thousand-dollar meal and his seven-hundred dollar wine. He relished the fact that he had the money to splurge like he was. His inherited businesses were doing him well. He had made a pact with himself that he would never get involved with human trafficking as that is what brought his father down. He, on the other hand, would stay with smuggling non-human cargo, drugs, and black market art works and antiquities. His biggest score was a painting he had acquired, sold for just over seventy million dollars at auction.

Knowing he was set for life, he still enjoyed the thrill and adventure of procuring merchandise and selling it for much more than it was worth, or as much as he could get. And because of that, he could binge like he was and eat a very expensive meal whenever he chose to do so. His meal this evening would run well over two-thousand dollars and he didn't mind at all.

*****

The next day, Salinas and Chogan had breakfast together and discussed what may have happened in Cheyenne. Conjecture was all they had at this point, but they would find out very soon. They would await the news about their two men, figuring the news would surely be out soon. Especially if the police had a significant amount of evidence to process.

"Out of all I have come up with to reason why they were arrested is the rental car," Chogan told his employer. "My contact had called and warned me, but too late I'm afraid. A big, flashy car like a Cadillac *Escalade* could be another reason. Why? Easily recognizable and traced. Perhaps if they had rented an old clunker of some sort, they may have fared better."

"That may very well be the reason," Salinas agreed with his man. "I will inform Renaldo that he will refrain from renting expensive vehicles for surveillance and such. The next time you speak with your contact, give them my thanks. Next order of business – have you found two suitable replacements?"

"Yes, el Jefe, they are on their way to Denver as we speak. I will meet them when they arrive and brief them while driving them to Cheyenne. I'm taking a personal interest in this venture now, and Renaldo will be taking a back seat. There will be no more mistakes, el Jefe."

"Very good; I like your style, Chogan. You have my blessing and please, have them continue to record the…events…for me. I do enjoy a good movie from time to time."

"It will be done as you say, el Jefe."

"Have you spoken with Renaldo?"

"Yes I have, and he is in Wheatland as directed. He did rent a blue Volkswagen Beetle for the job. People do not give them a second thought. I directed he be much more cautious with his movements, if any, and not to go out every day. I will have the two new men rent vehicles also, that way they will have three to work with. I believe this will cut down on their chances of being picked up. We must attempt to be very discrete."

"Absolutely. Discretion is what we want and need. They, and you, must be very cautious. The police must be very observant just now since we have taken six of their officers down. I am sure that is why Renaldo's men were captured. The whole of Laramie County must be on high alert," Salinas said with an evil grin.

Chogan did not add anything after that just continued his meal and keeping a cautious eye on Salinas.

✱✱✱✱✱

Bish pulled into the driveway at the house, climbed out and began unloading the Jeep. He was happy he'd gone to the cabin and wound down. He was tense, and worried about Anita. Six of his friends on the force had died in the last year, and now, with the capture of the two guys that were tailing the captain, he felt just a little better. The break at the cabin was at just the right time. His studies through the Bible helped immensely and he was significantly more relaxed than he'd been before his outing.

After unloading the Jeep, cleaning his equipment, and putting it away, he went inside and began putting his soiled clothing into the wash. By the time he was finished with that it, was close enough to lunch time that he cleaned up and made a sandwich to eat. He was sitting on the back porch eating when his cell phone rang.

"Hey, babe, I'm back," he told Anita.

"You okay?" she probed.

"Good to go…you got something for me?" he asked.

"Yeah, it's a boring assignment, but I figure while you do it you could do some research or something on your book at the same time."

"I could do that."

"You don't know what it is yet."

"I trust you and I'm bored to tears. What have you got?"

"Car watching and counting."

After a pause, "Come again…"

"Car watching and counting…what I mean is, watch, and count cars going by the department building on the north and south sides. You don't have to count our squad cars, just civilian traffic. You'll have a bank of four screens here in the squad room, a desk with plenty of room so you can do research and such on your book. I'll even get you a comfortable chair."

"When do I start?"

"Tomorrow good enough…I figure you need to recoup today."

"I'll follow you and Connie in. Sounds like an interesting and boring job, but I'm in. Already figure I can do the night counting first thing the next morning - can't be that much traffic in the evenings and nights. Uh, anything specific I'm watching or counting?"

"Every vehicle that goes by, then watch specifically for those vehicles that pass by regularly and/or frequently. Those we'll want to put a tag on and watch closer."

"Ah, I get it. Okay, sounds easy enough and I get a bonus since I get to be around you much more. I'm in."

"Good, I'll get the chief to put you on the part-time payroll and get you paid for this."

"Ohh, I get money, too?"

"I'll try my best, darlin."

"What do you two want for dinner tonight?"

"Can you make that maple, garlic chicken dish on rice, with peas?"

"I can smell it cooking already…sure thing, babe."

"See you later then…love you."

"Love you, too, bye."

Now that Bish had his work cut out for him, he finished his lunch and began making sure he had all the ingredients for dinner.

Chapter 17

It had been almost a month since Bish began counting cars. Everyone in the squad room was tired of him calling out 'blue bug' or 'red bug' or such as a Volkswagen went by. Another blue bug went by and when he turned to say it, he saw the looks he was getting and relented and kept quiet. He turned and noted the date, time, and direction the blue bug went; he then sorted his data on the Excel program and noted a blue bug going by five times in the last three weeks, almost at the same time and traveling in the same direction.

"Anita, get over here," he almost yelled. Anita quickly moved over to his desk as did several of the detectives, to look over his shoulder.

"What have you got, kid," Anita queried.

"Take a look at this," he said pointing at the computer with the Excel program. "This stands out don't you think?"

She leaned in closer to look at the data and slowly said, "Yes…yes it does. Have you got a shot with the license plate?"

Bish moved the cursor to another Excel sheet and said, "Yeah, I got it and I put it on this sheet. All of 'em I get are on here," he said, pointing again.

Anita grabbed his pen and the note pad he had, wrote the plate number down along with the dates and times the bug had passed police headquarters.

She ripped the page off the pad and said, "I'll be back soon," and left the squad room.

She went straight to the captain's office and when Tabitha saw her, picked up her phone, and informed the captain. "He said to go right in."

Anita opened the door and went in, and closed the door, saying, "Captain, you gotta see this. You know Bish has been counting cars for us..." He acknowledged with a nod. "Well, he got this today," showing him her notepaper.

After he'd looked at the sheet for several moments, he looked up at her and said, "Get a tail on this as soon as you can. You have an address yet?"

"No, sir, Pete is running the plate as we speak," she explained. "I figured you needed to see this as soon as possible as this might be our third party."

"I agree," the captain told her. "You know what to do – go do it."

"On it Cap," and she left his office.

When she got back to the office, Peter was waiting.

"It's another rental of all things," he told her. "Mike's on his way over to the agency with Andy, to get the paperwork and a copy of the surveillance camera video. Maybe we'll get lucky again."

"I don't think this is luck – its good investigative police work," Anita told him.

"That's right," Bish agreed.

Pete looked at him and smiled. "I suppose it is. Anyway, we're gonna get this person. We're gonna find that bug just like the Caddy and close this up for good."

The other two they had arrested with the Cadillac, were never going to see daylight again. The DNA evidence placed them at two of the murder scenes, the first and third. They were now under suicide watch with both a CPD patrolman and a county Sheriff's Department deputy watching the two. All of the Laramie County law enforcement (LE) officers wanted to kill the two, so they were under dual agency protection.

Every LE in the county as well as Albany County to the west, knew what those two had done to Nate and Trudy, not to mention what they'd done to Tim and Willie in Cheyenne. It was already a miracle the two were still breathing. The parents of Trudy begged the chief for the death penalty as did everyone else in the state. When the two were arraigned in court, they wore helmets and Kevlar vests for their protection as they moved from the police van to the courthouse under intense guard.

It was still a mystery if the two had had anything to do with Kevin and Barbara Lindsey's shooting deaths. No evidence could be found for those two murders save the bullet fragments - nothing. That investigation with the Albany County Sheriff's office continued, but still no evidence had been detected.

Everyone in the squad room knew the two would get the death penalty. There was no doubt with the amount of evidence they had on the two. They would at least get several life sentences without the possibility of parole each and be put in the darkest recesses of Rawlins, never to see sunlight again. That is what they all wanted – for the pair to suffer. And if the pair did get the death penalty, the state would make a fortune selling tickets for the execution.

Now they had the blue bug. Bish was the hero again having found the blue bug's habits troublesome. They now had a photo of the guy who had rented the bug, another fictitious name, and address. Every law enforcement officer, city, county, and state, was now looking for this blue bug. It would be a force bent for revenge when they found it. When the call came, it was believed every cop in Wyoming would respond, just to get a chance to shoot the guy.

The chief, however, had other plans and had given strict orders the guy was to be taken alive unless absolutely necessary to use force to protect oneself. To most of the old timers that meant to goad the guy into doing something stupid so they would have a green light to shoot.

The 1969 Chevrolet *Camaro RS/SS350*, painted in Daytona Yellow with black front to back racing stripes, slowly rumbled by the CPD heading west. It turned left on O'Neil Avenue, and then took another left onto West 18th Street. It went over the viaduct and turned west onto I-80, then at the I-25 interchange, turned northward.

Chogan was heading to Wheatland to have a meeting with his two new men and Renaldo. The drive north lasted a bit over an hour and Chogan pulled into the driveway just before dinnertime. He got out of the car and went inside without knocking.

Renaldo jumped up when the door opened, but upon recognizing Chogan, leaned on the kitchen table. As Chogan walked up to the three, everyone stood and shook hands with him.

"Have a seat everyone," Chogan began. "What's for dinner?"

One of the other two men said, "Pizza and wings being delivered soon, you came at the right time."

"Seems so," Chogan said with a smile. "We need to discuss a few things tonight, but will wait until the pizza arrives. Renaldo, I am truly sorry your men were arrested. I drove by the Cheyenne Police Department and there was a noticeable amount of officers loitering about the building. You suppose they have increased security or is that a normal observation?"

Renaldo thought for a moment before answering. "No, that is not normal. The three of us had been by there many times photographing the place and I have never seen any police outside unless they were getting into a vehicle. I agree with you – they are beefing up security."

"That is distressing," Chogan said looking at his feet and thinking. "I was hoping we might be able to get our men out, but now I do not think so."

One of the other two men said, "Way to dangerous. Perhaps we could hit them when they move them somewhere."

"We would have to rely on our inside contact for that kind of information," Chogan mused. "However, they just may be anticipating that kind of a move and may feed false information to see if they can detect our source. That would be very dangerous," he said, going quiet and thinking.

The doorbell rang and one of the men got up and went to the door. The pizza and wings had arrived. When he returned to the table with their dinner, Chogan was still looking at the floor in deep thought.

Renaldo got up and returned with plates, knives, forks, and a roll of paper towels. He set plates and utensils in front of everyone and said, "Dig in, gentlemen."

The three pulled slices of pizza and took a few wings each. Chogan remained still, staring at the floor deep in thought.

"Chogan…Chogan, dinner has arrived," Renaldo said to him.

He looked up and smiled and said, "So it has. Good, let's eat and he pulled a slice of pizza out of the box.

✶✶✶✶✶

While Chogan and his men were eating, Bish was serving his slow cooker honey glazed pork roast, with asparagus spears, green beans, and tomato wedges. They were drinking sweet tea.

"No luck on finding the blue bug yet?" Bish asked Anita.

"No, and that disturbs me," she answered. "Every agency has been looking and nothing. We're wondering if they guy has left, or maybe the car is parked in a garage somewhere…we just don't know. But every agency is looking."

"I haven't seen it go by again at the station," Bish said. "I did see a really cool Camaro go by the other day. It was yellow with black stripes, a great looking car."

"What year do you suppose?" Anita asked.

"Must have been a '69 or '70 I'd say," he answered. "It had that muscle car look, nice tires with mag wheels, back end jacked up some…just looked like it could take off and leave you behind in a flash."

"What's a mag wheel?" Connie asked.

"Chrome-spoked wheels we mounted our tires on in the old days," Bish told her. "They made our cars look far out."

"Far out…?" Connie said looking at Bish with a look of consternation.

"He means really cool, Connie," Anita said with a smile.

Bish started laughing and Anita followed suit.

"What…what'd I say?" Connie asked.

"Nothing, dear, it's just we're realizing we're getting older since the younger generation doesn't understand the language we used when we were young.

"So, what does 'far out' mean?" she asked.

"It means really good or very excellent," Anita explained.

"Good grief, I need to get a good dictionary so I can understand you guys," Connie said, taking another bite of her dinner.

Bish and Anita laughed again, but quickly settled down and continued eating their meal. It was nice to have company like Connie. The conversations more often than not led to laughter, especially when the difference in ages came to the surface. They had almost died the night Bish went on a rant about 'emoji's' and 'emoticons' and how the kids 'today' use them instead of language or just dialing and talking it out. Connie had actually fallen out of her chair she was laughing so hard. Bish didn't know whether to be embarrassed, angry, or laugh with the two women.

He almost bitterly said that the emoji's were sending the human race back to Egyptian hieroglyphics again, that the written language was soon to be outdated. He even said mankind was heading back to the dark ages and would soon be running around in skins, brandishing clubs and spears. Connie and Anita hurt they were laughing so hard that night.

The three finished their meal and together cleaned the dishes and straightened up the kitchen and dining area. They all three sat with another glass of green tea. Anita and Connie discussed a few of their plans they had the next day, and Bish announced he was going to stay home and write, that he was getting behind on what he wanted to put on paper. He said that one of the 'kids' could look at the screens all day and count cars. Anita and Connie laughed at him.

"What are you writing?" Anita asked him.

"I'm thinking that since I'm an old cop, I might just as well write about cop stuff, a murder mystery. or something, maybe a major heist or kidnapping," he answered. "I have experience with those."

"Boy, I'll say," Anita said.

"How far along are you on your book?" Anita asked.

"I've been doing some research and putting data into a research file in the computer," he explained. "I've begun character development, and since I know cops, I figure I can do a cop character fairly decently. Maybe an international cop of some kind," he said sitting back, thinking.

"I can see it now...*The Adventures of Tom Slick, International Detective Agent*," Anita said using her hands to quote the title. Everyone laughed.

Once the laughter died down, the three sat in their own thoughts. Bish finished his tea and stood, telling the ladies goodnight and giving Anita a kiss. He put his glass in the sink and went upstairs to their room. He indeed did have ideas for a book, and his mind was racing with ideas and thoughts. It took him a while to get to sleep.

Chapter 18

Anita and Connie left promptly at 0630 hours, after having a splendid breakfast made by Bish. He watched as they left the house and drove off. He got his AR-15 and nine millimeter, another cup of coffee, filling a thermos with the remainder of the pot, and ran up the stairs to get started on some of the ideas he had bouncing around in his head for his book.

In his library, he fired up his computer after sitting down. The particular computer he was using had never been hooked up to the internet, so it had never been infected with anything. He had bought several packages of 'thumb drives' to download his writings both for backup purposes and to use to allow others see what he had written, and those for others to see, were kept in an envelope. He had never shared anything with anyone as yet.

He brought up his *Microsoft Word* program and opened his notes for his book, and began typing furiously, setting thoughts to paper as it were. Idea after idea flew from his mind onto the virtual page. He paused long enough to sip some of his coffee then began typing once again. After almost an hour of 'mashing keys' as he called it, he stopped, sat back and looked over some of what he'd written, then got up and left his library. He had made a promise to himself that he would write for an hour, then get up and walk around for a while to get the blood circulation in his legs flowing again.

His doctor had explained that if he didn't do that, his legs would swell from too much fluid and he would begin to have problems. He had called the condition 'venous insufficiency' and told Bish the way to combat it was to move around, use a foot stool to rest his feet upon while sitting for long periods, and to drink plenty of water. Coffee was not advised, although Bish did drink coffee when he first started then switched to copious amounts of water afterwards.

So, he was up walking around the house to get the blood flow moving. He went downstairs to the kitchen, and filled his *Hydro Flask* with ice and water. Afterwards, he ran back up the stairs and stopped at the top, taking several deep breaths and doing several deep knee bends. He figured he was ready to sit and write again.

Just as he was about to sit, he looked out the window, his eyes picking up movement. He could see a yellow, 1969 Chevy Camaro pass in front of his home going east to west. He dropped to his knees, crawled over, and got his rifle and cell phone, quickly calling Anita and telling her what had happened.

"It had to be the one I saw at the station, babe," he told her.

"Are you safe?" she asked.

"Yeah, upstairs in the library with all my weapons," he answered.

"Stay there, we're on our way," she told him and abruptly hung up.

Bish checked his rifle and handgun, ensuring both were loaded and ready to fire. He moved over to the window and risked another look. He saw no vehicles. He moved back to the desk, leaned his rifle next to his chair after sitting, and made a few notes in the computer. He switched to the *Word* program and continued his writing for another minute and a half, when he heard the sirens coming. Hearing the screeching of the tires out front, he stood and with his rifle, went downstairs to welcome his detective wife home.

By the time he got downstairs to the front door, four cars had arrived, and nine officers were standing around watching for the yellow Camaro. Bish opened the door and Anita was standing there.

"You guys are fast," he said with a smile.

She gave him the look and with her hand and arm outstretched, pushed him back into the house. "You said the car was going east to west…?"

"Yes, ma'am," he answered.

Anita used her radio and ordered three of the five cars to go west and canvas the area and to take no chances with the vehicle, ordering them to call for backup immediately upon finding the Chevy.

Looking at Bish, she asked, "How much writing did you get done?"

"A bit, why?"

"Just wondering, what are you writing about?"

"Cops and robbers…you know the usual."

He got the look again.

"Chill out, babe," he said, smiling.

She just looked at him again and said, "I'm going now. I'm leaving Peter here with you until his shift ends. Connie and I'll take over then."

"Yes, oh maternal one, that's fine with me."

She smacked him on the chest with the back of her hand and said, "Behave."

Bish smiled and leaning over and gave her a kiss on the cheek.

"That's cheating, you know," she said, eyeing him with a demure look.

"Yes, it is," he answered with his own demure look.

"I gotta go back to work," she said, giving him a peck on the lips. "I'll see you tonight. Keep Pete happy."

"Yeah, right…what do you want for dinner?" he asked.

"Something spicy," she said, eyeing him.

"Tacos and wings it is," he said, giving her another kiss and backing into the house so she could close the door.

She did that, gave him a little wave, and turned for her SUV, where Connie waited. She got into her SUV, stuck her arm out of the window, and gave Bish another wave and he followed suit. All of the police cruisers left save one.

Bish closed and locked the door and turned to find Pete staring at him. "What?" Bish asked.

"Nothing, just that you two looked like you needed to go get a room somewhere, that's all," Pete said with a sly grin.

"I have a gun you know," Bish said jokingly. "Want some sweet tea?"

"Yes to the tea, and I have one, too," Pete said, patting his sidearm. "What are we doing today?"

"I'm writing…I don't know what you'll be doing except what Anita told you to do," Bish answered. "I suppose you could look out the windows down here and keep watch. That's what I'd do." Bish handed Pete a glass of iced tea.

"Thanks," Pete said taking a sip, then, "May I see your library? I've heard Anita talk about it and have wondered what it looked like."

Bish have him a quick, questioning look and said, "Sure, come on, I'll show you." With that, the two took to the stairs.

Bish waved Peter into his sanctum and said, "Look but don't touch."

"Spoil sport. Man, this is nice. I like the way you have the desk fronting to the window. I bet you stare out there a lot. This is really nice. Is it quiet?"

"Yep, fairly, until I turn on the music. Quiet enough for me."

Pete did a walk around of the room, pausing here and there to view a book or one of the many knick-knacks Bish had on the shelves. Small aircraft, small Indian pottery, several fossils Bish had found on his outings, and odd-looking rock or two, some foreign currency and coinage, a small pyramid copied from the Aztecs, and a few military looking bullets. Pete stayed longer at the shelf full of Bish's family photos.

"Your dad was in the Air Force?"

"Yeah, he was what they called a Chief Master Sergeant. The "Top Dog" in the Air Force enlisted corps. He retired with thirty-three years of service outta Warren."

"Wow…he still alive?"

"No, he got called home to the Lord in twelve from a stroke. I still miss him."

"I bet. I miss my father, too. I miss being able to call him for advice or just to man talk, you know."

"Yeah, I feel the same way, buddy. Dad always had good advice for me and I miss that, too."

"You have a swell set up here, Bish, thanks for letting me see it," Peter said as he turned for the door and stairwell. "I'll be down here watching."

"Thanks, Pete," Bish acknowledged. "What kind of music do you like?"

"Classics, country-n-western, rock…just about anything," Pete answered.

Bish put on some smooth jazz by Jeff Lorber. It was good to write with and Bish enjoyed it. When the music started, Bish pulled his keyboard towards him after sitting down and began typing. He began with the setting of his book, which was in Wyoming.

He was still typing and Mozart was playing when Anita and Connie got home. Pete looked at Anita, and pointing upstairs said, "He's been typing ever since you left. I'll see you tomorrow. Night, ladies," and with that he was out the door.

Anita looked at Connie and said, "Wonder what he's typing?"

Connie shrugged her shoulders and said, "I do too. We left almost five hours ago," she said with wonder written on her face.

"I going up to check on him, you stay here," Anita said and turned for the stairs.

She stood in the doorway to Bish's library and watched her man typing away. She was startled at how fast his fingers flew over the keyboard, not realizing how fast he could type. When she saw him pause for a moment, she knocked on the wall.

Bish jumped, startled, and looked back at her.

"Sorry, Bish, I didn't mean to startle you," she apologized.

"No problem, what're you doing back so soon?" he asked.

"Bish, it's almost six…Pete said you'd been at it for almost five hours. Need a break?"

"Yeah, I gotta hit the head and I need something to drink. Crap, I forgot to start dinner," he said to her with the deer-in-the-headlights look, shoulders drooping.

"We'll call out or go do a takeout somewhere," she said. "What are you in the mood for?"

"Chinese or Mexican sound good. I'll let you and Connie decide the fare. 'Scuse me, I'm heading for the john," but leaned over and gave her a kiss as he went by.

Anita called downstairs, "Connie…"

"Yeah?" Connie answered.

"Chinese or Mexican?"

"Chinese."

"Okay, call it in. Bish wants sesame chicken and I want Moo Goo Gai Pan Chicken, spicy, and get a side Pu-Pu Platter, too, please."

"Calling now," Connie called up.

Bish had come back from the john and was saving his last entry when Anita placed her hand on his shoulder and asked, "What were you writing?"

"The book…I'm done with the research and stuff and I'm putting it on paper so-to-speak now. I can't believe I was going for five hours. Time just slipped by. I'm gonna get a wind up clock and set it at an hour so I don't sit like that too long. And so I'll stop and make dinner," he said looking at her and smiling.

"Five hours' worth must make for an exciting opening, may I read it?"

"Not 'till it's done…not 'till it's done."

"That's not fair."

"Sure it is, don't want to spoil it for you."

"Just let me read the first chapter, how about that?"

"I'll think on it and let you know. Anyway, like I said, this is mostly background and scene development, you know, where it takes place, developing the characters…that kind of stuff…boring for right now."

"How far did you get?"

"I had just begun development of chapter six when you got me. Probably won't remember anything but that tomorrow."

She gave him a lover's tap on the arm and said, "Yeah, right, I'll bet you keep right on going tomorrow. I have one of those clocks if you really want one."

"I do, please. It should help me not get so focused that I lose track of time again. I can't afford to get the venous insufficiency the doc talked about. I gotta get up and move around."

"Well I do agree with that. Come on, let's get some tea and Connie and I'll go get dinner."

"Which is…?"

"Chinese and I told her to order a Pu-Pu Platter."

"Oh, yeah, I like those."

Chapter 19

Bish had thoroughly enjoyed his sesame chicken and his portion of the Pu Pu Platter. "Ahh," he said rubbing his abdomen, "I really like that food. Thank you ladies for cooking, I won't let you down again."

Anita looked at him while putting a forkful of her Moo Goo in her mouth and gave him a sly grin. Connie looked at him and said, in a stern motherly way, "You better not." All three began to laugh at that.

Bish had mixed the ladies some mixed drinks and took another healthy slug of his bourbon and *Seven Up*. "Well," he said scooting his chair back and standing, "I'm going back upstairs and write for a couple more hours. See you two in a while," and with that he turned for the stairway.

"Don't forget to get up in an hour and walk around," Anita yelled at him as he ran up the stairs.

"I won't," he yelled back. He sat at his desk and moved his mouse to reopen the work he'd been doing and began to type once again.

"It looks like you're becoming a writer's widow," Connie observed aloud.

"I hope not," Anita answered. "The way he's going, however, I just may become one. I haven't seen him so focused since he was a cop. I scared him almost to death when we came home. All I did was knock on the door. He was so engrossed in what he was typing into his computer, he had no clue I was there. I had to apologize to him," she ended with a nervous giggle.

"He had no clue, huh?" Connie asked with wide eyes.

"Not a clue," Anita answered.

"You need to talk to him about that," Connie began. "He could miss someone coming into the house and wake up dead, you know."

"Yeah, I'll have a talk with him. He should know better."

"He still on meds?"

"Yeah, but rarely uses them, and perhaps that is a good thing. He doesn't like the way they make him feel, all hung over, you know. He lives with the pain, even though it is getting better every day. We went on a camping trip into the Medicine Bow a while back and he even went on a hike with me. He did very well and didn't complain one bit, even though I saw him grimace a few times when climbing."

"I'm glad he's doing better. He appeared gaunt for so long, I thought he wouldn't make it for a while. We prayed a lot for the two of you."

"Thanks. That's good to hear and I appreciate it. He has improved quite a bit, but he needs time. I still think he's got at least another year or so before he's really back to what he once was."

"You really think so?"

"Yes, I do. I still see him grimace from time-to-time. And, he still drinks a little…shouldn't I suppose, but his doctor says a drink every now and then won't do him any harm. I'm still worried about him though."

"I'll keep him and you for that matter on my prayer list. I'll tell my Bible study folks, too. They'll pray for you guys at least weekly."

"Tell them I very much appreciate the prayer support."

"I certainly will."

"How often do you meet?"

"Weekly on Tuesdays, I don't always make it…work…you know, but I try. And the leader of the group emails prayer requests to all of us. He calls us prayer warriors - I kinda like that. He has a main prayer focus for the week, things like our country, our state, leaders, the church, you know, that kind of stuff, then there are the personal prayer requests from the church and from the folks in our group."

"What are you studying right now?"

"John's Revelation of Jesus Christ, and man, is it tough. I certainly don't understand all of it and he says there are things in the Bible, especially the book of Revelation, we're just not supposed to understand as yet, but will when God says it's the right time."

"Yes, Revelation is a tough one and fearful to a lot of people. I remember studying it some time back, and we learned that it was just what the title portends, a revelation of Jesus Christ. It's about Him, not us, and the gloom-n-doom stuff we read in it. Yes, it is a clear warning for all humankind, especially those that are not yet believers. It was really hard for me to understand that so many billions of people will be hard-hearted and turn from Christ, actually will reject Him. I just cannot wrap my head around that. I pray for them a lot."

"I do, too! I can't believe that either. So many lost, even after so many eye-opening plagues and disasters and they will still refuse Him. It's going to be so sad for a time. What do you think about the rapture?"

"Ah, a subject that many disagree upon…I hope it's pretribulation. I really do not want to be around to go through everything God is going to do during that time. But, there are so many good arguments for the three main thoughts on the rapture – pretribulation, mid tribulation, or post tribulation – I just pray it's before it all begins. But, if we have to live through it then so be it. We'll just have to make do and rely on our faith, and with that, face what comes."

"I certainly agree with you and I too, hope it's a pretribulation rapture of the Church. Our Bible study leader pointed out that the word church is used a lot in the first three chapters of Revelation, but not at all afterwards. He said that might mean the church won't be around during the tribulation."

"Yes, I've heard that point before. What version of the Bible do you use in your group?"

"The *New International Version* and I like it a lot. It's easy to understand. Our group leader is thinking about changing to the *New American Standard Bible* version. I went ahead and bought one and it too, is written in today's language and easy to understand. I like it also."

"I have both of those and enjoy them. I'm glad you like your study group."

"You should go with me some time, you and Bish both. I think you'd like it."

"I'm sure we would. I just might take you up on that some time. Thanks for the invite."

They continued their small talk for another hour, and then broke for their bedrooms. Anita stopped by the library and knocking, told Bish it was bedtime. He saved his document and got up and went to bed with Anita with no arguing.

*****

The following morning, Bish kissed Anita goodbye and gave a little wave to Connie as they left for work. Pete and Mike were walking up the sidewalk to the apartment as the two ladies were leaving.

"Don't let him do anything stupid today," Anita said with a smile.

"We're armed," Mike said smiling.

"We'll keep tabs on him for sure," Pete said as he gave her a hug.

"Hey, no hugging on my woman," Bish yelled from the porch.

"Jealous, huh," Mike threw at him.

"Nah, she's fragile," Bish answered with a snicker.

"I'll give you fragile," Anita yelled back.

"Promises, promises," Bish said with a smile. "Mornin' Mike...Pete...how's it goin'?

"We're here so probably bored silly sooner than later," Mike said.

"Yeah, right…come on in, guys," Bish motioned to them. "I just made a fresh pot of coffee so it should be done in just a few minutes."

"Now you're talkin'," Pete said as he entered the place.

"What's on the agenda today, boss?" Mike asked Bish.

"Me up in the library, writing is all," Bish answered. "We can sit at the table and BS a bit while we have some coffee though. I need to get caught up on all the cop gossip."

"Now that will be boring," Pete said with a laugh.

The three men went into the kitchen, got a mug of coffee, and then sat at the table and began their session, whose been transferred where, which cop has been promoted, who left, whose been hired or fired and why. They talked through three mugs of coffee before Bish said he needed to use the head and go write.

Upstairs, Bish fired up his computer and opened his book document, sat down, and began typing away. He was on a roll, and wanted to keep his focus for the rest of the day.

*****

Arriving at the office, Anita said good morning to her secretary and the rest of the crew. She gave out a few assignments and asked what the rest was doing for the day. She then gave them the daily safety briefing, along with a reminder to be alert and never alone, to not take any chances out there, and to make sure they read the daily-dailies.

At her desk, she no sooner sat down than the captain called and asked her to see him in his office. She got up and went there and was shown in right away. His secretary, Tabitha, was all smiles and happy so Anita figured the meeting was to be routine.

"Anita…how goes it?" Captain Carlisle asked as she sat down.

"Going okay, Cap," she answered. "Bish is a little preoccupied with his writing and that has me a little worried, but otherwise all is good."

"What's he writing?"

"All he's told me is it is a police mystery of some sort. He won't let me read any of it at all. He said I'd have to wait like everyone else."

"How's he feeling these days?"

"I think he's improved a lot. He still has a bit of pain at times – I see him grimace every now and then. He has meds but uses them sparingly. I think he's doing much better, color is good, and he's not looking so gaunt anymore."

"You must be feeding him well then," the captain kidded.

"No, not me, he's the chef around our place. Connie and I just about have to go on a diet he's been feeding us so well. Funny thing though, last night he was supposed to cook and was so engrossed in his writing he lost track of time and forgot to fix dinner. We ordered Chinese instead. I wonder if other writers are like that."

"Absent-minded…I'm sure they are," the captain told her. "I'm glad he's doing better, and please tell him I want a copy of the book, signed, when he's done. I'd like to read it."

"I'll be sure to tell him. So, what brings me down here this morning, Cap?"

The captain sat back in his chair for a moment, thinking, then said, "You know we got the DNA evidence back on those two we have downstairs?"

"Yep."

"That third grouping is a mystery. No history in the data base at all. So for sure there's a third guy out there. Blood type is O-positive and predominantly Hispanic with a little European thrown in the mix. The science types say with DNA certainty that this guy is thirty-five to forty years of age, has black hair, and dark complexion, well fed and healthy. They said he has no medical issues they could discern from the samples so he's not diabetic or anything like that. So, we're looking for one healthy individual."

"Geeze, Cap, you just described a third of Cheyenne," Anita said jokingly.

"Don't I know it," he answered. "But, we have a line on the guy and if we pick up someone, we're going to take DNA from everyone. Maybe we'll get lucky."

"What about those two downstairs…are they talking yet?"

"Not a peep, other than to say 'lawyer' all the time. The DA assigned that Montoya guy as their lawyer. I was there when they gave him his copies of the evidence file. I knew by his expressions that he knows he had a lost cause. Anyway, it strikes me odd that they are afraid. I'm sure their fear comes from whoever had them on the payroll. I'm thinkin' whoever it is has a long reach."

"That makes sense. It tells me whoever it is would get to them in prison, huh."

"Yeah, you're right. I used the name Enrique Salinas in front of both of them and there was no response. They're either well trained or didn't know a Salinas at all."

"I'm sure that case is closed for good."

"Yeah, me too; you got anything except that yellow Camaro running around?"

"No, and I have Mike and Pete staying with Bish for a while. Bish really got my attention when that thing went by our place."

"Me, too - I say keep Mike and Pete with Bish as long as this goes on. Just might be safer for the three of them."

"I'm glad you feel that way. I think I'll switch off with Tony and Steve a few times, just so Bish and all of them get new stories every once in a while."

The captain broke into laughter then, and after a moment said, "Okay, if you don't have anything else I don't either. Let me know if you get anything new or need anything, Anita. Be careful out there."

"Thanks, Cap, we'll be careful, and thanks again for the protection for Bish. I'm sure he appreciates it," Anita said as she stood to leave.

The captain actually stood and held out his hand for her to shake. She did so and the captain, hanging on to her hand said, "Anita, please be careful out there and tell your team to be as well."

"Thanks, Cap, I will."

*****

Back in the detective's office, she briefed everyone on her team what she'd learned from the captain and once again reminded everyone he was concerned for their safety and wanted to remind them to be careful out there. Once she was done, everyone went back to what they were doing and she finally sat at her desk.

*****

At the same moment Anita sat at her desk, Renaldo del Monte drove by the station house in a white Chevy *Impala*. He didn't even look their way, seeing what he wanted as he went by. He and Chogan were planning their next move, an event that was to shock Cheyenne.

Chapter 20

Chogan Black Cloud and Renaldo del Monte were in the white *Impala*, heading south on Interstate Twenty-five to Cheyenne. They exited at the Four Mile Road exit and turned east, coming to the curve to College Drive. They turned west on Lincolnway and then pulled into the Murdoch's Ranch and Home Supply store.

Inside, they placed duct tape, bailing wire, cotton rope, a box of black mechanic's gloves, a battery-powered drill with a box of bits, eye protection and face masks, and two rain suits. The checker took their cash and asked if they were painting something, and Renaldo said they were painting a garage. They took their merchandise and left the store, drove to Dell Range Boulevard and stopped for a late breakfast at Perkins.

While eating, they gave each other knowing looks and very evil grins. Both knew what was going to happen that night. Chogan had brought in two more men that would do exactly as told, no matter how bold or grotesque.

*****

Daniel Flores, Special Agent with the FBI, and his wife of twenty years were to go out for a nice dinner. They would be going to the Little Bear Inn for their anniversary dinner, and then to a well-known hotel in town to a suite he had rented for the weekend. Their son was staying with friends. Neither Flores, nor his wife felt the pin pricks from the darts that injected horse anesthetic into their bodies. Both fell at the door to the garage, unconscious.

Chogan's two men wrapped the two in heavy tarps and carried them to the Chrysler van, and unceremoniously dropped them into the back. They knew the two would be out for at least the next two hours, so didn't bind them. They did, however, search both and took everything from them, including Flores' service sidearm.

They stopped by Perkins and one of the two men reached into Renaldo's *Impala*, retrieving the bag of merchandise bought at Murdoch's. He climbed back into the van and they departed. Chogan pointed and smiled as he watched the two leaving the parking lot. Renaldo looked and too, smiled, then took another bite of his chicken fried steak.

✱✱✱✱✱

Bish, Anita, and Connie had just finished cleaning the evening's dishes and the kitchen and went to sit on the front porch with a glass of sweet tea with lime. The three sat in silence contemplating the evening, watching the birds collect their final tidbits of food for the night. A car drove past and Bish waved as it was a friend from down the lane.

"So, what happened that was interesting at the farm today?" Bish asked the ladies.

Anita said, "The Captain called me in and we talked about the progress of the investigation. Not really anything new. It seems to be a waiting game now. The two we have in custody are not talking and the District Attorney assigned the least experienced guy to their case he could find. He wants them to hang just like everyone else. I watched him read the evidence file and he shook his head the whole time, knowing without a doubt these two were going to hang. The DNA evidence alone is enough to convict."

"I spent a boring day doing your job, watching and counting cars," Connie said giving Bish a sideways glare. "It's better than a sleep aid."

Bish almost spit tea all over everyone when she said that. As it was, he was choking and laughing at the same time with

208

droplets of tea coming out of his nose. He had quickly bent forward trying not to get spit, slobber, and tea all over himself. Both Anita and Connie broke into laughter watching him suffer in his laughter.

The coughing and choking spell over, he wiped his face and nose and said, "I'll get you for that you little…"

"Now, now, you leave her alone," Anita chastised. "She's one of our best and I don't want you messing with her."

"Yeah, you leave me alone or I won't tell you about all the cars I saw today," Anita said with a grin. "You okay?"

"I'll live," Bish said, stifling another coughing spell. "It was funny, wasn't it?"

That brought another round of laughter. The three watched as another car went by, another friend that Anita and Bish both waved to.

The street they lived on was quiet tonight. They talked for a while longer then went inside to play a dice game they all enjoyed.

*****

The sun was still above the horizon as the van pulled off Happy Jack Road onto National Forest Trail 708 heading eastward. Three miles later, they eased down the rough two-track, through a narrow canyon. At the bottom they pulled up next to a large beaver pond. They were now surrounded on three sides by mountain, water, and forest. The only way in or out was the way they'd come in. They had seen no one – no campers, no hikers, no bikers – no one.

The two climbed out of the van and stood quietly, listening, and hearing nothing, then got to the task at hand. First, while the pair was still unconscious, they pulled them from the van and dragged them unceremoniously into the trees where they tied the two between some larger trees. Once their hands and feet were securely tied off, spread-eagle, the two began cutting their clothing off. Both stood back and admired the woman, nudging each other and grinning.

They went back to the van and retrieved the rest of their gear, dressed in the painter's garb, grabbed two lawn chairs and a bag of McDonald's food, went back to where the pair were tied off and sat to eat, watching for the two to wake. Neither said a word and ate their food quietly, waiting.

Agent Flores was the first to stir, quickly realizing he was bound began to struggle. The two sitting in the lawn chairs giggled, causing Flores to freeze. He looked up and saw the two apparitions with their masks, goggles, gloves, and white painter's overalls on and realized what was about to happen – he'd read the investigative report on the two they'd found in the Medicine Bow. Now his struggles became intense, knowing what was about to happen to him and his wife of twenty years. Thoughts of his son came to mind.

"Why are you doing this?" he asked the two. They just laughed. Flores pulled at his bindings, rope burning his wrists and ankles. He strained and tugged, all to no avail.

It was just a few moments later that Missus Flores began to stir, not realizing what was happening. She knew she was tied to something and began to struggle. "Daniel…Daniel what's happening?" she shakily asked.

"Keep quiet," one of the men said.

She looked up and saw them sitting in the lawn chairs and seeing something next to her, saw her husband struggling in his bindings – he was nude – and she suddenly realized she too, was nude. She began to whimper and cry, knowing they were in trouble. She began to pull and strain to escape her bindings.

*****

Three days later, a Friday afternoon, two University of Wyoming students hoping to have a quiet weekend of camping, hiking, and fishing, were sickened by what they found after beginning to set up their camp.

One of the two had heard an unfamiliar sound, one of birds arguing and fighting over something. He dropped what he was doing and walked over to the tree line to see what the birds were doing and began to vomit violently. His friend ran to his side to help, asking what was wrong and when his ill friend pointed, he too, became violently ill by what he saw.

After what seemed a long time, the two recovered enough to know they just might be in danger. One pulled his handgun and told the other to go call 911 as soon as he got a signal. Phone reception was not reliable where they were.

An hour later, a sheriff's cruiser came to a stop by the young man waving his arms. He was told to get in and the deputy, one Thomas Gerill, drove in the direction indicated by the UDub student. Arriving at the camp site, Deputy Gerill introduced himself and was told what they'd found and where, pointing,

Deputy Gerill was careful going to the scene, not wanting to disturb possible evidence, and was utterly disgusted by what he saw through the trees. He immediately went back to his cruiser and radioed the sheriff, telling him to alert the coroner of two bodies like the ones found earlier in the year and to send help. Once the sheriff told him he would get everyone rolling, Gerill began to interview the two UDub students, taking their statements. Once that was completed, he told them to pack their gear and wait at the top of the canyon. He would remain watching the site.

✱✱✱✱✱

Late that afternoon Anita answered the phone, "Cheyenne Police, Detective Anita Bishop speaking, how may I help you?"

"Hi, Detective Bishop, it's Deputy Gerill from Albany County," TJ Gerill answered, rather subdued.

"Oh, howdy, TJ, how are you?" she asked.

"Not so good ma'am. We have two more murder victims like the ones we found earlier in the year. The scene is out on National Forest Trail 708. It's exactly like the other two in every detail."

"Oh, Lord God, no," Anita said. Then after a pause, asked, "Do you have an ID yet?"

"Yes ma'am, an Agent Flores, FBI, and his wife," TJ answered. "Ma'am, it was really bad what they did to them. We know it was two people as there were two different sizes of footprints. The sheriff asked me to call you and let you know. We've already notified the FBI, State Police, the Laramie PD, and now you. We'll get all the reports and photos to you as soon as their available."

Anita asked, "Who found them?"

"Two UDub students out for a weekend of camping, hiking, and fishing," Gerill answered. "They're not doing so well and we have them with a counselor right now. Both were sickened by what they saw. They had no involvement, just in the wrong place…you know."

"Poor kids…you think they'll be okay?"

"I hope so. I got 'em by the shoulders and prayed for both – I've seen both of them at church – and asked God to take away what they saw. I know they'll see that in their minds for a long time, but never hurts to ask, you know."

"Yeah, Tom, I do. Well, if you don't have anything else, I'll let you go. Thanks for contacting us. I'll go talk to the Captain and probably the Chief and I'll let them know your office will send us what you can when you can. You might expect a call from the Chief to the Sheriff though."

"I figured that, too. I don't have anything else for you other than the notification so I'll say so long. You take care and say howdy to Bish for me."

"Will do, Tom, and God bless."

"Thanks, bye-bye."

Anita hung up and called the Captain and was told to get to his office immediately. She waived for Tony and Steve to follow and shortly afterwards walked into the Captain's office and told them what she'd gotten from Gerill. All three were disgusted and the captain said he knew both Agent Flores and his wife. He smacked his desk and said, "I want a task force developed. I gotta go talk to the chief. Anita, you come with me – you two," indicating Tony and Steve, "get back to the office and brief everyone."

They broke with everyone going their ways. At the Chief's office, they were ushered right in and briefed him. He too, knew the Flores' and hung his head in prayer for a time. After a few more minutes of quiet contemplation, he asked, "You have a plan or direction yet?"

"That's why we're here, chief," Captain Carlisle said. "With an okay from you, I want to start a task force, with the feds, state and both Albany and Laramie county sheriff's deputies. I want to go hunting for these nuts, and I want everyone on board. Would you do the calls?"

The chief called for his secretary and told her who to contact and asked for them to either come over or call in for a face-time session. She began at once, and within fifteen minutes had everyone save the Albany County Sheriff on the line. Deputy Dave Malone was on for Albany County.

After two and a half hours, the meeting adjourned with a Wyoming task force developed of four FBI agents, two State Troopers, four Albany County sheriff's deputies under TJ Gerill and David Malone's supervision, two Laramie County sheriff's deputies, and Anita's team. She had even arranged to have Bish on the force as an intelligence expert to gather evidence and information for the task force.

The new task force went to work immediately. Everyone was at their respective offices working to do one thing – bring to justice those responsible for these heinous acts.

The next morning, Anita, Connie, and Bish all walked in together to the detective squad room. Anita's first move was to assign Steve and Tony to take apart every scrap of information regarding Enrique Salinas. She told the group she had a feeling about the man and wanted every possible lead pursued to a termination point. She felt they were missing something so she had them going over every scrap of information. She especially wanted them to go over financials and known associates and their financials. Something was there, she just knew it. Bish joined the two in their quest.

Mike and Pete took the rookies under their wings and had them searching phone, mail, email, and paper records from the case. Within an hour, they had seven computers up and running, going over every document collected, every phone number, every mailbox and known addresses Salinas had. The FBI provided every email known to have come from or to Salinas or any of his known associates. It would take months to go over everything.

The task was so daunting the Cheyenne team loaded four thumb drives of information and sent them to the Albany County Sheriff's Office for Gerill and Malone and their friends to go over. Together the four spent hours upon hours poring over the information received.

In all, the task force had twenty-two people working the issue. The two they'd captured were grilled over and over. They were kept separated and under constant guard. Not only did Anita's people grill the two, the FBI and Gerill and Malone did also. They would tag-team the two for hours on end, attempting to break them.

Their lawyer even attempted to get them to talk, explaining they may receive some semblance of leniency, possibly staying a death sentence. The two prisoners looked tired and worn out and wanted nothing more than to be left alone. They knew leniency was nothing for them as they would be killed in any prison sent to spend their time. Better to keep quiet and die when sentenced than to be killed horribly in a jail cell.

*****

It took nine days of constant hounding by the task force when one of the two broke, begging to give the cops what they wanted just to be left alone. Anita and the lawyer were called immediately.

The questioning began straightaway and the guy sang like a rapper at a half-time show. He told them the how and where they'd committed the murders, everything taped for the judge. The poor lawyer kept shaking his head as the guy kept talking even after the lawyer said not to.

The main question was never answered – who wanted the murders committed. The guy absolutely did not know and his accomplice remained silent. The questioning went on for several hours, the interviewers asked their questions every way they could and the man answered the same way.

It was two in the afternoon when they stopped the session. The man was fed and given a soda for a reward. The tape was played while Tabitha fed it into a computer, officers surrounding her desk listening. After she completed entering the interview, she printed the document, gathered and stapled the sheets, and went with Anita, Captain Carlisle, and the guy's lawyer to the holding cell. There, she handed the document to the lawyer, who had the man sign it in front of the watchful eyes of the group, and then Tabitha signed it, notarized it, and handed the document to Carlisle.

Carlisle took the document and made ten copies of it, gave two to Anita and the rest he laid on his desk after giving two other copies to the man's lawyer. "Anita, good job in there," Carlisle told her with a smile. "I wish we could have gotten the other name, but what we have is great. They're running that name, Renaldo del Monte, through the data base…we should know soon."

"I hope we get something for him; that might lead us to whoever is running this crap," Anita said. "Still, I don't have a good feeling about the name. We may not get a thing is what I'm afraid of."

"Come on, Anita, get positive on this," Carlisle prompted.

A knock on the door and Pete came in with Mike, "Nothing on the name…nothing at all," Pete said handing the printout to the captain.

"Darn, at least he put another nail in their coffins," Carlisle said while reading the sheet. "I wonder if the name and that third set of prints go together…."

"We wondered the same thing, Cap," Mike added.

"Okay, guys, keep at it," Anita told the pair and they left the captain's office.

She sat in a guest chair and rested her head in her hands. The captain sat also. They were like that when the captain's phone rang and it was Albany County Sheriff's Deputy David Malone with information about the most recent murders. The captain listened intently and after several long moments, said, "Send it to us immediately and thanks to all of you for what you do," and hung up. He sat quietly for a moment, Anita looking on, and finally said, "DNA says there were two of them which verifies the evidence found at the scene, both from south of the border anywhere from Mexico to Peru. So, I guess we're looking for another pair of dudes fitting about the same description as the two we already have."

"Sounds right, Cap," Anita agreed. "Want me to BOLO them?"

"Malone already did the tri-state, and it's out on the wire," the captain said. "Anita, please have the group go over everything with a fine-toothed-comb again. I'm going to brief the chief."

She stood and said, "Will do, Cap, see you later," and turned for the door.

Everyone was hard at it doing as the captain instructed, going over every shred of evidence again, and again, and again, looking at every detail as if they'd never seen it before. Pete and Mike even had photos spread out on the conference table with one of those World War II-looking magnifying glasses on stilts to look at fine details of every shot. They were seeing nothing new, however.

Anita went over to Bish and said, "Come on, champ, I want lunch and you're buying."

"Me…you're the money bags these days," he complained.

"Come on, sucker, we're going to Tortilla Factory," she said pulling his arm. The Tortilla Factory was one of their favorites.

As they sauntered out the door, Pete called to them saying, "Bring back a taco sixer for me 'n Mike."

"In your dreams," Bish said with a snicker, knowing full well he and Anita would do just that, bring the guys a six-pack of tacos, chips, and salsa.

"I want to sit and eat," Anita said as they pulled into the parking lot.

"Yeah, me, too," Bish agreed.

Inside, they were seated at a table in the middle row of tables, one with a nice view out the windows, and one inside the place. They could see everyone. Cops always felt better when they could see well.

The server brought out their meals and as they ate they spoke of little other than the weather outside. It was a pleasant day, a nice one for Wyoming. Bish had sweet tea with lime and Anita had hot tea. Bish had just received a refill on his tea and froze in mid sip.

Anita looked up just as Bish froze and saw the look on his face. She knew it was his cop look and read the danger. She didn't react by turning to look, but saw his gaze quickly switch his gaze to her eyes.

"What is it?" she quietly asked.

"Guy and a couple of dudes just came in and I got a bad case of déjà vu," he replied. "The guy looks like Salinas."

Anita's eyes got big. "You're kidding," she said.

"No, I'm not - almost loaded my pants."

She chortled, and said, "I gotta go to the restroom. Where is he?"

"Farthest booth to your right as you turn to go to the ladies room."

"Be right back, lover" she said getting up and heading for the ladies room. She gave the booth a quick look as she went by and saw what Bish had seen. She, too, was amazed at the resemblance. She made it look good by staying in the ladies room for a while, and took another look as she passed returning to their table.

"Well...?" Bish asked as she sat.

"You're right, the guy has an uncanny resemblance to him, so much so he may be a relative," she said incredulously.

"My *'spidy-sense'* is still going off," he said.

"I know, I saw it in your face when you first saw him."

"It's way too uncanny. He has to be related. I wonder if he's a son or something."

"You think?"

"We need to get back. See if you can photograph the guy with your phone as we go by. We gotta tell the guys about this. I'm gonna order that sixer for Pete and Mike." He got up and went to both pay the bill and get the six-pack, chips, and salsa ordered. He was watching the three in the booth out of the corner of his eye, also.

He saw Anita get up and her phone was in her hand as if talking to someone, but it was actually on video and she had it to her right ear as she went by the booth, hoping she got the three of them on video as she passed. As she reached Bish, she changed the phone to her left ear and tried to get them again.

Bish paid out, collected the sixer, chips, and salsa, and the pair left the restaurant. Back at the office, they gave the food to

Pete, and called the team together and told them what had happened. Anita pulled her phone and hooked it up to her computer and pulled up the video. She indeed had caught the three on film. Those on the team, who had been on the Ladies of Cheyenne rescue, were just as amazed as Anita and Bish were.

Anita froze the frame on each face and printed hard copies for the team. She made extras and with Bish in tow, went to the captain's office to report the incident. Captain Carlisle was just as amazed and said as much.

"We gotta find these guys again and put a tail on 'em," the captain said to the pair.

"I don't have anything going, I can go back and watch for 'em," Bish volunteered.

"What do you think, Anita?" the captain asked.

"Go…stop by the office and get a radio and tell Mike 'n Pete what you're doing," Anita said in answer. The captain nodded to Bish as he left.

Bish got heavy on the gas pedal going back to the Factory. He was pulling into the parking lot when the three sauntered out the door and got into a parked Toyota *Land Cruiser*. They, along with Bish, turned south on South Greeley Highway and went to Terry Ranch Road, turning westward. They pulled onto Interstate 25, heading north. Bish called it in to Anita and she told him to follow, that she would have Mike and Pete pass him shortly and take over the tail. He described the vehicle they were in and continued to follow northward.

Ten minutes later, Mike and Pete flew past Bish and pulled in behind the Toyota. Bish pulled off at Chugwater and went to the Soda Shop for a real soda fountain root beer float. Back on the highway, he called Mike and Pete informing them he was back on the road. They said the Toyota was still heading north and to keep pace, they would call if they needed him.

It wasn't long when they radioed Bish saying they were pulling off at the first exit in Wheatland. Bish copied and said he'd do likewise. Mike gave him a play-by-play as to where

they were. When the Toyota pulled into the driveway of the
rental, the pair of detectives drove past without looking. Mike
radioed Bish and told him and asked if he would do a drive-by
and take some video of the place.

As Bish went by, he had his phone up just enough to film the
place as he passed. He went up another mile or so and turned
around. He shot stills as he went past this time, as many as he
could tap the button.

He radioed Mike and Pete, and told them he was heading
back to Cheyenne. They told him they were at the city PD and
inquiring about the place, who owned it, who was renting it if it
was a rental, and so forth. With that information in hand, they
called Anita on a landline and told her what they had. She got
the number where the two were and told them to wait there and
to make sure they thanked the Platte County folks assuring them
the CPD appreciated all the help.

After she hung up, she phoned the captain and gave him a
quick rundown on the information. He told her to have the men
return to Cheyenne, that he would call the Platte County folks
and ask their assistance on surveillance of the place and the
people within.

Anita called Mike and told him to return to Cheyenne. The
Platte County folks were more than willing to stakeout the place
and report movement, the sheriff alluding to the fact they were
bored outta their minds right then. He also said he had a rookie
that was in some hot water and this is just what he needed to do
to cool off, laughing all the while. The captain felt sorry for the
poor kid, but, he had to learn.

With everyone back in Cheyenne, Mike and Pete went back
to work in the detective's office, Bish kissed Anita on the cheek
and went home to cook dinner, tagging Tony and Steve to

follow along. They were still taking no chances with each other's lives.

Anita waited on a call from the captain telling them what was happening in Wheatland. She knew they just might be on to something, especially after seeing Bish's face at the Tortilla Factory. It had looked like he'd seen a ghost or something, but even after she'd seen the guy, the resemblance to Salinas was uncanny. Maybe this joker was related to him in some way. She was waiting on information from the Platte County folks on who had the place under surveillance, and being anxious, got up and began to pace.

Chapter 21

Roberto Salinas, Chogan Black Cloud, and Renaldo del Monte pulled into the rental house in Wheatland, little knowing they had been followed. Between Bish and the two detectives from Cheyenne they had done their jobs well and had not been tagged by the three men in the vehicle. The Platte County Sheriff's Office had taken over the surveillance of the home and would inform Cheyenne of any movement or other vehicles that might visit the place.

The three had one of the other men make them some tea and they were sitting around the small table in the dining room eating chips and discussing next moves. Renaldo said he would still like to target the captain and his wife. That would upset the masses terribly, and make the population of Cheyenne tremble. It would send a clear message that no one was safe.

Chogan argued for the Bishops as they were the reason his father, Dante Black Cloud, was no longer among the living. His reasoning was much the same as Renaldo's as killing that pair would most certainly instill fear into the city of Cheyenne.

Roberto Salinas ate his snacks in silence, listening to the two argue their points. He smiled from time-to-time envisioning what his crew might do to the unlucky person or persons who would be next to enjoy the treatment his men would apply. He looked at Chogan, nodding as Chogan talked about what he would do to the Governor's pets, the Bishop's.

Anita and the captain were happy. They'd finally had something new on the case. From the captain's office, they'd contacted the other agencies involved and updated them, including providing stills of the three men's photos for their files along with assurances of additional information as it came in.

Anita went back to her office and as she sat down at her desk, her phone rang, "Bishop speaking," she answered.

"Hey, Anita, Larry up in Platte County, how's it goin'?" the deputy asked.

"Not bad here, what's up?" she asked.

"The rookie just called and reported the garage opened and a yellow Camaro pulled out and drove to Phifer Airfield, dropped a guy off who got into a private aircraft and departed to the east. The Camaro went back to the house."

"What year Camaro?" Anita asked, motioning for Mike and Pete to come over to her desk.

"Older model probably late sixties, or early seventies he said. He also said it had a hood scoop and looked cool."

"Is the rookie still watching?"

"Yeah, he's on the place…why?"

"The Camaro is a hit. It's on our list of vehicles to watch for. We have the owner under suspicion of being involved in some way with the recent murders. Tell your rookie great job and he deserves a commendation for this. It's big. Keep close watch on that place if you will. I'll be in touch," and with that, she hung up, quickly briefed Mike and Pete, and headed for the captain's office at an extreme pace.

Captain Carlisle rubbed his chin as he contemplated what Anita had just told him. He looked at her and grinned, knowing they had a firm lead now and would work it to death. "I love concrete," he began, beaming. "They still have someone on the house?"

"Yes, Cap, the rookie is still on it," Anita answered.

"You think the kid is reliable?"

"He's the one that got all of this information, Cap," she answered.

"Call the airport – I want to know who was on that airplane…go," he ordered, still smiling.

Anita jumped up and at a brisk pace went back to her office, called her friend with the Cheyenne branch of the Federal Aviation Administration (FAA) and asked him to look into it and get her a name. She told him why it was so important and he said to give him ten minutes.

She hung up and waited, most of her crew watching her.

Her phone rang at eight minutes and it was her FAA rep. "Passenger was one Roberto Salinas out of Denver. Plane has turned south for destination Rocky Mountain Metropolitan Airport, Denver, Colorado; it's out on the west side near the mountains. It's actually in Broomfield, Colorado, but is listed as a Denver resource. No other information on the passenger. Good enough?" he ended.

"I owe you a steak dinner with all the fixin's," she promised and hung up.

She motioned for Mike and Pete to follow her as she sped once again to the captain's office. No fanfare, she and the two detectives went right in, closed the door and she said, "Captain, I think it's Salinas' son, the name of the passenger on that aircraft was one Roberto Salinas."

There was total silence in the room with numerous wide-opened eyes. The captain looked at her as did Mike and Pete, not believing they might be facing a revengeful son of Enrique Salinas. One they didn't even know existed until that very moment.

After several long moments of silent contemplation, the captain picked up the phone and called the Chief, requesting an emergency meeting of all the players on the task force, including Albany and Platte County folks. The captain pulled the phone away from his ear as the Chief yelled for his secretary, Frances, and told her to make the calls. He told Carlisle he'd call him back as soon as he could and hung up.

Within minutes of the Chief's call, vehicles pulled out of agencies all over southeast Wyoming, running Code 3, and as fast as possible converging on Cheyenne for the meeting.

Carlisle looked up at the three and said, "Okay, get everything together you think we'll need for this meeting. Everything! And put it on thumb drives, one for everyone. Get to it."

The three jumped up and left the captain's office at almost a run. Back at her office, Anita got everyone's attention and gave the orders. They all jumped to it, collecting data, and loading it onto one drive, which they would copy when they had everything together. They were ready within a half-hour, and had ten thumb drives full of information, both the current case and everything they had on the *Ladies of Cheyenne Rescue* case and Enrique Salinas.

Anita called the captain and said, "We're ready for the meeting, Cap. Who from here do you want in the meeting?"

"You, Mike, and Pete, and I want you to recall Steve and Tony, and tell them to bring Bish. If he gives them any trouble, they can arrest him and drag him to the meeting," he told her.

Anita burst out laughing and everyone in the room looked at her like she'd lost her noodles. "Yes, sir, I sure will," and hung up. "Mike…Pete…contact Steve or Tony and tell them to come back and to bring Bish either voluntarily or under arrest and drag him in in cuffs. The captain wants all six of us in the meeting." Both Mike and Pete laughed and got on the phone right away.

Mike gave Anita a thumb up and said Bish was coming along peacefully. Another round of laughter filled the squad room. Anita called the captain and relayed that Bish was coming in peacefully and heard laughter from him. He told her the meeting would be in a half-hour in the Chief's conference room and to bring everyone and the drives with her. She thought that a quick turnaround time for the meeting with so many agencies. She supposed this was important enough to have speed as an ally.

She collected the drives, Mike, and Pete and headed for the Chief's office. She radioed Steve and told him to meet them at the Chief's office. The six of them got together and after Bish gave her a hug and a kiss, went into the Chief's building.

"Geeze, she never gives us hugs or kisses when we get to work," Steve said with a grin.

"Nor will I ever you shmuck," Anita quipped.

"Better not," Bish growled.

"Down boy, down," Anita said, grinning.

"You sounded like a wounded bear with that growl, Bish," Mike said with a grin.

"Yeah, and I eat meat…especially fresh meat," Bish growled out giving him a stare.

"Settle down, boys," Anita commanded. They'd all heard that tone of voice from her before so they all clammed up right quick.

The elevator opened and they stepped out into the foyer of the Chief's floor and his secretary Frances, pointed to the conference room and said to go right in. She also said the only folks they were waiting for was the Wheatland people and they were six miles out and coming fast.

They went inside and found the FBI, State Police representative, Laramie County Sheriff, Albany County Sheriff's deputies Malone and Gerill, and Jennie Best from the Emergency Management Agency (EMA) sitting around the table. Heads nodded and some hands waived as Anita and her guys came in. They pulled chairs behind the captain and sat down. Anita handed him the small bag with the thumb drives.

Another fifteen minutes went by and the door opened with the Chief leading and the two men from Wheatland following.

"Welcome everyone," the Chief began. "I suppose you all know why we're here. Detective Bishop, would you brief the team please?"

Anita stood and said, "Certainly, sir. Our information comes from a rookie Platte County Sheriff's Deputy. He was placed on stake out at a home in Wheatland where we tailed a suspect that looked almost identical to Enrique Salinas." That brought a stirring and murmurs from the team. "The rookie contacted us after he'd followed a yellow, late sixties yellow Camaro to the local airport and watched as a man got into a small plane that took off to the east. An informal inquiry to the FAA revealed the name of the passenger on the aircraft as one Roberto Salinas (which brought wide eyes and gasps). We've since run the name and found out this is the son of Enrique Salinas." Now the murmurs and stirring became intense.

"Okay, everyone, settle down," the Chief called for and got. "Anita, continue please."

"Yes, sir; based on this information, we began researching. The aircraft landed at Rocky Mountain Metropolitan Airport in Broomfield, near Denver. We have no information regarding the passenger after that. This is all new to us so we haven't begun a formal investigation on this Salinas as yet. My team has put together every scrap of information we have on the current investigation and on the *Ladies of Cheyenne Rescue* and Enrique Salinas on these drives," she said motioning to the captain to hand out the drives.

He took one out of the bag and passed it along. After every agency had taken a drive, Anita sat down and waited. The Chief looked at Captain Carlisle and said, "Daryl, how do you want to proceed?"

Carlisle stood and said, "Sir, I believe we need to first find out where Salinas is located in Colorado and put a 24/7 tail on him. We need to continue the surveillance of the home in Wheatland and follow those people wherever they go, not letting them out of our sight. We have the two in lock up with one giving us information, and I feel if we tell him we know he works for Salinas, he'll sing even more. We possibly may get some vital information from this source and I further feel we should act on that as soon as possible. If we garner any new information from that source then we'll act accordingly and make immediate notifications to all of you. I'm sure we'll get more answers from the people in Wheatland, but as of now we have no evidence to support an arrest so that'll have to wait. That's what I have for now, sir, ladies and gentlemen."

The Chief was quiet for a moment and looking up at Anita said, "Anita, call your friend with the Air National Guard and see if we can get that drone again. If so, have them go to Wheatland and pull surveillance for us. They can stay aloft for days and monitor any vehicle that leaves. Also, call that FAA guy again and see if he can get any local information on that passenger that deplaned in Broomfield. If he won't play ball, give the chore to the FBI," he told her pointing to the Feds. "Once we find where Salinas is, we'll arrange with whomever in Colorado for surveillance assistance. Daryl, I like your directions so get 'em in motion, especially on those two we have in custody. Use the photos of Salinas and those other guys that were with him. We just might get lucky with this."

"Albany," he said looking at Gerill and Malone, "You're on standby. If you would please, contact the federal forestry folks and see if they'll assist with beefed up surveillance of the Medicine Bow. I know that's a big area to cover, but whatever they can do will be a big help and greatly appreciated.

"Ladies and gentlemen, we don't want any more deaths," the Chief said, pausing for effect. "Please brief everyone concerned about these people and their possible involvement in these gruesome murders and that they need to be extremely cautious. These people are in all likelihood armed to the teeth and very dangerous. Take no chances. I'll brief the Mayor and the Governor and request a shoot on site authorization."

The FBI guys nodded, knowing they would be asking their leaders the same.

He looked down at the tabletop, and after a moment looked up at the people in the room, making eye contact with each and said, "Use your best judgement out there and above all be careful." After another moment of looking around the room, a room so quiet one could almost hear their own heartbeats, the Chief said, "You have my authorization to shoot to kill."

That statement reverberated around the room and still, not a sound was made. He looked at each person and finally said commandingly, "Get to it."

Everyone in the room jumped up and headed towards the door. Out in the hall, Anita corralled Malone and Gerill from Albany County and asked them about the airport out there and if they had a contact. They did, and she asked that they be alerted to watch for a private aircraft from Broomfield coming in and to notify the Sheriff's Office if one did. Both said they would take care of that. She shook their hands and gathering her team, headed back to their office.

Chapter 22

Salinas woke smiling, eyes opening to the view through the picture window in his bedroom that faced the west. The morning sun had set alight the eastern slopes of the Rocky Mountains and the view he had lying in bed was spectacular. The sunlight created brilliant greens and dark, menacing shadows in other areas. The lime-green leaves on the aspen trees radiated the light and the white contrasted brilliantly with the black streaks on the aspen trunks. This was one of the reasons he built his home on this spot.

He was also happy knowing that his men were handling Cheyenne so well. He knew these things took time, and every time his men caused another death or two, the community feared all the more. This is what he wanted – Cheyenne, especially the police, to fear the unknown.

At this point he assumed Cheyenne had no idea who was committing these heinous crimes. He knew his first two henchmen were captured and imprisoned, but continued with the assumption they knew very little about his ongoing operation.

He reveled in their fear. It thrilled him. The sociopath in him was being well fed by all the mayhem not to mention the sadistic psychopath side he had. He was ecstatic with what he was doing to the people and cops of Cheyenne. He basked in the knowledge. If his men can get a hold of Carlisle and his wife…he tingled with the anticipation of what would come.

Salinas was indeed mad. His obsession to deal death to those who caused his father's demise went beyond obsession. That made those who were involved with that operation all the more in mortal danger. His men were just as unbalanced, willingly going to great lengths to make their captives suffer in so many ugly ways before death. Salinas drooled when he was told the details of the murders, lavishing in the misery so freely given, and had watched the videos over and over and over. He and his henchmen were evil personified.

✶✶✶✶✶

Anita woke to an unusual smell. She was confused as it smelled like sausage cooking, but different and she could not place the difference. She noted Bish was out of bed and knew he was cooking something special for breakfast. Getting up, she thought she had to see this. After cleaning up and brushing her teeth, she went downstairs to get a cup of coffee and see what the love of her life was preparing.

Connie came out of her room as Anita hit the bottom of the stairs and said good morning, and asked what was cooking. Anita told her she didn't have a clue but would be asking Bish in just a moment. Together they went for their morning coffee.

Bish, smiling, greeted them with a hearty good morning and a steaming mug of coffee. Both added creamer. "What in the world are you making for breakfast?" Anita asked him.

"I call it my Breakfast Pizza and you're gonna love it," he answered. "It'll really kick-start your day 'cause it has hot salsa cooked into it along with fresh jalapeno shavings. It has hamburger, sausage, fresh bread, cheese, green peppers, onion, salsa, jalapenos, and eggs. Like I said, you're gonna love it."

"Sounds different," Connie said. "And good morning by-the-way."

"Thanks, it is a good and beautiful morning out there, you should go see," he said motioning to the back door. Anita and Connie turned that direction while Bish continued cooking. All the 'fixin's' pre-cooked, Bish spread the bread dough in a buttered casserole dish, then placed the ingredients on top of the dough. Next, he covered the mix with grated cheese, using a four-cheese mixture, and for the final touch, cracked, and scrambled eight eggs, pouring the eggs over the entire contents of the dish. He placed the dish into the oven and cleaned his mess. He poured himself another mug of coffee and joined the ladies on the back porch.

"Breakfast will be served piping hot in forty-five minutes, girls," he announced, sitting on a step and taking a sip of his mud.

"My mouth is watering already," Connie declared.

"Mine, too," Anita agreed. "Where did you get that recipe?"

"It's mine…I invented it about fifteen years ago," Bish answered. "Remember when we tried pulling duty with the fire department? I was tasked with breakfast one day and since there were a dozen of us in the firehouse, I made two of these just off the top of my head. There wasn't a morsel left when all was said and done. And I got rave reviews for the dish. They all wanted the recipe," he said laughing at the memory.

"Well, then, I'm ready to try this," Connie said. "If a bunch of fire dogs enjoyed it then I know I will."

Bish chuckled again then asked, "What will you ladies be doing today?"

"You mean what will the three of us along with everyone else be doing today?" Anita corrected. "We'll be doing police work. Investigative work – you know, digging for facts and suppositions about Salinas and whatever he's doing these days. We have to find this guy and all of his men including those in Wheatland. We need to end this and it's gonna take all of us to make that happen."

"Yeah, okay, we'll get on it soon enough," Bish said looking her in the eye. "We'll get 'em, but we can't let it dominate us. We gotta let go or it'll eat us up, and that means we'll make mistakes that'll get someone else killed. And I for one don't want to see that happen. We've lost enough good people already," he ended, his eyes clouding over and suddenly looking sinister sitting on the step.

Nothing else was said until the stove alarm went off. Bish jumped up and going inside, turned off the alarm first, and then shut off the oven. He got a pair of hot pads and pulled breakfast out and set it on a hot plate stand on the stovetop. It bubbled.

Bish took three plates out, opened the drawer, and pulled three forks and a serving spatula, and a butter knife. He set the table, and going back into the kitchen, used the butter knife to cut the breakfast dish into portions. He served each of the ladies after returning to the dining table, and then himself. Connie said the blessing and they dug in. All three ate two helpings.

"Man, that was good, Bish, thank you," Connie said.

"Yes indeed, that was good," Anita agreed.

"I'll freeze those other portions and we can have them some other time," Bish said pointing to the casserole dish. "We can enjoy another good breakfast then."

"Boy, I'll say," Anita said. "Now I know what you mean when the fire house guys ate every morsel. Whew, I ate too much as it is. I'll have to take a long walk later and drink lots of water."

"You and me both, sister," Connie said, patting her distended but firm abdomen. "Bish, you out did yourself with this one. That would even make a swell dinner sometime, especially on a camping outing."

"It would taste great on a camping trip, huh," Bish said filing that away in his brain for later use.

"Come on, folks, we need to get ready to go," Anita said pushing back from the table. The three got up and got ready to go to the station. Bish wore his sidearm and mags and would from now until this mess was over with. None of them were taking any chances. And with what the Chief had said in the meeting the day before, everyone wanted to be the one that made the shot that ended the killing spree.

*****

"Eight murders in as many months, and six of the people police officers,' the captain ranted. He was really miffed. He was pacing his office like he was measuring a football field. Hands clasped behind his back, he moved from wall to wall.

"Why doesn't Colorado find this guy? Why can't the feds find this guy? I know this guy is behind all this, why won't they go get him?"

All these questions bounced off the walls of his office, unheard by anyone else. Tabitha would turn once in a while and look at him and wonder if he was okay. She'd ask if he wanted coffee or something and usually be run out. He was definitely in a mood and she didn't want any part of it.

"Get Wilson in here," he shouted to her, using Anita's maiden name instead of Bishop.

Tabitha didn't hesitate and dialed Anita's number and gave her the message. Anita arrived two minutes later and Tabitha motioned for her to go right in and as she went by said, "Be careful," and gave Anita a knowing look.

Anita knocked.

"Get in here," the captain almost yelled. "Anything new?"

"Nothing as yet, Captain, but we're trying," Anita told him. "Every agency has all their people working on finding out where Salinas is. We're working on facial recognition on those other men that were in the car with him - nothing yet. And we're trying to run the ownership of that yellow Camaro, too. We're working every angle we can think of, Cap."

He stopped his pacing and looked at her, finally softening somewhat and said, "Good job. Keep at it and tell everyone I have complete confidence in their abilities. Bish here?"

"He's here; we have him counting cars again," she answered.

The captain chuckled. "Okay, get back to it. If you get anything let me know quickly, please."

"You'll be the second to know, Cap," Anita said and turned to leave. She gave Tabitha a thumb up as she went by. When she got back to her office, she relayed the captain's sentiments to the team and got on the phone. She called her favorite florist and ordered a chocolate basket with yellow roses for Tabitha. She knew that would help with her during this trying time.

"Well hello there," Salinas said after listening to the person on the other end of the burner phone. "We have not spoken for some time. What is new?"

"They know it was you in Wheatland, saw you get on that plane and had the FAA do a check and found out it was you. They know about the Camaro, but not the other cars and they have Wheatland staked out. You might want to consider a break for a while."

"Thank you, I just might consider that," and he hung up. It had been quite some time since his contact in the CPD had contacted him with useful information. This was indeed excellent information.

He called Chogan and told him to break camp, using a taxi service to leave. He told him to have his team go to Belize for three weeks of vacationing and to spare no expense. He explained why and said things needed to settle down for a while. He would be going elsewhere and would call when he wanted them back on the job.

Chogan agreed, hung up and told his men what was happening and to pack immediately. They went out the back and had a taxi meet them on the corner of the next block over to the north, the taxi taking them to the Cheyenne Municipal Airport. They took a flight to Denver, then a connecting flight to Merida, Mexico, where they changed planes once again and flew to Ladyville, Belize. A car took the men to a seaside chateau Mister Salinas had rented for their pleasure.

Salinas had his car take him to Denver International Airport, where he boarded a private jet that whisked him to Isla de Providencia, a small island of the Catalina's belonging to Columbia. He had leased a lodge on the southwest side of the island. For a young man fresh out of college, it was a paradise indeed, and since he had the money, he enjoyed it to the fullest.

✶✶✶✶✶

After a week of no activity at the home in Wheatland, the observing officers decided to see for themselves and strolled up to the door, clipboard in hand, and knocked. There was no answer and they heard nothing. Looking in the windows, they saw the house was empty and immediately called it in.

"What do you mean they're gone? Gone where?" Captain Carlisle yelled into the phone. He listened as the Platte County Sheriff explained they had no clue how the men got out without being seen. After a few more minutes of conversation, Carlisle said he'd be contacting the FBI and see if they wanted to enter the home, print the place and set listening and tracking devices.

After calming down some, he also said, "And please keep your men watching that house. Maybe they'll see those guys returning. Thanks for the news," and hung up.

"Tabitha, please ask Anita to come down," he said to his secretary.

Anita as always was quick to respond and sat as the captain motioned. He told her the bad news and told her to warn her team that someone just might be in danger and wanted everyone to be on their tiptoes and watching for threats. He made her assure him they would be at least doubled up for protection. He contemplated aloud that he wished the National Guard had that drone of theirs working in Wheatland, but it was on missions elsewhere.

Back in her office, she briefed her team and asked if any of them had any ideas on where the men might have gone. No one had a clue, and all of them wondered how they got out of that house without being seen. She told them she didn't want conjecture at this point, but told them to continue to work the issues they did have. She told them if the FBI did an entry on the home in Wheatland, they would be getting the information first, and she wanted her team to act on it rapidly. If the feds did go in, they would be processing the place for prints and DNA.

She directed Steve and Tony to go and grill the two they had in lockup once again. Any information just might be helpful at this point. She asked them to talk to the pair about places they'd gone for vacations and such. When they asked why, she said she had a hunch was all.

*****

Down in the holding cells, Steve and Tony had the guards pulled the first man and put him in an interrogation room. He was chained to a holding ring set solidly in the floor – he would not be going anywhere. The room also held a stainless steel table that too, was firmly bolted to the floor.

Steve and Tony dragged in two chairs and sat across from where the man stood. They looked the man over while they stood there, then sat down and just stared at him for a time.

The man, finally curious about why they had him asked, "What is it you want with me?"

"We're supposed to wait for your lawyer," Tony quietly answered.

"No need, I dislike him as it is," the man said.

"So you don't want your lawyer here while we question you?" Steve asked the man.

"No," he answered with finality.

"You will have to sign a statement to that…is that okay?" Steve asked.

"Yes, I will sign," the man said.

Tony got up and knocked on the door. When the guard came up to the barred window, Tony asked for a waiver form and a pen. The guard came back with the paper and pen, opened the door, and waited as a witness while Tony had the man sign the form. Afterwards, Tony, Steve, and the guard, all signed the paper making it a legal, binding document. Taking the form, the guard smiled at Steve and Tony, and then left the room, relocking the door as he left.

✳✳✳✳✳

Five hours later, Tony and Steve had asked their questions many times over. The man was having trouble standing and was obviously getting confused due to dehydration, so the two detectives knocked on the door and told the guard they were done and to take him back to his cell, give him some water, and a sandwich. He had earned the reward.

The two went back upstairs to the office and reported to Anita, telling her the guy had said they had had several vacations, one to Cancun, and another to Acapulco, Mexico. They had been to Barbados and to Belize. She quickly called the captain and he instructed her to call her contact in the FAA and have him see if any aircraft from the local area, Denver, or Broomfield had set a flight plan to anywhere in the Caribbean. She made the call and the guy said to give him a half hour.

He was true to his word as just over a half hour later he called her and said a private aircraft had flown out of Denver for Isla de Providencia. She asked where that was as she'd never heard of the place. He told her where it was and that it belonged to Columbia. This immediately set alarm bells off with her knowing Columbia was a major drug distribution country.

The FAA representative then told her about another aircraft with three men that left Cheyenne to Denver, then to Mexico, and finally to Ladyville, Belize. She thanked him profusely and said she owed him a second steak dinner somewhere. He would be more than happy to oblige. She chuckled, said her thanks again, and said goodbye.

Anita sat at her desk and wondered if these were the men in question. She picked up her phone and dialed the Platte County Sheriff's Office. A deputy answered and after the introductions, she asked if anyone from the FBI had been out at that house. Not that they knew of. She thanked him and after hanging up, called the Feds and asked if they were sending a team up to the place. They were indeed, and would be going up the following morning. The strange thing…they asked if she wanted to tag along. She said she would get back to them in a few minutes and rang off.

Captain Carlisle was more than willing to let Anita and one other detective tag along on the trip to Wheatland. He asked her to especially look for written documents, anything that might firmly tie Roberto Salinas to the place or to the men residing there. Any information would be beneficial, but the captain wanted specifics if they were to be had.

Anita talked the captain into allowing Bish to accompany her to Wheatland. She called him and his first words were, "Road trip!" He would be happy to go because he'd been holed up for so long. She warned him about the FBI, that they would be in charge of the scene, and to not get pushy with them. He just laughed at her but said he would be on his best behavior.

Anita got up and went to Steve's desk and told him she would be out the following day and that he would be in the leadership spot while she was gone. He didn't press and agreed saying he would take care of business in her absence.

Chapter 23

The following morning found Anita and Bish headed north on I-25, passing Chugwater and the open prairie to the east. They arrived at the house that had been under surveillance just after 0900. The FBI forensics team was already on site as was the Platte County Sheriff's deputy. He was leaning on his cruiser parked in the driveway.

"Howdy," the deputy said as Anita and Bish walked up. "Y'all up here for the fracas?"

Anita responded saying, "Yes, we're from Cheyenne. They in there yet?"

"Yes, ma'am, they sure are, a whole passel of 'em," the deputy answered. "I never seen so many feds in my life. Must be ten of 'em in there. They are all dressed in coveralls and wearing gloves and masks 'n stuff."

Bish poked Anita and said, "May as well just wait out here until they give us clearance to go in."

"I suppose," she said and leaned against the cruiser. "I'm Chief of Detectives Anita Bishop and this mug is Sam Bishop, my other half and a part timer with the department."

The kid offered his hand to Anita to shake and said, "I'm Deputy Tony Morris, nice to meet ch'all," and held his hand out to Bish after Anita shook his.

"We got a Tony working with us, too," Bish said shaking the proffered hand. "Where are you from kid?"

"I'm originally from Bradley, Arkansas, got this job instead of cowboying," he answered. "I think this is the better deal."

"Me, too," Bish said. "You cowboy much in Arkansas?"

"Yeah, rode two small ranches down there, not really big places like y'all got up here, but enough fence line riding to ruin a good day."

"Did my share of that after high school here in Wyoming," Bish told him.

"What made you become a cop?" the kid asked.

"I was witness to a robbery at a bank when I was younger…they shot the security guard – just wounded him – and were stopped as they left the building by the Cheyenne Police. I watched a cop come into the bank and stop the guards bleeding, probably saving his life. That's when I made my decision. I wanted to help folks out like that."

"Yeah, I 'speck that'd do it. I just figured being a deputy would be a lot warmer in the winter, sittin' in a cruiser like this one with the heater runnin'."

"Now that's a sound decision," Anita said with a smile.

The kid pointed and when the two from Cheyenne turned, they saw several of the overall-clad feds coming out of the house. Anita waived to one of them and he sauntered over. "You the folks from Cheyenne?" he asked.

"Yes, Detective Bishop and…temporary administrative employee Bishop," Anita answered sending a thumb towards Bish.

The guy gave them a funny look and she added, "He's my other half and a retired CPD detective."

He nodded his head and asked, "What may I do for you?"

"Is it possible for us to go in and take a look? We'll glove up," she said.

"You'll need booties, too, but shouldn't be an issue," he said. "Looking for anything specific?"

"Paperwork, especially anything about the home," she answered.

"We found some paperwork in the desk in the dining room and there's another desk in the front room to the right as you go in. You can take a look at those, and photograph what you might need. Don't take anything as that might alert them, you know."

"We'll photograph what we need," Bish said, patting his camera bag.

"I'll tell the guys you're heading in," the agent said turning.

"Thanks," Anita said to his back.

"Booties and gloves," Bish said turning for their cruiser to add booties to their kit. Ten minutes later they were inside rummaging through the paperwork, gloves, and booties on.

"I'm not finding anything worthwhile," Bish said from the dining room desk.

"Me neither," Anita said from the front room. The pair had been at it for almost an hour going over every document they saw. Anita opened the bottom right drawer and found another stack of papers, mostly billing statements for power, water, gas... What did catch her attention was a letter in an envelope addressed to a Chogan Black Cloud from the women's supermax prison in Canon City, Colorado.

"Bish - look at this!" Anita practically yelled.

Bish hurriedly moved to her side and said, "What 'cha got?"

She handed him the envelope while she read the letter inside. It was from Isabella, the woman who took care of the captives that Enrique Salinas had. She told this Chogan character that she was sorry his father was killed along with Enrique and told him how proud she was that he was taking care of business in Cheyenne. Anita could only assume the letter meant the murders. She quickly laid the two pages out and told Bish to photograph both and the envelope. He quickly did so.

Anita returned the letter and the envelope to the drawer after going through the rest of the paper. She closed it and said, "I think we have what we're going to find. Let's check and see if they found anything in the bedrooms."

Together they moved down the hallway to the bedrooms and found the feds in the master. "Find anything interesting like paperwork, letters, that kind of stuff?" Anita asked the first person she saw.

"There's some letters over there in the night stand," the agent replied.

"Mind if we take a look?" she asked.

"Be out guest," he answered and went back to what he was doing.

Bish opened the drawer and withdrew several letters, two from the prison in Colorado, one from a resort in Barbados, and another from a private home on the island where Roberto Salinas supposedly was visiting.

"Photograph everything and let's get outta here, my stomach is growling," Anita said.

Bish pulled his camera and began taking photos and while he was doing this, Anita asked the agent, "Any place around one could get a fair meal?"

"Yeah, over on sixteenth; a diner that does a pretty good family fare of home-cooked meals. Good food," he answered.

"Cool, thanks," she said and watched as Bish finished taking his photos. Together, they thanked the agents and left for the diner.

Inside they found the place homely and comfortable. They chose a table by the window. She had the chicken fried streak with green beans and fries and he had a burger with onion rings. They both had sweet tea. After they'd eaten, they got refills on their tea and sat and discussed the letters.

"You have the drive?" Anita asked.

"Yeah, and I backed it up before we left so we have what's on the camera and two drives with everything," Bish answered.

"Good, you ready?" she said.

"Yeah, let's boogie," he said getting up and helping her. He drove on the return leg and it turned out to be a quiet ride. When they'd gone over the hill past Chugwater, he said, "I'll make hard copies as soon as we get back. How many you want?"

Anita thought a moment then answered, "Four of each should do - one for the captain, one for me, and two for the team to go over."

"I'll make five, one for me to go over real good," he said. "I gotta feeling this is gonna help us out some."

"I have the same feeling, darlin'. I'm still amazed we found out Salinas has a kid running around. Makes me wonder if there are more."

"Me, too."

"So the new tidbit of info is that Chogan Black Cloud. We're dealing with two wanting revenge. Where did they wind up sending that guy Sims, Salinas' butler?"

"He's in Rawlins, I'm hoping in a hole in the ground. Why?"

"I wonder if he's tried to contact Roberto Salinas, that's all."

"I didn't see anything from him in any of that stuff we looked at so probably not. Maybe they don't let him write letters," he ended with a chuckle.

"Bish," Anita chided.

"Okay, maybe they didn't really know each other, after all a butler doesn't mix with the boss's friends. Maybe that Black Cloud dude was one that Sims didn't get along with."

"Sounds plausible; still I want to look into it. We might get in touch with Rawlins and see if Sims has written anyone else. We just may get something from it. I'll give 'em a call in the morning," she said as Bish parked the SUV in her spot.

In the office, Bish said, "I'm gonna go do those photos for you. See you in a few," Bish said turning for his computer.

Peter came over to Anita's desk and asked, "You get anything useful up there?"

"As a matter of fact, we did," she answered with a smile. "Here, take a look at this," and she brought up the photos of the letter and envelope from Isabella to Chogan Black Cloud.

"Whoa, I'll say," Pete exclaimed after reading it. "So we may have two revenge motivated people coming after cops?"

"That's exactly what Bish said up in Wheatland," Anita told him. "I'll run a disc and hard copies down to the captain in just a bit. Bish is running the hard copies now. On the way back from Wheatland, I had a chance to do some thinking while watching the prairie go by. I think this son of Salinas and the son of Black Cloud are gunning for anyone that had anything to do with the *Ladies of Cheyenne Rescue*. If you look at all the murders, every one murdered had a direct impact on that operation. Dalton and Smith were one of the sniper teams, Adams was on the SWAT Team, Flores was the FBI representative on the SWAT Team assault group, and Lindsey was in charge of SWAT at the time. Trudy and Barbara were just in the wrong place at the wrong time. That's what I'm thinking."

"Why does that make so much sense?" Pete asked rhetorically. "I think we ought to go down there and grill those two in the lockup one more time and present these names to them and watch their reactions. Maybe we'll fabricate a story, something like we killed or captured that Black Cloud guy and he's singing. Maybe they'll open up even more."

"I like it," Anita said. "Take a copy of the letter down with you and show them. Maybe that'll loosen their tongues. When they see we have that, it'll give credence to the story. You and Mike get together and make up the story and run it by me before you go down. I'll alert the captain when I see him and get the green light. Scoot."

"Yes, ma'am," Pete said, smiling and turning for his desk.

✶✶✶✶✶

Later that afternoon, Anita with the captain's approval, told Pete and Mike to go see the pair."

Both left the office with evil grins on their faces. Cops enjoyed playing suspects against one another. The first guy kept his mouth shut once again. They had yet to get him to open up. The second, as soon as he saw the letter and was told Black Cloud was dead, he opened up completely, even began crying.

They went back to the first guy, used the letter this time along with the news of Black Cloud's demise, and dropped a few bombshells from the second guy's diatribe. That got a visible change in the guy's face. He softened quickly and told them the other two guys they'd brought in when they were captured were probably in Belize. He said that Roberto Salinas was most likely in Barbados as that was his favorite place to go.

Pete and Mike didn't say anything about Isla de Providencia where they already knew Salinas was. The guy told them about Renaldo del Monte - that was news - and told them he was the middleman between Salinas and Black Cloud. He would make the contacts with either of those two and get instructions, passing those along to the 'hired help' as it were.

Mike asked for a description of del Monte and brought in a police sketch artist to make a composite drawing. That took another two hours, but had a fair likeness of the middleman. They took the drawing to the other guy and he agreed that it was a good drawing.

Pete told the artist to get it to Chief of Detectives Bishop as fast as possible. They finished questioning the first guy, had the guard give both a soda and a sandwich as a reward for helping out, and left for their office.

Anita was waiting at the door. "Great job getting those two to open up, that composite is already out on the wire. We'll have the Denver and Broomfield airports and ours watching closely for this guy. We're looking for photos of Salinas and Black Cloud now, but nothing as yet. Bish is on it if you want to help him. Again, great job you two."

The two went over to Bish and began a search on their computers, first looking for the names, and next trying to match photos to those names. It would be a tedious evening.

Chapter 24

"Anita!" Pete exclaimed staring wide-eyed at his computer screen.

Her head jerked up from what she was doing to look at him and saw the expression on his face and said, "What've you got, Pete?"

"I got Salinas on camera, a video from the Denver airport – come see," he said over his shoulder.

She and about half the room got up and went to Pete's desk to see what he had. "This was taken the other day when they all left the states," Pete explained. "You see him getting outta the limo here, at the ticket counter here, and walking down the concourse here to the private aircraft area here. Then we see him leaving the terminal under escort out to a private jet. That's gotta be him," Pete said looking up at Anita.

"Put that on several discs and make half-dozen hard copy photos of the best shot of his face," Anita told him. "We'll run this down to the captain and see what he wants to do." As she was moving back to her desk, she turned and said, "Pete, check that video we took of those at the Tortilla Factory and see if that composite matches one of those two that were with Salinas."

"Got it, boss," Pete said and got busy downloading the videos onto several discs and making photograph copies of the guy they presumed was Salinas. Once he had everything together, he brought up the video Anita said and bingo, the composite matched one of the guys!

"Anita!" Pete yelled.

She scooted back to his desk and said, "What have you got?"

"That composite matches this guy," he told her, pointing to his computer.

Anita bent down, looked closely at the frozen photo on the screen, and compared it with the composite…and smiled. "Great work, Pete."

She gathered all the information, and together with Pete went to see the captain, giving him the discs and photos. Anita had Pete explain what he'd found and went through the videos and the composite with the captain.

The captain's phone rang and it was the Cheyenne FAA representative and told the captain that at a Detective Peter Donaldson's request, he had checked on the destination of a private aircraft that left Denver airport and asked the captain if that was authorized. The captain said yes it was and to give him the information. The rep said the plane went to Isla de Providencia and off-loaded one passenger and returned to Atlanta to pick up another passenger.

The captain about wet his pants and thanked the rep profusely. Hanging up and turning to Pete, he said, "Great job, this is him for sure. The plane went to Isla de Providencia and dropped off one passenger. It's gotta be him. Keep at it and run everything you can on this guy. Great job, Pete. Anita, this is terrific. Your team is doing wonderful work. I'll run this up to the chief. Great job you guys."

Back in their office, Anita said to the team, "Okay everyone, we're fairly certain – 90 percent – that this is Salinas," holding up the photo, "and this one is Black Cloud," holding up the other. "Send them to everyone on the task force and put another call into Denver to keep an eye out for both, especially with their facial recognition programs. We wanna know when they come back to the states and put a tail on 'em. Connie, you and Bish start running down compounds and expensive homes in the Broomfield area and see if we can figure out where this guy lives. Get to it."

The room, for a moment, went frantic as people moved to start the process of tracking this Salinas down. Main focus was contacting Denver police, the Denver airport police, and attempting to find where this guy lived in Colorado. Anita sat back in her chair and smiled, having very good thoughts about her team going through her mind.

Her phone rang and when she answered, it was the FBI forensics team that had gone over the Wheatland home. They had processed several DNA samples and run every finger print they'd found and had matched both with two people – Chogan Black Cloud who had an interesting rap sheet, and the other was Renaldo del Monte, also with an interesting sheet. Two other sets of prints and one DNA sample were not on file. He said he would finish his report and send her everything they had. Anita thanked him and hung up.

Things were beginning to move, not as fast as she and everyone else wanted, but the case was progressing. This she was happy about.

It was close to the time when everyone began to leave for home and Anita called the room to silence. "Great job today everyone. I know we're moving on this and making progress, but that doesn't mean we're outta danger. Remember to pair up and keep situational awareness. I don't want to lose anyone else. Stay on your toes and stay alive." She gave a wave of her hand towards the door for those about to depart to carry on.

✳✳✳✳✳

Anita, Connie, and Bish arrived early the following morning and were surprised to see the room bursting with activity. Mike, Pete, Tony, and Steve were already there and going full blast. When Pete noticed Anita, he gave her a wave to come over to his desk.

"Morning, Pete, what's up?" she asked.

"Morning, I, uh, well, I've fractured a few laws – I think – and maybe a few international ones, but I hacked into a few of the hotel and resort registry systems and found out that Salinas has a thing for Barbados, just like his dad did. This resort," he said pointing to one on his screen "is the obvious favorite as he's been there at least five times in the last four years. He's been to Belize a few times also, and I've tracked the rest of the names we have and guess what…"

"What," Anita said, smiling.

"That Chogan Black Cloud…is in Belize right now. Seems he and two other fellows checked in at the same time a couple of days ago." Anita bent down to look closer at what he was pointing to on his screen. "So now, I've got two more names and photos of all three from the security cameras. These resort folks should make better passwords for their places; it was too easy to hack in."

"Great job, Pete, and I'll overlook the *fractured laws* this time, but don't make a habit out of it. If anyone asks, you had permission to do this for the task force. Use my name. Make half dozen hard copies of the photos and dump what you have to disc. We gotta go see the captain as soon as he gets in," she told him and turned for her desk and the phone.

"Tabitha, good, you're in," Anita began. "Good morning, too. Hey, I need to see the captain as soon as he gets in…yes, it's very important…okay, thanks, lady, see you in a bit."

"Pete," she called out, "be ready to go see the captain in a few minutes."

"Got it, boss," he returned with a thumb up.

Tabitha called and said the captain was in and for Anita to come on down. She got up, taking her mug of coffee with her, and motioned for Pete to follow. He grabbed the photos, the discs, and his mug and followed her.

"Morning Cap," Anita said entering his office.

"Morning, y'all," Carlisle answered. "Have a seat and let me have it."

"Sir, this morning, Pete here, under my direction, was able to retrieve vital information regarding the task force's investigation. It involves the activities of Salinas, his henchmen, Black Cloud and two others. He was even able to download photos from hotel security systems of the three henchmen," she told him and motioned for Pete to turn over the photos and discs to the captain.

First thing the captain did was view the photos, then inserted the disc in his computer and clicked on the info file. He read the headings on the spreadsheet program and then took in the dates. After a few minutes, he looked up at Anita and Peter and said, "I don't want to know how you got these, but since you," he said pointing at Anita, "said he was under your direction, I'm going to accept these. So, we know Salinas is on that island that belongs to Columbia, and now we know these three are in Belize…"

Anita and Pete knew he was being rhetorical so they didn't comment. They waited, sipping coffee, as now the captain was deep in thought.

Carlisle sat up straight and practically yelled, "Tabitha, bring me a cup of joe and get the chief on the horn, please."

She made the call and after transferring the chief to the captain, she poured him a mug of coffee and took it in to him. He thanked her and continued to explain the new information to the chief.

"Yes, sir, Detective Bishop authorized the action…yes, sir…yes, sir…yes sir…" and that's the way the conversation rolled for several more minutes.

Anita and Pete looked at each other with concerned looks. Pete shrugged his shoulders and looked back to the captain.

The captain hung up the phone and looked at the pair. "Well, I guess we won't be hacking into *anything* anymore will we…"

They definitely knew that was rhetorical and didn't comment, but kept their eyes glued to the captain.

"Share the photos and discs with the task force. You," he said pointing at Pete, "get your partner and run the stuff to the feds, sheriff, state, and over to Laramic to the Albany County Sheriff's Office…go."

Pete jumped up and took off.

"You…" he smiled, "are a sneaky chick, you know it?"

"Yes sir," she answered with a devious grin.

"Good work, kid, now get," he said with a wave towards the door. Anita smiled and left.

****

"Deputy Malone and Deputy Gerill, how's it going?" Pete said as they entered the office. They all shook hands and sat in the small conference room.

"We're doing well," Malone answered for the pair. "What brings you guys all the way over here from the big city?"

"These," Pete said, handing the envelope with the photos and disc over to him. "Got a computer handy?"

"Yeah," Malone said and reached down for his laptop.

Pete explained what they had as Malone and Gerill looked over the photos and the material on the disc.

"Gee whiz, guys, how'd you come by this?" Gerill asked.

"We're not at liberty to say," Pete said. "Just know we were authorized to go after the information. What do you think?"

Gerill was first, saying, "I've seen both of these guys," pointing at Salinas and Black Cloud, "I think it was at the rib place over by the Hilton. I was having lunch with my pastor and these two walked in. My *spidy-sense* tingled when I saw them. I figured it was just the cop in me."

"I've see Salinas around somewhere myself," Malone added. "I can't remember where, but like you," he said nodding to Gerill, "my cop sense went off and I took notice."

"You think Salinas might have a place around here?" Mike asked.

"Couldn't tell you – I know his daddy did - but we'll begin looking and let you know," Gerill answered.

"Well there went the afternoon," Malone said. "We'll get on it as soon as we're done here."

"Speaking of ribs," Mike chimed in, "where is that rib place?"

"I'm hungry, too," Gerill said standing. "You guys follow us and we'll go get some."

"That's great," Pete said standing.

They discussed the case some more while eating ribs and drinking root beer. They shook hands and promised to keep in touch, and Mike and Pete took off for Cheyenne. Gerill and Malone went back to their small conference room and began making calls trying to see if Salinas or Black Cloud owned, leased, or rented a place in Albany County. They did remember that Enrique Salinas had a place northwest of Centennial, but also knew it was seized and then sold at auction after the rescue in Laramie County.

"Bingo," Malone said. It had been two hours since lunch. "Salinas has a place in Albany of all places, a cabin on the northwest side, just north of the South Fork of the Little Laramie River. Had it for two years. Wanna go check it out?"

"Yeah, let's tell the sheriff, he may want to go," Gerill said.

The pair of deputies got up and went to see the boss. He told them to go, but to armor up and be prepared for anything, to radio when they turn in to go to the place and when leaving. He would have a backup unit with two more deputies in Albany if needed. The pair thanked the sheriff and left.

Both armored up and each had their M-4 rifles and extra magazines loaded and ready to go. They checked all their equipment, got into Gerill's Sheriff's Office SUV and left for Albany. It was 1600 hours.

*****

"Captain?" Tabitha said.

"Yeah."

"Albany County Sheriff on the horn for you."

"Thanks...Carlisle, how's it goin'...? You don't say...they're going now...want us to help out...I can have my two detectives turn around and code three it to Albany...will do," he said hanging up and going to his radio station. He got ahold of Mike and Pete and directed them to turn around and head to Albany, and for the one not driving to call him. He then called Anita and told her to get down to his office. She flew in a moment later just as the captain's phone rang.

"Pete, Captain Carlisle here, the reason is Salinas owns a cabin on the northwest side of Albany. Malone and Gerill are on their way up there to check it out and might need all the backup they can get. You're authorized code three all the way, but I'd say kill the noise a couple of miles out. Yeah, I authorize it and the Albany County sheriff asked for the help so get on it."

He hung up and told Anita what was going on. Now it became a waiting game and both officers were tense waiting. They knew that Mike and Pete would get to Albany in about forty-five minutes as they had just reached the Summit when they got the call.

"Want me to get another team ready to go?" Anita asked.

"No, Albany has another team responding. Mike and Pete are insurance."

✻✻✻✻✻

Malone made the radio call in to the sheriff letting him know they were on site. Gerill crept forward with his SUV, the gravel crunching under the tires on the two-track leading to the cabin. When they could see the place through the trees, Gerill stopped and turned off the cruiser. They waited, watching and listening. Malone gave Gerill a tap and they got out of the rig with their rifles, charged the weapons, and eased into the trees.

They separated by about ten yards and moved abreast of each other towards the cabin. It was a small place, just a weekend place by the looks of it. A stack of what looked to be two cords of firewood was on the porch to the right of the door, and just did cover about a third of the one window on the front.

Both stopped when the trees ended. They waited, listening, and watching for movement, especially at the window. Seeing or hearing nothing, Gerill gave the signal and they moved in unison, creeping towards the place. There were no cars or trucks around so they figured the place was vacant, and they soon verified this as they mounted the porch.

Malone actually knocked on the door, making Gerill jump.

"Quit that," Gerill said.

Malone chuckled and stretched over the stacked firewood to peer through the window. "Don't see anyone, wanna try to go in?"

"Let's make a circuit first then try," Gerill directed, he going left and Malone right.

In the back was a small shed, probably holding a snow blower, gardening tools and such. There was a back door to the place and Gerill tried the knob. It was unlocked!

Both swung their backs against each side of the door and waited. Since the door swung in, both looked at each other wondering if anyone would come out or begin shooting. After several tense minutes, Gerill looked around the doorjamb and peered inside. Nothing was moving so he motioned for them to enter, he going left and Malone to the right.

After clearing the place, they went through every drawer, closet, and cabinet. Gerill even tapped on the walls searching for secret panels. Malone used his rifle butt to pound the floorboards looking for hatches to underground areas. They found nothing like that.

They read all the paperwork they found and those they thought relevant photographed. It was 1830 hours when they called it quits and radioed in to all parties that all was well. The other pair of Albany County deputies left Albany to go back on regular duty.

Mike was doing one hundred thirty miles per hour and preparing to turn south on Highway Eleven when they got the radio call to stand down and return to Cheyenne. "Ah, crap, we never get to have any fun," Mike complained taking his foot off the gas and shutting the lights and siren down,

Pete said, "You did get to drive almost ninety miles at over a hundred though. Isn't that enough?"

"I suppose," Mike answered in a forlorn tone. "It was fun, wasn't it?"

"Yeah, I did get a kick outta that even though I wasn't driving. I loved seeing the faces as we swept past."

"Come on, I feel so good dinner is on me, and we need fuel," Mike said pulling a U-turn on Highway 130. They headed back, fueling in Laramie, then on to Cheyenne having decided to have dinner at *Pour Decisions*, a restaurant that catered to a wide clientele. Mike and Peter both liked the fried chicken sandwich with roasted jalapeno, onion rings, and a fresh root beer. They pulled in at 2000 hours. Afterwards they would head home for a well-deserved rest.

Chapter 25

The sunrise the next morning was a typical Wyoming spectacle with oranges, reds, yellows, and a beautiful maroon color shadowed by the clouds. It was one of those pieces of art that only God could paint. And, as usual, it only lasted ten minutes or so.

"Did you see that sunrise this morning?" Anita asked as she, Connie, and Bish walked into the office. Several 'yes' answers came out as she moved to her desk. Only four of her crew was in.

"Bish…Connie, you two work on the Colorado issue today if you would," Anita told them. "We need to find out where Salinas lives down there and get a stakeout on it."

"Will do, boss," Connie said. She and Bish went to their computer stations and began the task.

"Pete…Mike, if you would, please contact Albany County and see if they got anything out of that cabin that might be useful."

"On it, boss," Mike said and picked up his phone to call either Gerill or Malone. Pete poured the pair a mug of joe and sat at Mike's desk, handing his partner his cup. They both clinked mugs and took a sip. Mike quickly swallowed when Gerill answered. "Hey, TJ, this is Mike over in Cheyenne, how's it goin'?"

"Hey, doing well, and I want to say thanks for your effort in getting to Albany yesterday," Gerill thanked him. "We really appreciate the support."

"We had a blast hauling it all that way," Mike said.

"I bet; I know I'd enjoy it. How fast did you get?" Gerill asked.

"Better 'n one-thirty near the Laramie Airport…we were really hauling it. Glad we didn't hit an antelope. That would have been a mess."

"No kidding. So what do you need?"

"The boss asked me to call and see if you got anything outta that cabin you went through."

"Ah, yeah we did get some documents copied…hang on while I get 'em," and Mike could hear the phone being put down on the desk and paper rustling.

It was just a minute later when TJ came back on and gave Mike the overview. Mike had put the phone on speaker and Pete was listening in.

"The only real interesting thing Dave found was an envelope from Colorado, addressed to Salinas. It was a utility bill from a place near Broomfield."

Anita, Connie, Bish, and half the remaining crew jumped up and surrounded Mike's desk. "What's the address?" Anita practically yelled.

"Anita, that you?" Gerill asked.

"Yes and everyone else has surrounded Mike and Pete wanting to hear this," she said.

Gerill gave the address and it was like the principle walked into the room as everyone, save Mike and Pete, dashed to their desks to begin research on the address given.

"Wow, that cleared the room," Mike told Gerill.

"You're kidding," TJ said.

"Nope, you couldn't have gotten them to move that fast with anything else. I'll say thank you for all of them," Mike said.

"Me, too, thanks," Pete dittoed.

"You're welcome, and you guys come over for some ribs again real soon. Talk to you later," and TJ Gerill rang off.

"Man, I've never seen them move that fast," Pete said quietly. "I 'bout jumped outta my skin."

That got a chuckle from Mike, who said, "Yeah, you always were a frady cat."

"Shut up you…you…cop," Pete chided.

✱✱✱✱✱

The address was actually west of Broomfield, in Eldorado Springs, off Colorado Highway 170. The bill was for just over seven-hundred dollars for one month so the home had to be a large one. Mike brought up *Google Earth* and after some searching, found the place and it indeed was huge. It had a paved driveway, what looked to be a connected three or four-car garage, several out buildings, and a fenced in area that looked to be a garden of some kind with a green house.

"This guy must be loaded if his utility bill is around nine grand a year," Andy the rookie said. That's a third of what I make in a year."

"Yeah, and look at this place," Clint, another rookie, said pointing at the image on the computer screen. "I could get comfortable living in a place like that."

"I bet he can see for miles with that place up on the side of that mountain like it is," Andy commented.

"I bet he has some wild parties up there, too," Clint added.

"Okay, knock it off you two and get back to work instead of ogling someone else's home," Anita sternly said. The two rookies moved quickly to their desks. Bish couldn't help but snicker and he got the look from Anita.

The crew was hard at it and things appeared to be coming together. Now if they could only link Salinas with the murders. And what about this Black Cloud dude – is he involved as well. And the Renaldo del Monte…what's his involvement? Too many questions still remained unanswered. Too many holes remained and to be able to fill in the blanks they needed to find Salinas, Black Cloud, and del Monte to come up with answers.

Anita sat back in her chair and sipping her coffee, went into deep-thought mode. She was running everything they had through her thought processes, attempting to find a missing link or two.

Bish looked at his watch and saw it was getting close to noon and his stomach was growling. He turned in his chair and looked at Anita and she had the thousand-yard-stare going and clutching a mug of coffee. He knew the look and decided he could wait a bit longer. He knew not to interrupt that train of thought, as it would bring repercussions that he didn't want.

He went back to his task at hand. His stomach growled again and he noted it was seven after twelve, so he turned and saw Anita still staring. He shook his head and said her name.

She startled and almost spilled her cold coffee. She looked at Bish with a wondering look and he pointed at his watch. She looked at the clock on the wall and her eyes went wide. She didn't realize she had been in deep thought for so long. She took a sip of her coffee and cringed at the coldness of the fluid, gave a grimace and looked at Bish. He was smiling.

"Time to go to lunch according to the clock and my stomach," Bish said. "Where to today?"

Anita got up and going to the sink, poured the cold coffee in and rinsed her mug. "How about *2 Doors Down?*" she answered.

"Deal, I like their fries," Bish agreed. "Connie, you ready for lunch?"

"I'm going out with Clint, Tom, and Andy for lunch today if that's okay," she answered.

"That's fine, kid, we'll see you later," Bish said getting up to leave. He took Anita's arm and they left.

At the restaurant, Anita chose the mushroom Swiss burger with fries and Bish ordered a bacon cheeseburger with fries. They both had sweet tea.

"How far along are you on the book?" Anita asked.

"Haven't done much lately since I've been helping on this case with you, but I'm on chapter twenty," he replied. "I figure I'm about midway through the story. I have to begin the thinking process for the ending."

"Will it be exciting?" she asked.

"I'm trying for that. I'm sure it will affect every emotion known to man, and that's what I want. I want the story to move a person, you know. I want them to feel the emotions as they read. I want them to hunger for the next line, the next paragraph, and the next page...does that make sense?"

She looked at him not saying a thing. She realized he cared about the reader, those people that would read his work. Finally she said, "I think it does. What you just said tells me you're more concerned with the reader's emotions than you are about your book."

"I feel that writing a book isn't just putting an idea on paper or in cyberspace. I'm not in it for the money, I really want the reader to enjoy what I write, so much so that they experience an emotional attachment to the characters and the story itself and feel emotionally involved. I want the reader to ask 'what's next, who is doing what and why'. Why did this happen or that?"

"I think it will be a wonderful book."

"You don't even know the story line so how can you say that?"

"Because you care. Not only about the words you're putting on paper, but you're more concerned about the person that will be reading your work. I wonder if other authors are just as concerned."

Their lunch came and that ended the conversation. Bish inhaled his burger and fries and the server refilled his tea twice.

"Man, that was good and I was starving," Bish said with a satisfied smile.

"Yeah, right...starving...sure," Anita said sarcastically. "You ready to get back to it?"

"Yeah, I have a string or two to follow. You know, those computers are useful to a certain point."

Anita looked at him as he wiped his mouth for the last time and took a last swig of his tea. "What's that supposed to mean?"

"Computers...they have so much information in them to use. They're great for doing research like we're doing and like I'm doing on my book. But, there is so much information it takes time to go through it to find exactly what one needs. For us as cops that's not good, the slowness of the process finding the right information. You know what I mean?"

"Actually I do, and I feel your frustration. I do wish there was a faster way to get the correct information. Even using the search engines and inputting exactly what one is looking for just doesn't cut it as it still gives thousands or millions of findings to view."

"Information overload is what I call it. Too much of a good thing I guess. But we'll do the best we can with what we have. Come on, toots, lets hit the road," and he got up offering Anita a hand as he did so.

They left and walked back to her SUV. "What a beautiful day," she commented. "I wish we could just keep on walking for a while and enjoy the outside time together. I'd rather be up at your cabin, you know?"

"Our cabin - and yes, I know what you mean and I wish the same thing. I think I should put some kind of power in up there so I can write. The laptop dies after a day or so without a recharge. I guess I could have a crew come in and put in a sceptic system and a toilet, too. I bet I could get a well drilled easy enough up there, especially with the creek the way it is. Maybe I can run a line directly from the source of the creek - you know it's over by the cliff - and we'd have at least cold running water most of the time."

"That sounds nice and with the new bedding arrangements I want to make, the place will be just about perfect."

"Come on, let's take that walk. We'll get back to the office in a while. Let's enjoy the day and the weather," Bish said, taking her hand in his and pulling her towards Lincolnway. They crossed and went to the Cheyenne Depot Plaza in front of the old railroad depot and they strolled in the sunlight enjoying the heat and the mild breeze, a rare thing in Wyoming.

Both were smiling and swinging their hands back and forth as they walked around the plaza. The moment was a happy one for the pair, even though they didn't realize they were being watched.

The guy was sitting on a plaza bench, pretending to read a book, but keeping a wary eye on the two cops smiling and strolling around. He wondered what they were doing, but kept watch anyway. That was what he was being paid to do. Just watch 'em.

Chapter 26

Anita was driving. "Why so quiet all of a sudden?"

"Did you see that guy watching us?" Bish asked. "Either he was amused at seeing a couple walking around holding hands, or he was 'watching' us," he used his hands to quote the watching.

"I did notice him, but I figured the former, he was just reverential seeing us strolling hand-in-hand."

"My *spidy-sense* tingled, though."

"Uh oh," Anita said, smiling.

"Knock it off. I really got a creepy feeling about that guy. I don't think he was just amused. I wish I coulda got a picture of him. Mike and Pete would have run him down." He looked at his wife driving and added, "Any tails?"

She looked in the mirror a few times and after a moment said, "Green VW Beetle about five cars back in the left-hand lane. We'll see when we make the turn to the station."

When she made the turn, she watched in her mirror and sure enough, the bug turned with them, although still five cars back. She made the left onto the street the station was on and just before she turned into the underground garage, she saw the bug follow once again.

"The bug turned with us again," she said to Bish as she grabbed her radio mike. "This is Delta six-one; we have a lime green Volkswagen Beetle following us. I need a unit or two to make contact and tail the bug."

"Charlie one-one, he heading west?" a patrolman asked.

"Yes, just about to pass the station garage entrance."

"On it."

"Charlie nine, one-one I'll run west and intercept if he turns," a second patrolman said.

"Copy, thanks."

Anita and Bish stayed in the car listening to the two officers. Charlie one-one picked up the bug and tailed him. When the guy made a turn to the south, he reported this to Charlie nine and she intercepted as the bug turned west on Lincolnway. The guy turned north onto I-25, and Charlie nine asked if she should continue the tail.

Anita answered, "Charlie nine, authorized to the northern Cheyenne border. Contact me then, please."

"Copy, Delta six-one."

Ten minutes later Charlie nine contacted Anita and said, "He's still heading north; I'm turning off on four-mile, copy?"

"Got it Charlie nine, thanks for the support," Anita said, then picked up her phone and contacted Laramie County Sheriff's Office (LCSO) and asked for a tail, and that if the bug went into Platte County, to contact the PCSO and ask they continue the tail.

"No problem, Anita, I'll get a unit on it right away," the LCSO dispatcher said.

Forty-five minutes later, a PCSO deputy called Anita and told her the guy pulled into the garage of the house they had been watching for so long. They noted the yellow Camaro was still in the garage also.

"Thanks a million, deputy, that's great news," Anita said smiling. "Mike…Pete, get over here please." When they got to her desk, she updated them and directed them to get the videos from the cameras around the plaza at the depot. She and Bish would be able to ID the guy, especially Bish. The two detectives hustled to the task. Anita sat back in her chair, deep in thought.

She called the captain and updated him, telling him about the tailing and what PCSO did and told her. She told him she had Mike and Pete on the videos from around the plaza and maybe they'll be able to get a good photo of the guy and see if he's one of them they already had on file. She said she would never doubt Bish's *spidy-sense* again. The captain laughed and told her he would contact the chief.

Meanwhile, Mike and Pete got four videos from the plaza and began watching. They called Bish over when they saw the pair move into the view. The three watched as Anita and Bish went by the main door of the depot, and saw the man walk over and sit on the bench. They tried zooming in and the images were too blurry and grainy to view. The second video had the same result.

The third however, showed a clear image of the man from his right side. They could also tell he was definitely watching the two sauntering around the plaza and not reading the book he had out. A noise or something caught the man's attention and he looked in the direction of the camera and they got a full-face view. Mike made hard copies of the both the profile and front-on shots for everyone.

The three pulled the other photos of the men under surveillance. None of the photos matched this new character. They had a new face for the task force, and immediately went to Anita with the revelation.

"Great job, guys," she told them. "How many copies did you make, Mike?"

"A dozen of each, you want me to get 'em ready for distribution?" Mike asked.

"Yes, please, and the faster the better," Anita said. He turned for his desk and Anita told Pete and Bish she would take them down to the captain as soon as they were ready. "Bish, Pete, please run the photo through facial recognition and see if we get anything."

They turned for their desks, but Anita stopped them asking, "Did you notice if the guy touched anything while he was sitting there?"

"Not really," Bish answered.

"Then look again and if hc did, get Norman's guys on it please."

"Will do, boss," Pete said and turned again for his desk.

Bish smiled at her and gave her a wink, then turned.

"Bish…" He stopped and looked at her, "I'll never doubt your sense again."

He smiled again and went to view the video with Pete.

*****

When Mike delivered the prepared photos to Anita, she left for the captain's office. There, he took them and looking at his set, said he didn't recognize the guy. Anita told him Pete and Bish were watching the videos again to see if the guy touched anything so they could send Norman's guys out for prints and maybe latent DNA samples. Carlisle told her that was a good idea and if she need his support with Norman to let him know right away. She left his office satisfied. He would deliver the rest of the photos.

As she walked into the office, Bish was motioning for her to come over. "He touched the side of the bench with his right hand when he sat down. Norman is coming up to look and said they'll go right away."

That's when Norman walked in. He, Anita, Pete, and Bish watched the video together and Pete pointed out everything for Norman.

"Anita, we'll go right now, if that's okay with you," Norman said. "Well vacuum the area, too, for DNA samples. I'll let you know as soon as we get everything together."

"Great, Norm, I know your team will do a splendid job, thanks," she told him and he turned to leave. "Mike, Pete, and Bish, the captain said great job. He's happy we picked up on this."

All three told her thank you and went back to work. She went to her desk and sat down. Now it was a waiting game once again.

"Did they see you?" Salinas asked the new guy.

"No, sir, unless it was just in passing," he answered. "All they did was walk hand-in-hand around the plaza, and then drove back to the station."

"Did anyone follow you?" Salinas asked.

"No, sir, I was very careful."

"Very good, you did well," Salinas said and hung up. He sipped his Vodka Collins with lime drink and sat back on his Chase lounge to enjoy the relaxing sun. With that phone call he decided he would have Black Cloud and his men return to Wyoming the following day. He would remain on the island for another week or so, as he was very much enjoying his holiday.

His servant on the island brought his lunch out, tuna salad sandwich with pineapple spears, apple slices, and tomato wedges.

"I'll have another one of these, please," Salinas told him.

"Certainly, sir," the man said and turned to do Salinas' bidding.

Salinas took a bite of his sandwich while looking out to sea. He marveled at the blue-turquoise expanse of the Caribbean Sea, the white water swells undulating. It was soothing to sit there and watch. This was his kind of paradise. He liked and very much-enjoyed Barbados, but they were not as open to lustful longings as this island. Barbados was a predominantly Christian nation and didn't condone such behavior.

He took another bite of his sandwich as the servant delivered his fresh drink. "Thanks," he said with a mouthful of tuna. The man bowed and quietly left. Salinas continued to enjoy his lunch and the scenery.

Once he ended his meal, he pulled his phone and dialed Black Cloud's number from memory. Once he was connected, he said, "Chogan, I want you to return to Wyoming tomorrow. Call the plane and have them come get you."

"It will be done as you say," Chogan answered and listened as Salinas hung up. He dialed the private aircraft company and arranged for a plane to meet them the following day and take them to Wyoming. They would land in Casper, rent a car, and drive to the home in Wheatland. They would await further orders there.

*****

"Any word on Salinas from Colorado yet?" Anita asked as she walked into the office.

"Nothing as yet," Mike quickly answered.

"Anything new from Wheatland or the Platte County boys?" she asked.

"Nothing," was the answer from Pete.

She stood in front of Mike's desk, thinking, and finally asked, "Anything from Norman yet?"

"Another no, Anita" Bish answered. "We're still waiting. They got back a little over an hour ago and are working the prints they pulled. We'll know soon."

"I hate this waiting," she said unpleasantly.

No one said anything to that statement. They all hated the waiting. It was time wasted to all of them, but it was unavoidable. When Norman was ready with the information, he'd share it.

Anita's phone rang and she practically ran to her desk to answer, "Detective Bishop."

It was the captain, "Anita, any word from Norman yet?"

"No, sir, I just asked that question myself," Anita told him. "I'm sure he and his team are hard at it, captain."

"I hate waiting," he told her, exasperated.

She chuckled.

"What are you laughing at?" he asked her.

"I'd just said the same thing, sir," and chuckled again. "We're all anxiously waiting and wish it was now, you know."

"Yes, I know exactly what you mean," Carlisle agreed. "Keep at it," and hung up.

Anita hung up her phone and looking at the team said, "That was the captain and he's frustrated, too."

That brought a few chuckles from around the room.

"Bish, call PCSO and see if they have anything new on the house," she asked.

"On it," and he turned to make the call.

A few minutes later he went to her desk and said, "Nothing new at the house in Wheatland, but they're still watching. The deputy said they see someone walking around inside every now and then, but no one has left lately."

"Thanks, babe," Anita said smiling at him.

"Babe…?" from Pete. "Babe…you don't look like a Babe," he said sarcastically.

"You're just jealous you dweeb," Bish shot back.

"I agree," Anita said and chuckles arose around the room. Pete, however, was smiling. All in good fun and it helped to break the tension seemingly beginning to be taut as a bowstring in the office. Levity was a healthy pill to swallow in a situation such as the team had before them.

"Who's watching traffic?" Anita asked.

"Me," Connie said, raising her hand like a student in class.

"Is anything strange going by out there?" Anita asked.

"Only Bish," was the answer, which brought laughter from the entire group. Bish gave Connie a look, but was grinning all the same.

"Bish, would you get me a refill, please?" Anita asked holding out her mug.

He took her mug and said, "Sure, babe," giving Pete a look. Pete was smiling and shaking his head.

Bish returned a moment later with her now steaming mug of joe. She thanked him and he went back to what he was doing.

Anita's phone rang, "Detective Bishop." Her head popped up and her eyes got big. "Thanks," and hung up. "Okay everyone, that yellow Camaro is south on I-25 right now. That was the PCSO deputy watching the house. He said there were three people in the car and tailed it until it hit Laramie County.

Pete…Mike…I want you two out to the north side of town post haste and tail these guys. Tony…Steve…I want you at the I-25/I-80 interchange and take over if they exit there. You four keep in touch with each other out there and be careful. Move it.”

The four detectives jumped to their tasking grabbing their M-4s and ammo as they left the office. No taking chances out there.

Anita looked at the five that were still in the office and said, “Tom…Clint…I want you two ready to move out at a moment’s notice. Get your weapons and ammo ready and make sure you have your armor on. I don’t want anyone hurt out there. Connie…Andy…you two have the office. Continue your investigating with Bish helping.” After a moment, she motioned for Clint and Tom to scoot, which they promptly did.

Bish was looking at Anita, nodding his head in agreement with everything she’d just done. Connie looked downcast, not being included in the action portion. Tom was wide-eyed, the rookie still in him, watching everything happening so fast.

Anita picked up her phone and called the captain, explaining everything that had just happened and her actions, which he approved. He wanted to know about safety and she told him she had reminded all of them to have their armor on and weapons, including their M-4s, ready to go. He approved and said he’d call the chief and the other task force members and for her to be ready for calls from them wanting information or to help.

When she hung up, she looked up and Bish was standing in front of her desk, giving her a bit of a startle. “Oops,” he said. “Sorry, I didn’t mean to startle you like that. I think you’ve done this perfectly, getting the guys out to tail these dudes. Pete and Mike’ll get ‘em. Anything you want me to do specifically?”

“A hug would be nice, but…” she said with remorse.

Bish moved around behind her and put her in a bear hug anyway. She tensed for just a second, and then relaxed and laid her head back into his shoulder, enjoying the moment. Connie smiled and Andy looked away.

Chapter 27

Pete and Mike followed the yellow Camaro to the Wyoming southern border on I-25, where they stopped and called it in to Anita. The Camaro didn't even stop, but continued south. The two detectives watched until it disappeared out of sight. Anita told them to return to base and to tell Tony and Steve to do the same.

"Rats, I so wanted to have a high-speed chase today," Pete complained.

Mike was using the radio to tell the other two detectives to head back to the office and why. He looked at Pete when he was done with the call and said, "How about a burger…on me."

"Sure," Pete answered. "I vote for *Sanford's.*"

Mike laughed and said that was going to be his suggestion, and that's where they went after informing Anita.

They ate their meals in relative silence as they were a bit dejected by not having the chase. All cops wanted a chase, to be in the action, or to be in exciting action of some sort. It was a rare day when these officers had any 'real' action to speak of. Sure, they investigated the odd break-in, or a suspected burglary, but they rarely had any action that was super exciting.

The pair finished their bowls of Jambalaya and sweet tea and left to go back to the office. Taking the long way around to the station, they drove in silence. Both had the windows down as it was another of those pleasant Wyoming days from a weather standpoint.

*****

Chogan Black Cloud was driving, heading to Denver, Colorado, to meet up with Roberto Salinas when he arrived later in the day. He had Renaldo and one of the henchmen in the car with him.

Salinas would be landing in just a moment at the Pueblo, Colorado, Memorial Airport. It was a very small airport, just barely capable of handling a private jet like the one Salinas was in. Allister would have is limousine waiting for him and would drive him to his home in Eldorado Springs. He had planned this so that he and his men would sit down to a very good meal an hour after he arrived.

Once the plane landed on runway one-seven South, it quickly taxied to the space near the control tower, where Allister stood waiting next to the lemo. As the plane stopped and down-spooled the engines, the hatch came open and the co-pilot stepped out and went towards the rear of the aircraft, opened the storage hatch and took out Salinas' luggage. Allister was Johnny-on-the-spot to carry it to the lemo. Once it was stowed, he stood, waiting next to the car.

Salinas deplaned after several minutes, shaking the co-pilot's hand and walking to the limo, where Allister greeted his employer, opening the door for him and closing it after Roberto was inside.

Getting in himself, Allister asked, "Where to, sir?"

"Straight home if you please Allister," Salinas said, picking up the Denver newspaper.

Allister did not reply to that, but put the limo in gear and pulled out, turning right on Highway 50 and heading west, turning north on Interstate twenty-five a short time later. It took almost three hours to reach the Eldorado Springs home, as traffic in Colorado Springs and Denver was atrocious as usual.

But, arrive they did and safely. Chogan met them at the door and helped Allister with the luggage, taking it straight to Salinas' bedroom. Back downstairs, the two found Salinas, pouring drinks of Macallan eighteen-year-old scotch. He handed a glass to each of the four men, including Allister, who was most surprised, and said, "This is for a successful Wyoming excursion."

Chogan said, "Here, here." They all sipped the very good scotch.

"Now, I am sure you are wondering why I wanted all of you to meet me here, so I will get right to it," Salinas began. Allister beat a hasty retreat from the sitting room when his boss began, knowing what was to be said was none of his business. "I want Wyoming to forge ahead. Chogan, were, or are, those men in Wheatland watching anyone just now?"

"No, sir, they're staying quiet as much as they can, what with the information you received before we went on…vacation," Chogan answered.

"That is understandable," Salinas said. "Get them on their toes and have them put someone under surveillance. You three will do the same beginning tomorrow morning. Go back to Cheyenne and put as many on the list under your watchful eyes as you can. Please contact me before you take any action."

Chogan half raised a hand and Salinas nodded to him indicating to say his piece, "Sir, if I may suggest, our men just may run into a situation where sudden and decisive action needs to take place, especially if we can take another one or two quietly…is that permissible?"

"Most certainly and I will reward them handsomely for the effort. I believe the military calls that a target of opportunity," Salinas said with a chuckle. Chogan and Renaldo chuckled as well. "Take as much time as you need as I want this job done with finesse and silence whenever possible. Money is no object so acquire what you need to do the job properly."

He looked at the three men seated before him and since they said nothing, he told them to meet him in the dining room in two hours for dinner. Allister already knew to have dinner prepared and ready to serve at six that evening. Salinas turned and strolled to his bedroom as he wanted to take a hot, soaking bath before dinner. Allister had already set his tumbler and decanter of scotch near the tub. The three were on their own until dinner.

The office was quiet with everyone working their own portion of the case. Keyboards could be heard with the tapidy-tap of fingers dancing across letters. Anita looked up from her computer and note taking and saw everyone doing the same or on the phone with someone. Bish was glued to his screen watching and recording traffic. She grinned, but it was a grin of satisfaction knowing her team was hard at work attempting to find a way to apprehend these murderers.

She went back to her own work. She had the utility bill copy they'd received from Deputy Gerill from Albany County, and was working that angle. Since it was a Colorado utility company, she would have very little influence attempting to contact them as they would most likely not cooperate with her at all. She caught Bish's attention and motioned for him to come over to her desk.

"What's up?" he asked as he moseyed up.

"You still think that contact you had with the Colorado cops would help us again?" she asked.

"I'm sure they would, especially since I asked the Chief to send a thank you letter to her supervisor," he answered. "I'm sure that has some butter left."

She handed him the utility bill copy and said, "Please ask them to get what they can from the utility company on this, you know, the usual who, what, where, questions and whatever else you can scrounge from them. I'm sure it'll help the team."

"I got it…okay, I'll give 'er a call," he said with a smile and turned for his desk. He made the call immediately and the young lady answered right away, and, she said she would do what she could if Bish faxed the utility bill to her. He hung up, gave Anita a thumb up, and then faxed the bill to the cop in Colorado.

He had requested that she ask all the usual questions and to add anything outta the box she could think of, that it was vital to their ongoing investigation into the police murders in Wyoming. She had been sincere when she said she would do all she could and get back to him as soon as she could. He thanked her profusely and hung up.

After he'd faxed the bill, he went back to watching and logging traffic. He figured it'd be hours or maybe even a day or two before he heard from her again.

✳✳✳✳✳

The following Monday morning Bish got the call. His contact in Colorado gave him everything they already had, and told him Salinas paid a little over two and a half million dollars for the place. Sadly, they didn't really get anything new. She did ask him if Anita would like them to put a watch on the place. Sure, he said to her and thanked her for everything.

He was about to hang up when she said, "Bish, before you hang up, I went up there and looked around myself."

"Yeah…?" he said.

"Yeah, and I saw eight men enter the place and one was definitely Salinas," she told him.

He turned towards Anita and began snapping his fingers getting her attention and waiving her over.

"That's great, go on," he said into the phone.

"I hung around a while and got several photos of a few of them men that went in with him…want me to email 'em to you?"

"If you do, I'll owe you a steak dinner with all the fixin's somewhere nice, so please do," he told her.

"On their way to you - hey, tell Anita I said hi, will ya?" she asked.

"She's right here, hang a second and you can tell her yourself," he told her, switching the phone to speaker mode. "Go ahead, you're on speaker."

"Hey, Anita, how's it going, lady?" the Colorado officer asked.

"If we'd solve all these murders I'd be doing a lot better, but for the most part, fine…how about you?" Anita said.

"I'm doing great. Hey, if you ever get tired of Bish, send him my way, will ya?" she asked.

"Naw, I'm keeping this one," Anita said, then laughed.

"Hey you guys, I gotta go. Bish, I'll let you know where Anita and I want to go for that steak, ya hear?
," she said as a farewell.

"You just say the word and we'll make it a night out for the three of us," Bish said with a smile. "Bye-bye."

After he'd hung up the phone, he pulled up his email and saw the file from her, opened it and saw pictures of four men. He, with Anita looking over his shoulder, enlarged each photo and made hard copies.

Anita took the first set and took off for the IT guys so they could run facial recognition on them. Bish made another ten copies of each for every office on the task force. He had them ready when Anita came back and taking them told the crew she was going to see the captain.

On the way out the door she said, "Bish, thanks for this," and disappeared around the corner.

He smiled and went back to watching traffic.

*****

"Morning, Captain," Anita said entering his office.

"Morning, Anita, what's up?" Carlisle returned, smiling at her.

"Bish has a contact with the Colorado police and she came up with something new," handing him one set of the photos.

The captain looked over each photo and said, "Get these up to IT for facial…"

"Already there," Anita broke in.

"Good, those the other sets for the task force?"

"Yes, sir," she answered handing him the packet.

He took the envelope and peered inside quickly, then set it aside, saying, "I hope we have 'em on file. They give Bish anything else?"

"Not really, she did say Salinas paid over two point five million for that place he's staying in down there," she answered.

"Whew, if I had that kind of money I wouldn't be working here," Carlisle said with a faraway look.

"You and me both, buddy," Anita agreed. "I'd be up on a mountain somewhere watching Bish write a book or something."

"Yeah, how's he doing with his writing by-the-way?"

"Right now, not at all, since he's been volunteering and working here with us so much. He'll get back to it when we finish this."

"He writing a cops and robbers thing?"

"Yeah, and won't let me see any of it yet so don't ask 'cause I don't know."

The captain laughed. "Okay, you guys keep surprising me…keep at it, lady, now get," he said with a flick of his hand.

"We're on it, boss," she said leaving.

Chapter 28

They were able to get identities on three of the four faces the Colorado contact provided photos of. All three are what is called career criminals, each with long histories of convictions, or in other words, a long rap sheet. All three had convictions for assault and battery. Captain Carlisle and Anita made the assumption the fourth man would also have a similar rap sheet.

"Are the Colorado people still keeping an eye on Salinas' place?" Carlisle asked Anita.

"As far as we know and as far as their resources will allow," she answered. "She called Bish this morning and said they had seen movement, but it was to go get take out at a local restaurant. As far as they know, none of the eight men have left the home and not returned."

"I'll have to give their captain a call and thank him or her for their assistance. Are our people keeping alert?"

"Yes, sir, everyone has doubled up and is not going anywhere alone. Bish was complaining about his neck hurting, saying it was because his head is always on a swivel these days."

Carlisle laughed and said, "No, I won't authorize disability for that."

Anita chuckled and said, "He's already disabled enough. I'll massage his neck muscles…he'll be okay. Shoot, mine hurts, too. I don't feel comfortable even going out for lunch at *Two Doors Down,* much less going anywhere else. It's not too bad going shopping with the three of us together, one or two of us are always watching."

"Three?"

"Yeah, remember Connie is staying with us through this mess."

"Ah, yes, I remember. She holding up?"

"For now, as we all are. Tensions are high for all of us. More for a few and I'm watching them. I think they need a down day and I may give them all a three day weekend, one set Friday through Sunday, and another Saturday through Monday, and follow up with the others the next weekend."

Carlisle interrupted with, "Do it, and do it starting this weekend. How are you, Connie, and Bish holding up?"

"The stress is building, but we're doing okay…why?"

"I want you to take one yourself. You and Bish go somewhere. Can Connie take her time with someone else?"

"Sure, I'll see to it. Bish will appreciate this."

"What will you two do?"

"He'll probably write, knowing him."

Carlisle laughed.

"I'll probably hibernate in a hot bubble bath with a bottle of wine."

"Why does that sound appealing?"

Anita laughed. "I thought that was just a girl thing."

"No, since I put that six foot jet tub in for the wife, I think I've used it more than her. I added a heat pump and it keeps the water at whatever temperature you set it. I keep it at around one-oh-eight for me. And those jets on my knees…ohh, does a body wonders."

"Jet tub, huh…that something like a mini hot tub?"

"Ohh yeah."

"Hmm, maybe when Bish sells his first million books or so he'll put one in for me," Anita said thoughtfully.

"I'll mention it to him," Carlisle told her. "You need to get on back up there. I'll see you later."

"Yes, sir, see you," Anita said and left the office.

Upstairs in her own office, Anita called a meeting. Everyone sat around the big table and wondered what she was going to tell them.

"Good news," she began. "Those three we ID'd, all had long rap sheets. That is the good news. The better news…Connie…Andy…you take a three day weekend beginning Thursday night (Anita knew those two had a thing). I don't want to see you back here until Monday morning. Mike…Pete, you two take a three dayer beginning Friday night and I don't want to see you until Tuesday morning. This is with the Captain's blessing. Clint…Tom…yours will be next Thursday through Sunday. Tony…Steve, next Saturday through Monday. Bish and I will take the following Friday through Sunday."

"I want all of you to relax. Get some good food in you and some good rest. Don't go anywhere alone – Captain's orders. Take your weapons with you and keep your cell phones handy. If something breaks I'll have to recall you. Any objections?" Everyone shook their heads negatively. "Okay, then, back to it," and with that everyone broke to their own desks, smiling of course.

That night, as the three of them ate, Connie thanked Anita for the upcoming time off.

Anita said, "No problem, kid," and Connie blushed just a little bit. Bish kept eating so he wouldn't bust a gut.

Officers were not supposed to date each other - that was the rule. However, Connie and Andy had hit it off when they first met and had been together since. Anita knew this and most likely everyone else in the department knew it, but everyone kept tight-lipped about it.

✻✻✻✻✻

"Gentlemen, I bid you welcome to my home," Salinas began the meeting. "I hope you find everything satisfactory, if not, please see Allister and he will make things right for you. Now, the reason I have called you all together. Mister Black Cloud here," placing his hands on Chogan's shoulders, "is the foreman. He is in charge in my absence. His decisions in my stead are final and binding, is this understood?"

Positive head nods all around the room.

"Good. Now, I want a very dramatic ending to the issue we have in Wyoming. Chogan will give you the particulars, but I want whatever you do to be messy. I want it to shock the people in Laramie County, Wyoming, and specifically Cheyenne. I want them to cower in fear. I want them so nervous, they won't go out. I want them astounded with distress," he said then looked at Allister and asked, "Does that make sense?"

"Yes, sir, you want them scared to death or worse," Allister answered.

"Yes, precisely that," Salinas said smiling.

Several of the men shifted nervously in their seats.

"If I may, what is meant by this?" a man from Venezuela asked.

"To frighten them so much they're afraid to even come out of their homes," Chogan explained.

"I see," the Venezuelan said.

Salinas, in a dangerous sounding voice said, "Fear…abject terror…I want their angst to be so bad they shake in their beds. I want the news media to have nothing on except the reports of your actions. They must be spectacular and so fearsome that anarchy will break out. Criminals will run rampant. The teen hoodlums will go wild, beating people at will, damaging property, stealing cars…," the look on Salina's face became almost maniacal and drool formed at the corners of his mouth. The men looked at him in wonder and a few had reservations about what they had been hired to do.

Salinas continued, "I want their police force so overtaxed that we can work unhindered. Is this clear?" he said looking around the room at the expectant faces and seeing nods from everyone. Salinas looked at Chogan and nodded, turned and left the room, wiping his mouth with his sleeve. Chogan waited several minutes, allowing the men to process what they had just heard.

He stood and began, "Our employer is dedicated to this task do you not agree," it was rhetorical. "You have the address of the home we have in Wheatland. Soon we will advise you of another in Cheyenne. Do not consider these places to be safe (he let that sink in for a moment). If you chose to do so, you may rent another place or even a hotel room somewhere. Do not let anyone else know where it is."

"We can only assume they have our other two brothers incarcerated somewhere. Both have not been heard of for some time. We do not want anyone else captured. That is why I tell you to be cautious in all you do, even keeping your whereabouts quiet and to yourselves. Do not think for one moment these police are not smart. They are! These people even have drones as Mister Salinas said they used one when observing his father's home. You must be cautious in everything you do. But make no mistake, gentlemen, Mister Salinas is most serious when it comes to their treatment once you capture one or two of them. No mercy and let your imaginations know no limit."

Chogan rose announcing the end of the meeting. The men broke and went their way in the spacious home. Two went into the kitchen and made themselves a sandwich with chips, poured some iced tea, and then went and sat on the back veranda.

The rest went to their rooms. There, they reviewed information provided by Salinas. It was in a dark-blue pocket folder and included photos of the targets. Each photo had attached a synopsis about the target – age, height, weight, where they lived, where they worked, who their loved ones were and more detailed information regarding each. The material covered practically everything the men would need to accomplish their mission.

These six new men were recruited from the dregs of the washed-out foreign military services. One was from Iran, one from Venezuela, one from Syria, one from Brazil, one from Britain, and one from France. All spoke English as that was a requirement for acceptance on this job. All had completed their country's specialized training, but these men were not service oriented specimens and were booted for unruly or abnormal behaviors.

They were hardcore. Each would follow orders as they were being well paid for their particular talents. They rarely spoke to one another or to Mister Salinas. They did speak with Chogan as they knew his background from the Mexican Army special forces, thus he was one of them. Besides, Mister Salinas and Chogan was giving the orders. And the order for the day was to review everything they had on everyone who was a target in Cheyenne.

They studied maps of Cheyenne and the surrounding county, also those of Albany and Platte Counties. They reviewed road maps of all three counties as well. Found where the 'safe house' in Wheatland was. They studied where local airports were located for use in urgent departures. Mister Salinas said he would have aircraft waiting at these during the operations for use when and if necessary.

At dinner that evening, questions were asked and answered. The men would be leaving in two days' time and travel to the safe house in Wheatland. From there, they would begin operations. With the other three men already there, nine should suffice. Chogan had assured Salinas this would be so. Weapons and other gear had been acquired by the three there. They had traveled around the state of Wyoming and into Nebraska to acquire tools and materials for the tasking. All would be waiting in Wheatland.

The dinner over, questions answered the men left the dining room and went their separate ways. Several went to their rooms, gathered prayer rugs, and met on the back veranda, which had been swept clean earlier. The five faced east, towards Mecca, ensuring the *mihrab* with its niche facing the proper direction or *qibla*. They began their prayer time.

The other man watched TV in his room, watching a *Jason Bourne* movie and eating a bag of microwaved popcorn. He was drinking some of Salinas' eighteen-year-old scotch. Feet up on a desk, he was a happy camper.

$$*****$$

Salinas called Chogan into his suite. "I want you to leave immediately and go to Wheatland. Take any vehicle you wish...not the Bentley. I want you to ensure everything is ready. Make sure those three twits have all the supplies and equipment necessary for this," he directed.

"I will leave immediately and contact you tomorrow in the usual manner," Chogan said.

"Be careful, Chogan," Salinas commented in a not-too-friendly manner and with a flick of his hand dismissed Chogan to his tasking.

Chogan gave a slight bow and left the room for his own to pack what few things he had. He would stop by the armory before he left and select a few to take along. He felt he always needed to be prepared for any contingency, especially when employed by a sociopath.

Chapter 29

The dawn in Wheatland, Wyoming, broke with a dismal mist falling, heavy overcast, and temperature hovering just over the freezing point. The Platte County Deputy Sheriff shifted uncomfortably in his cruiser's seat, attempting to keep warm in the miserable weather and not succeeding well. He was positive the ten men now in the home he was watching were very comfortable as he could see a steady stream of smoke rising out of the chimney.

Yes, ten men. PCSO had watched as first one man in a Toyota Land Cruiser pulled in, then two hours later, six more men in three vehicles pulled into the drive the day prior. They had not left the premises since arriving. Cheyenne had been notified and by end of day, every police agency in Wyoming, Nebraska, and northern Colorado had been also.

The task force had gathered to discuss the new information and found it to be worrisome at best. Ten men affiliated with Salinas meant danger in the first degree. Who, where, and when were the prevailing questions with no answers at all. Warnings to all law enforcement personnel were handed out to be very observant for the near future, to sing out if any suspicious activity was taking place around them, their families, or homes. Every effort would be made to protect each other during this time.

The alphabet soup mixture of agencies sat off to one end of the conference room and pretty much kept to their selves. They spoke in hushed tones and when specifically asked a question, gave the typical government speak, or one syllable answers. However, one could see the angst in their faces, the stress building. A few of them had been on the rescue and were therefore targets…along with their families.

There was no question that they would all support each other if and when the time came. Police were after all, family to the ninth degree, no matter which agency a cop worked for or with. Family was family and no one messed with an officer's family without having the full measure of police forces coming to bear against the offender.

✱✱✱✱✱

Bish was gazing out his library window, ticked off that he couldn't be included on the task force team – excluded because he was no longer a cop. Yes, it made him somewhat angry, but he understood their reasoning and tried his best to keep his cool, but…. He moved back behind his desk and continued his writing.

He'd been sent home close to ten that morning and after pacing some, made some coffee and once it was ready, poured a mug and went upstairs. He brought up his computer to begin writing, but instead went to the window to stew some more.

What a lousy turn of events, he thought. He looked at the screen and it began to depress him. He kept writing even though his emotions seemed to be getting to him. He wanted to cry…he wanted to scream…he wanted to beat the walls at his misfortune. Being hit in that firefight was a bummer. He never thought he would be wounded like that. And almost dying still weighed heavily on his mind from time-to-time. He still had restrictions from the wound and that bothered him, too.

The screen seemed to tuck into itself so he stopped tapping on the keyboard and just stared at it. The house was quiet. He hadn't turned on any music when he got home as he usually did. He thought about that now, wondering if that would change his mood, and thought about what kind of music to put on. He chose some smooth jazz by Foreplay.

Sitting in his chair, he leaned back and listened to the soft tones emanating from the speakers. He was beginning to relax and get comfortable with the sounds, and woke up sometime later, drool running down the right side of his chin, his neck hurting from his head tilting on his right shoulder for who knew how long.

He coughed, wiped his chin, grunted a few times, and stood. Dizziness set in and he knew he needed something to eat and some water. He was very thirsty.

He stretched and moved around some to relieve the stiffness, then headed downstairs to the kitchen. He opened the fridge and looked around deciding on a cold, leftover pork chop. He grabbed the mayonnaise also. He would make a pork chop sandwich. Yes, a slice of cheese to help it along…and pickles, lettuce, and a slice of tomato.

After building the sandwich, he cut it into halves, from corner to corner, placed the portions on a paper plate and went to the back patio. The glass of water balancing the sandwich plate while he opened the door.

Other than the birds chirping in the neighborhood, he ate in silence. He was alert, eyes constantly moving from space to space, searching for anything out of the ordinary.

This is no way to eat having to constantly be on the lookout for sickies wanting to kill us, he thought to himself. Stress while eating was not a good bedfellow he knew, but he ate his meal and drank his water in silence.

Afterwards, he called Anita, "How's it going?"

"Still hashing out a few things…eating just now," she answered.

"I ate the pork chop for lunch," he confessed.

"I figured you would…the usual?" she asked.

"Yeah, the works and pickles, too," he said.

"Yuk," was the comeback.

"You just don't know how to eat like a man, that's all," he chided.

"I'll get you for that comment, you chauvinist," she taunted.

"You like having a chauvinist around and you know it," he shot back, then, "But I'm a gentlemen chauvinist, huh."

"Yes, you are that, a gentleman that is. What are we going to do for dinner?"

"I haven't been thinking about that yet. I'm done writing for the day so I guess I can come up with something. How about going out to eat somewhere?"

"Really…in our current predicament? You want to go out to eat…"

"Just a suggestion. We've got some chuck roast in the freezer. I could pull that out, thaw it and cook it slow in the Dutch oven with some taters, onions, and carrots, mix some gravy and fix some rice. Have some corn with it. How's that?"

"My mouth is watering. I'll tell Connie. You wearing your gun?"

He crossed his fingers quickly and said, "Most certainly, always at hand."

"Liar."

"What…you want me to pull it and rack a round or two for you?"

"Go get the beef, sugar. I'll see you in a few hours," and she hung up.

The task force had met all day. As they all departed, one could see all the heads and eyes moving in every direction checking the area for threats. Neither seeing nor perceiving any, they entered cars and left to their next destinations.

For Anita and Connie, that was home for a home-cooked meal. When they entered, the house was permeated with the aroma. Both of their mouths began to water.

"Hurry up ladies, soups up," Bish yelled out of the kitchen.

Both hurried to drop coats, weapons, and purses, wash their hands, and sit at the table. Bish was bringing out the last of the meal as they sat.

"You're gonna love this," Bish said. "Connie, would you say the blessing, please?"

Thirty minutes later, their stomachs full, they sat back and enjoyed sweet tea with lime. The chitchat finally moved to the

294

task force meeting with Bish asking the question…what went on.

Anita answered, "We discussed many things. I think the most interesting was the fact that the FBI wanted to put out a decoy to attempt to draw in the killers to try and capture them. That even drew a few chuckles, especially from the Wyoming folks."

"I bet," Bish said with a laugh. However, that thought stayed with him.

"Salinas has not moved from the other place as far as we know," she continued. "The men in the house in Wheatland have been out, but for supplies - groceries and such – but no movement towards Cheyenne. We cannot figure out what they are waiting for."

"Maybe orders from Salinas…you have the house bugged?" Bish said.

"No, not that I know of anyway," Anita answered. "That would be nice though. We're just not sure what they're up to and because of that unknown, we all need to be on our toes all the time, and for you, buster that means keeping that sidearm on all the time you're awake – got it."

"Yes, ma'am," Bish said sheepishly. "I need another box of ammo if you can arrange it. I've got a few extra rounds here, but if I get into a fight, it'll go quickly."

"I'll fix us up," Anita told him. "The alphabet folks are providing a load for everyone and I'll latch onto a nice box or two for us." A box in the alphabet soup environment was a thousand rounds, so having two thousand rounds of nine-millimeter ammo in the house would last them a while. He already had a few over six-hundred rounds in the house for his AR, seven fully loaded magazines and one bandolier with somewhere over four-hundred rounds stuffed in it.

"That should do us, darlin'," Bish said, smiling. "Those alphabet soup guys are nice."

"Yeah, right," Connie quickly answered.

"I agree," Anita said. "I'm sure they want something in return."

"Maybe the collar rights with the media," Bish said laughing.

"They can have it after the last time," Anita said.

"That was a mess and I hated every minute of it that I was conscious for," Bish agreed.

"You lucked out missing most of the frenzy. But, you did suffer after you woke up," Anita said.

"Yeah, I wanted to strangle a couple of those folks, but thanks to you, I kept my cool," Bish said.

"No more of that," she added. "I'll give the media frenzy to the feds any day. By the way, how are you feeling? You seem to be moving around much better."

"I'm much, much better and I've been exercising more, limbering up. I can even bend over and touch my toes again. I'm gonna talk to my doc and see if I can begin jogging again."

"You sure you're ready for that?" Anita probed.

"I think so and I promise I'll start with slow, short distances and wait awhile before any LSDs (in this case LSD stood for Long, Slow Distance). I don't want to push it and have a setback, you know?" he said.

"We'll see what the doc says. When do you see him?" Anita asked.

"Tomorrow morning."

"What! Bish! Why didn't you tell me sooner?" Anita chided him.

"You were busy and I didn't want to worry you. Look, the doc is gonna give me a clean bill of health and charge the county a pretty penny to say so. I'm fine. It'll be okay," Bish tried to say convincingly.

"What time do we have to be there?" a stern looking Anita asked.

"Ten and yes, I do want you there," Bish told her.

Connie had sunk into her seat and sat silently, bug-eyed, watching the fireworks.

"You're going in with us tomorrow morning and we'll go see the doc together," Anita said with finality.

"Sure, whatever you say," Bish agreed.

*****

They were out of the doctor's office by eleven, and no, Bish was not going to be jogging anytime soon. The practitioner had given Bish a list of activities he could do, and first on the list was to rest, and secondly, lay off the alcohol. Bish's lab work was not up to par. The doctor did say that Bish had shown improvement, but he still had a long way to go.

Bish had asked if he could continue to write and the doc gave him the green light for that activity, reiterating he needed to get up and walk around every hour or so to improve his circulation. The doctor said that walking was very good for Bish and should be a daily activity and that he should strive for at least ten-thousand steps a day.

They had almost reached Anita's SUV when she said, "So, what are you going to do?"

"Well, lay off the booze, walk some, and write I suppose," he answered morosely.

She didn't say another word as she unlocked and climbed into the driver's seat and started the rig. Bish got in, fastened his seatbelt, and kept quiet. Anita fastened her seatbelt, put the SUV into gear, and pulled out into the slight traffic on House Avenue.

To start, Bish asked, "Remember what we talked about with the cabin the other night?"

"What, the sceptic and power issue…yeah, why?" She answered keeping her eyes on the road.

"For rest, you mind if I go over there for a while? I'd be spending most of my time in the county seat, getting permits and such to get the work done," he said. "Since our land is surrounded on three sides by National Forest lands, I may even have to go to them for permits, too."

She kept quiet, but he could see she was thinking about it.

"I think I'd even have 'em drill for water," he continued. "I've talked with a few folks over there and the good stuff is down about four-thousand feet or so. One company I talked to would give us a deal, if we went that deep, and only charge fifteen bucks a foot instead of the current rate of twenty-five. That'd still be a pretty expensive hole, but I feel worth it for the good water. And with it, we can have hot and cold running water as I'd have 'em put in a propane system for us with a hot water tank. You'd have lights, a toilet, and a bath."

She didn't say a word, just kept driving until they got home. She dropped him off and said as he closed his door, "I'll think about it," and drove off.

Bish stood there watching her SUV as it went away. He shrugged his shoulders knowing she was ticked off about something, turned and went inside, locked the door, and went upstairs to write.

Chapter 30

Two weeks later, it was a Tuesday, and Bish was once again waiting in the Albany County Seat building. This time he was to finalize the paperwork for the permit to dig the well. Everything else was going splendidly. The plumbing company was just waiting for the well to be dug to set the septic system and run the plumbing to and inside the cabin. The electrical company was already dropping poles in the ground to run power to it. They'd already had a team inside running line and putting in an electrical panel that included a thirty-amp outlet in case a friend brought a camper up to visit or go hunting. The electrician said he'd have power by Friday that week. Neat.

"Mister Bishop," the lady called out.

Bish got up and sauntered over to the counter where she was and said, "I'm Samuel Bishop."

"You're all set, Mister Bishop," she said with a smile. "Here's the paperwork you'll need to show the drilling company supervisor. It says here," and she pointed to a spot on the papers, "that they are authorized to go down to five-thousand feet if necessary – I don't think they will, everyone else up there are down around two to three – and says that you have ninety days to complete the project. Should only take a week or so. Happy?"

"Yes, ma'am I surely am, and thank you very much," Bish told her with a healthy smile.

"You're certainly welcomed, sir, and I hope everything works out for you," she ended turning for someone else's paperwork.

Bish looked over his paperwork for a moment and satisfied, left the office, deciding to go to *Born in a Barn* for lunch. He was smiling as he left the building and thought he'd call Gerill and Malone and ask them if he could buy them a burger. Both agreed and met him there for lunch.

The burgers were great as always, so too were the fries. After being highlighted on the TV show *Diner's, Drive-in's, and Dives*, the place seemed always packed. It was no different this day, as the three had to wait for a table. Hallelujah, the uniformed deputies had priority and got them to the head of the line and were seated in ten minutes.

"So, what brought you over to this neck of the woods?" Dave Malone asked.

"I've got some land and a cabin up in the Medicine Bow, near Albany, and I'm putting in some power and stuff," Bish explain.

"Ouch," Gerill uttered, "there goes a billfold or two dozen."

All three chuckled.

"Yeah, it'll be a chunk of change, but will be worth it in the long run," Bish told them. "I'll get most of it back when I decide to sell the place."

"How long have you had the place?" Dave asked.

"A few years – bought it on a whim," Bish tells him. "I was a bachelor cop then saving every penny for who knew what and I saw this add about the land. On a whim, I called the number listed on the advertisement and the realtor invited me over for a tour. I fell in love with it and made the deal that day. For a long time, only the realtor and I knew I owned the place. I just didn't tell anyone. After a year, I began to build a cabin, you know, a little at a time. I built the foundation first, then the floor and so on. It's a one-room affair with an old-fashioned fireplace I built out of rock from my property. Keeps the place warm and I made a pullout rack that I put a six-gallon stew pot of water on. I put a faucet in the pot down on the bottom. I fill the pot with water on the rack; push it in over the fire and wha-la, hot water at my disposal. Coffee, tea, freeze-dried meals…whatever. When it gets low, just add more water."

"Wow, that's neat," Gerill, said, smiling. "What a novel idea."

"Yeah, I like that, too," Malone agreed. "Did you make a log cabin bed?"

"Nah, I have these sleeping mats I put down along with my sleeping bag, that's it," Bish tells them.

"Why the power now?" Gerill asks.

"I'm married now," Bish said and that brought laughter. "Really, I'm bringing in power, having a septic system put in after the drilling is done for the water. It'll be real up-town when I'm finished. The plumber is a carpenter, too, and he's helping me add on a bathroom replete with a toilet, sink, and a small tub with a shower so Anita can take a bath if she wants."

"How much land?" Malone asks.

"Forty acres. It's surrounded on three sides by National Forest and Albany is to the northwest from the cabin, about a half-mile. That's the nearest neighbor."

"Wow, sounds peaceful," Malone says.

"It really is. Sitting on my front porch sipping coffee or something, I've seen elk, deer, and moose walk right into my front yard. As long as I stay still and quiet, they hang around for a while. Just a while back, Anita and I were sitting there having some iced tea when a doe with a new fawn walked in. I thought Anita would faint. Her eyes were huge watching the pair."

"Ah, what a privilege, and a sight granted by God," Gerill mused. "I bet it was a swell moment."

"Man, you just don't know. I'll never forget her eyes and after they'd moved off she was talking about the moment ninety miles an hour, you know?"

Laughter from the two deputies.

"I hope you two have many happy moments like that up there," Malone said earnestly. "It sounds like a perfect place to go rest and enjoy the outdoors."

"Yeah, it is," Bish, said, but his mood suddenly changed and Gerill noted it.

"What's the matter, Bish?" Gerill asked.

Bish looked up at him and had a very serious look on his face. He looked at his two friends before he spoke and finally said, "You two know what we're going through…you've seen it firsthand. The murders that is."

Both nodded, saddened by their memories.

"Can I ask you two something; off the books and the record?" Bish suddenly asked.

The two looked at each other and both nodded affirmatively.

Bish looked at his empty burger basket for a moment, forming his thoughts, and finally said, "The other day, after Anita and Connie came home, Anita was talking about the meeting with the task force."

"We were both there," Malone stated.

"Good. Anyway, she said that one of the FBI guys made a comment about a decoy, you know, someone making themselves vulnerable, but with plenty of protection around to keep them healthy."

Both said they remembered the talk.

"The next day," Bish continued, "I got to thinking about that and the cabin and figured that would be a good place to spring something like that. And I'd make good bait," he said looking at both and making eye contact.

Both Gerill and Malone sat back in their booth benches and stared at Bish. Both knew what he was saying. Both knew how dangerous it would be.

Bish squirmed on his side of the booth, held up his empty tea glass so the server would refill it, and kept quiet until she had. After taking a sip, he looked the two deputies in the eye again and said, "Now, I wouldn't want to rush into something like this. I know it'll be extremely dangerous, to say the least. But, up at the cabin, I would put in some booby traps and such. And with the right guys helping me," he implied by nodding to the two of them, "we could have a real good chance of cleaning the clocks of these murderers. I'm saying I'd take the time to really plan something like this out and really be prepared."

It got very quiet at that table suddenly. Bish could see the thought processes going full blast in their minds and he wondered if they were sizing him up to be a maniac or something.

After what seemed a long time, Gerill was the first to speak up. "Where's your place, exactly?"

Two hours later and at least two pitchers of iced tea, the three got up, leaving a healthy tip for the server, paid their tab and left, each to their own vehicles. Bish headed to the drilling company to give them the paperwork and let 'em know they were cleared to work. They already knew where to drill, the spot chosen on a previous survey. Bish had given them written permission to work the property even with him not being around.

Gerill got into his sheriff's office SUV, radioed base that he was going to patrol near Albany, and headed for Wyoming Highway 130. He would turn south on Highway 11, and go to Bish's place and look around.

Malone, in his SUV, went back to the Sheriff's Office. He would patrol Albany in a day or two and take a look also.

The planning stage had begun and only three people knew about the operation and they would keep it that way. Bish had already told them about his writing, and now that power was going into the cabin, he'd be having an excuse to go there more often, not only to write, but to prepare.

Gerill had told Bish that he had been in the Army and was a Ranger, and was trained on booby-traps and such and that they would put in a bunch. Malone said he would take care of weapons and ammo for the operation, that he had a very good supplier in Centennial who would go over backwards to assist on an operation like the one they had in mind, even going so far as to help out since he was a Korean War veteran. Bish agreed.

✻ ✻ ✻ ✻ ✻

Once back at the cabin, Bish cleaned up the place, packed the Jeep, locked the place up tight and headed to Cheyenne. He'd left Gerill on his own after giving him a penciled map of the forty acres.

Back in Cheyenne, Bish unloaded the Jeep and headed for the jet tub. He was tired and somewhat worn out after his dealings with government, even the small government of Albany County. It was still a wearisome process. He stopped by the fridge first, found a pitcher of sweet tea, poured a glassful, adding a slice of lime, and went upstairs.

He fired up his I-pad music on the playlist he called 'Morning Relax', an assortment of soft jazz style music from many different artists. He then started the water in the tub, and once satisfied at the heat he wanted, let it run while he disrobed. He went into his library and fetched a book titled, *How to Make War*, by James F. Dunnigan. It said on the cover that it was a 'comprehensive guide to modern warfare'. Just what he needed to read he felt.

Back in the bathroom, he pulled a hand-towel and a washcloth, set them and the book on a small table they had next to the tub, and then eased into the hot water, giving an audible 'ahh' as he sat down. He relaxed until the water got above the jet openings then turned on the jet system and the heat pump. The pump would keep the water at the temperature he'd set the water for as long as he remained in the tub, and today that was just about 108 degrees Fahrenheit. A few minutes later he turned off the water when it reached what he called 'his level', then lay back, and relaxed, allowing the jets to massage his tired muscles for a bit.

He startled, having just about fallen asleep in the soothing bath. He shook his head to clear the cobwebs, took a healthy slug of his tea, donned his reading glasses, and picked up the book to review. He saw several chapters he would read back in his library and take copious amounts of notes to share with Gerill and Malone. He figured Gerill could write the book with what he knew about war after his tours in the desert.

He sat the book aside, took another big slug of his tea, and then slid down as far as he could in the hot, turbulent water. A satisfied smile creased his lips and he closed his eyes to savor the heat and massaging movements of the water.

He heard the front door open and knew Anita and Connie had arrived. They didn't expect him until the following day, so he, in the tub, would be a surprise. He heard Anita call up the stairs, "Bish, that you up there getting cooked?"

"Yes, darlin', it's me," he answered. "I'll be down in a bit," he followed and went back to savoring the water.

✳✳✳✳✳

"He'll probably be up there another hour if I know him," Anita pondered aloud. "We may as well think about something for dinner. What say, kid, what are you in the mood for tonight from the delivery world?"

Connie looked askance, thinking, and after a few minutes said, "How about Olive Garden? They don't deliver, but will bring it out to the car as you drive up."

"That sounds fine," Anita said. "I'll order lasagna for Bish and me. We can order one large salad to share, get some bread sticks. My mouth is watering."

"Lasagna is what I was thinking about also," Connie said, smiling. "I'll give 'em a call and order three lasagna meals, a large salad for three, and bread sticks. My treat tonight, since you guys have treated me to a safe haven her in your home. The least I can do."

"Thank you, that's nice," Anita said, smiling. "Go ahead and call it in and I'll alert the whale in the tub upstairs."

Connie laughed as she pulled her phone.

Anita went upstairs, knocked lightly on the door, and when Bish said 'yes', she opened the door a crack and said, "It's me, sweetie."

"Better be," he said looking at her.

Anita smiled looking him over in the tub and said, "We're ordering lasagna dinners from Olive Garden and will be leaving in a few minutes to go pick the order up and bring it back. Don't drown now, you hear?"

"I'll be here and clothed when you get back," he said with a grin. He lay back for another few minutes of relaxing time in the tub.

Chapter 31

"He's going to his cabin again, el Jefe," Chogan told Salinas.

"How do you know this?" Salinas asked.

"He's loading his Jeep with equipment, enough that it looks as if he'll be staying awhile," Chogan began. "He goes there to be alone and write."

"He is writing…what?" Salinas inquired.

"We do not have that information, el Jefe," Chogan told him.

"That is thought provoking," Salinas, spoke more to himself than Chogan. "If you can find out, do so…if not…no matter. Will you have opportunity with him?" implying would Chogan's crew take Bishop at the cabin.

"I thought you wanted us to wait on he and his woman, to the last." Chogan stated.

"Yes, I did," Salinas, answered. "However, what kind of statement would it make to her and the community if he is killed in a manner befitting his position?"

"It would be a strong statement indeed," Chogan replied with a sneer.

Salinas sat deep in thought and eventually, looking at Chogan, said, "No, I prefer the two of them be taken together. Is there any indication she will be accompanying him?"

"None, el Jefe."

"Sad. So, have two of your best tail Bishop to his cabin and have them watch."

"It will be as you say, el Jefe."

"Chogan, have them take photos for me. I want to see the place. Tell them they may stay in my cabin on the northwest side of Albany. Give them the map and key. They may stay as long as needed. Thank you," Salinas said, and that ended the conversation.

Chogan gave a nod of his head, turned, and left the room. He pulled one of his burner phones, called his men in Wheatland and gave the two their marching orders, with explicit understanding they were to do no harm unless directly threatened. They understood the orders and told Chogan his orders would be carried out to the letter.

*****

Bish had quite the load in the Jeep. The poor beast struggled on the hills along Happy Jack Highway. He stopped in Laramie at the Yamaha dealer and ensured the All-Terrain Vehicle (ATV) he'd ordered was in. It was. It was a beauty, the same color as his Jeep. Bish had them deck the thing out, with a six-foot plow blade, eight-thousand pound winch on the front, a locking trunk-like cabinet in the back, dump-truck style bed, and had them make the thing legal to drive on the road if necessary. He'd also ordered a full cab for the thing with windshield, doors, and rearview mirrors on the wings, a horn, and turn signals. It even had the capacity for towing light loads. Bish was quiet pleased and told them he would be back the following day to pick it up and the new trailer with it.

After he'd paid the bill for the ATV, he went to the local ranch and farm store and bought five, six-gallon gasoline cans. Having an extra thirty gallons of fuel available for the ATV would come in handy. He also bought two, one-hundred foot ropes, an axe, a shovel, a high-lift jack, a fire extinguisher, an ammo can (for nuts and bolts and such), a spool of bailing wire, a roll of duct tape, an emergency stove and cook set, several freeze-dried food packets, and survival matches. He also picked up two, four-packs of ratchet straps, and a large bundle of bungee cords. These items would go into the 'trunk' he'd put on the ATV. He knew they would come in handy on occasion.

One could not put another item into the Jeep after he'd placed all of the items just bought into the vehicle. He could barely fit. He chuckled as he pulled out of the ranch store parking lot and made his way to his property. He barely gave the ratty-looking Ford, a second thought as he pulled out.

Once at the cabin, he pulled the Jeep right up to the porch steps and began unloading his haul. It took him over an hour and afterwards, he parked the Jeep in its place in the trees and back in the cabin, started a fire. He also turned on the pump for the new well, the propane also, and lit the hot water tank, smiling all the while. He was happy with the improvements they had put in, as even turning on a light was a joy.

Everything put away, he started his dinner, which for tonight would be one of the freeze-dried meals. It happened to be one of his favorites - *chicken and rice*. Too, the pouch held enough food for two, so he would have enough for his lunch the following day. He would have a heated hoagie bread loaf and iced tea with his meal.

While he waited for the water to boil on the fire, he thought about the materials he'd brought. They would have to wait until the day after tomorrow as he was too tired to start something this night and tomorrow he would be picking up his new ATV and trailer. He would fill the gas canisters also and tie them down to the trailer with the ratchet straps.

He found himself very tired after eating, so threw two more logs on the fire, and turned in. Still sleeping on the mats and sleeping bag.

*****

The two henchmen followed Bish all the way to Albany and watched as he turned onto the two-track leading to the cabin. Satisfied, they retraced their way into Albany proper and turned onto Mister Salinas' lane to his cabin turning in for the night. The next few days would be challenging for them.

*****

The following morning, Bish was up early making a breakfast of eggs, bacon, toast, and an apple. Of course, a mug of steaming hot coffee. He sat out on the front porch and as he ate, he watched the birds, chipmunks, and squirrels frolicking and foraging for their morning meals. He had always enjoyed sitting on the front porch quietly and watching the animals. It was peaceful.

He'd cleaned and put away the dishes, brushed his teeth, and taken a shower. He felt the shower was much better than the lukewarm sponge bath he usually had. Afterwards, it was a smiling Samuel Bishop that loaded the empty gas cans into the Jeep and set off for Laramie. He figured he wouldn't return until early afternoon with his new toy, the ATV.

In town, he first went to the ranch store and bought another pair of work boots. His pair at the cabin were just about done in. As he left the store, he noted it was just past nine, so the dealer would now be open.

There, the dealer showed him his new ATV already sitting upon the trailer. The plow blade had been stowed against the front rail of the trailer. They had already tied down the ATV with ratchet straps and the dealer showed and explained to Bish where and how they should be properly used when trailering the rig.

The dealer helped him back the Jeep up to the trailer and hook up, ensuring for Bish all the lights worked properly. Bish set the emergency brake and got out, thanking and shaking the hand of the dealer. He was excited to get back to the cabin and run around Albany and elsewhere in his new ATV.

His last stop before Albany was a gas station. The one he liked happened to be right at the turning point onto Highway 130. He pulled in and got the gas cans out, as he would fill the Jeep, the ATV, and the six cans.

As he began filling the cans, the owner, Jerry, came out and said, "Hey, Bish, what 'cha got there my boy?"

Looking up, Bish smiled and said, "Got a new toy, Jerry. What'd ya think?"

Jerry walked around the trailered rig, gave a whistle, and said, "Ain't she a beaut! Same color as your Jeep, too. That's nice. You're gonna have a blast up there with this thing, man."

"I think you're right, Jerry. You'll have to come up sometime and take a ride with me. Maybe we can zip up to Rob Roy and do some fishing."

"That's the ticket – fun 'n fishin' – you betcha. I'll be happy to come up sometime." Jerry knew about the land, just didn't know where exactly.

"Next time I'm in for fuel we'll set something up, how's that?"

"Sure, sure. Man, you're gonna have a blast with that. Well, gotta get back in there, you be careful with that thing, ya hear. See ya later, Bish," and he went back inside.

"See ya later Jerry, and thanks for the gas," Bish said as he filled the last can. He stowed the six, full gas cans on the trailer, tying them down with bungee cords. He pulled his receipt, climbed in the Jeep, and set off for the cabin.

✱✱✱✱✱

Bish stored the gas cans in a shaded area behind the cabin. He took one, and added it to the supplies and equipment he'd already stowed in the ATV, strapping it down with bungees. He looked at what he'd done, figured it was all in and stowed securely, gave a devious smile, and climbed in, adjusted the five-point harness belt system to his body, inserted the key, and started the ATV.

He revved the engine a few times, smiling all the while. He freed the emergency brake, put the thing in gear, and slowly drove it off the trailer. He resisted the urge just to take off, instead parking the new vehicle, and parking the trailer and Jeep. Once that was done, he gave the cabin a quick check. All was right, so he got back into the ATV, set his harness, put on his sunglasses, started the beast and took off down his two-track.

Bish couldn't help it, yelling a great 'yee-haw' as he sped down his trail. Once out to the main road, he turned to the left and headed up the mountain into the National Forest. He had already made up his mind to go all the way to Rob Roy, and to stop by Lake Owen on the return trip.

He slowed when he saw the moose, watching the big critter as it munched who knew what outta the boggy area it was standing in. It looked Bish's way, but paid him no heed, probably curious at what was making all the racket. Bish smiled, waved, and sped on.

He reached Rob Roy Reservoir in twenty-five minutes. He stopped just over the bridge, unhooked the harness, and got out to stretch. It was a beautiful, sunny day. Of course, the Wyoming wind was up a bit, but he paid it no mind and walked around the ATV, looking at his equipment, ensuring it was still secure. Satisfied, he stretched again, looking to the south over the expanse of the water and savored the scene.

*****

The two henchmen watched as Bish sped past, giving it another five minutes before moving towards the cabin. The leader pointed to the right, sending his partner that direction, while he turned to the left. They would meet somewhere in back of the cabin and talk about their next move.

It took a long twenty minutes for them to rejoin. They spoke in low tones, just barely above a whisper. They knew there was no one else in the cabin and hoped no one else was expected. The two approached the cabin, looking in the windows and even mounting the front porch and checking the door – it was locked. They looked at the Jeep – it, too, was locked – and walked around the front of the cabin.

"When the time comes, this should be easy," the leader said.

"Yes, I feel the same," the second agreed. "How do you want to take him when the time does come?"

"I think he'll park the ATV over there, so when the time comes, we should set up nearby," the leaded said. "We'll need to be concealed very well as this man in no stranger to his surroundings. I have watched and he always checks the surrounding area before he goes into the cabin. I think that once he and the woman turn for the cabin, that's when we shoot – both of us at that instant – ensuring a proper hit and dosage."

"They'll drop quickly, right?"

"Yes, my friend, they will not reach the porch. Anyway, once he and the woman are down, we'll have our fun." Both laughed.

The leader, satisfied with the reconnoiter cut two thick branches off a pine tree. These they would drag behind them as they walked down the two-track effectively erasing their footprints. The man, Bishop, would not be the wiser. The pair made their way off the property and hiked back to Salinas' cabin.

✶✶✶✶✶

Bish felt like a kid again. He was screaming down National Forest Trail 500, heading east, the direction of his cabin. However, he made a crazy, sliding turn onto NFT 513, and then another onto 517, and sped to Lake Owen. He pulled into the trailhead and parked near the fishing pier. He released his harness, got out, and stretched again. He was exhilarated.

He walked down to the fishing pier, more to stretch his legs than anything, and leaned on the railing, looking to the southeast, inhaling deeply the fresh air. He saw an eagle and watched as it soared, most likely looking for a trout for its daily meal. He turned to the north and knew that as the crow flew, his cabin was about two miles distant, over some very tough terrain.

He leaned against the rail on that side and inhaled the air once again. At that moment, he was a very happy man.

Shaking off the melancholy, Bish went back to the ATV, set his harness, and backed out of the parking slot. He floored the beast and sped, what he would call break-neck speeds for dirt, back to the main trail, 500, took a right, and headed home at full tilt. He was cruising at fifty-eight miles per hour when he slowed for the hairpin turn just before his two track.

Bish slowed for the right turn onto his lane and at once noticed something out of the ordinary. He stopped the rig, letting it idle, and he scanned the area. He didn't see anyone, but something was amiss. Something was wrong but he couldn't put it to mind what it might be.

He undid his harness and slowly climbed out after setting the brake. Being cautious, he moved slowly down his lane, scanning both sides of the trail as he moved along. He craned his neck, looking up the two track, and could not see anything out of the ordinary. He stood listening, only hearing the ATV idling to his rear and the birds fussing over whatever. After a few minutes, he shook his head and turned, and that's when it hit him – no tire tracks.

The tracks he'd left when he pulled out that morning were not there and he knew the wind wasn't up that much to have erased the knobby tire tracks the ATV left behind, those he specifically looked at as he pulled out that morning just to see what they looked like in the sandy soil.

He knelt down and looked closely, even moving at a duck-walk back up the trail a ways, looking for something to tell him what happened. He came across a partial footprint, and looking at it, determined it to be a boot, one with cleated soles, possibly combat boots, or such. He backed off and went back to the ATV, hooked his harness, backed out of his two track and headed for Albany. He didn't have phone service near his cabin, but they did near the Albany Lodge.

Since it was close to lunch, he went inside and ordered a sandwich and chips with iced tea. While waiting for his meal, he called Deputy Malone.

"Deputy Malone," Dave said, answering his phone.

"Hey, it's me, Bish…how's it goin'?" Bish asked.

"Hey, brother, I'm good, how about you?" Malone returned.

"I've had company up at my cabin," he began and gave Dave the rundown on the day's events.

"Have you been up to the cabin yet?" Dave asked.

"No, figured I'd give you a call first," Bish answered.

"You have your sidearm?"

"Always."

"Might have known. No, just kidding, but good thing you have it. Want me and TJ to zip up there and give you some backup?"

"Not sure, I'm at the Albany Lodge – ordered a sandwich – and was wondering if someone was up at the cabin waiting for me. I don't want to put you guys out."

"No, TJ is just around the corner, actually. He was patrolling Centennial and Albany today, so I can get him on the radio and send him around. You'll at least have backup, you know."

"Okay, I'll wait for him here. Tell him if he gets here fast enough, I'll spring for lunch."

"Oh, you know what's about to happen now (laughter from both). I'll give him a call. Be careful my friend."

"I will, and Dave, thanks loads buddy."

"Any time, friend, any time. Talk to you later."

Now Bish sat back and sipped his tea, waiting for TJ to arrive. And arrive he did, in less than ten minutes. He sat across from Bish, and the two just looked at each other. When the server came to give Bish his sandwich and chips, TJ said he'd have the same and tea.

After she left, TJ said, "How'd you know someone was at your place?"

Bish explained the morning's events in detail and TJ agreed on his assessment.   TJ knew Bish was an experienced investigator so didn't second-guess him.

"Here you go, TJ, sugar – how ya doin'?" the server said with a big smile.

"I'm doin' fine, Darla, how about you?" TJ asked.

"Much better now that I've gotten to see you today," she said demurely.

"Well I'm glad your day is a good one," TJ said. "Thanks for the lunch," and with that he took a bite of his sandwich, the clear signal she needed to go back to work.

The two ate their lunch quietly, enjoying the tea. When they were done, TJ asked, "I'll follow you up to the cabin. You're driving that blue ATV out front?"

"Yeah, that's my new toy," Bish answered. "I'll let you and Dave know where the key is if you come up, you can take it for a spin. It's nice," Bish said with a grin.

"You had a blast zipping around in that this morning didn't you," TJ said.

"You bet I did," Bish said with a grand smile.

"Come on, let's do this," TJ said and rose.

Bish got up, grabbed the check, and after paying, set his harness, backed out and headed home with TJ on his six.

Bish stopped just before the spot where the boot print was, set the brake and motioned for TJ to come look. Bish pointed out the print once TJ walked up. TJ knelt down and looked at the print, and then scanned around area looking for anything else out of the ordinary.

"Hang here for a sec," TJ said, "I'll be right back. I want to cast that print." He went back to his SUV, got the casting material, set the form, mixed the ingredients, poured it into the form, and waited for it to set. It would take five minutes or so. While the casting was doing its thing, the two looked around the area, even going off the track into the woods and looking around.

TJ came out with two pine tree limbs that had obviously recently cut with a knife. "Looky here – found these back there about ten yards in," holding out the limbs to Bish. "I figure they cut these up near your cabin and used them to try and cover their tracks coming out."

"Makes a lotta sense," Bish said. "See anything else?"

"Not to speak of. Saw tracks in the grass, you know, grass bent over, but nothing of interest."

"Okay, on to the cabin?"

"Yeah, that's the next step. I'd go ahead and pull your weapon and don't put your belts on. Just drive slow."

"Let's do this," Bish said, throwing the limbs in the back of the ATV, getting in and pulling his sidearm, ensuring it was loaded and ready to go. He started the rig, looked back at TJ who gave him the signal to go, and the pair eased up to the cabin.

Bish shut the engine off and it was suddenly very quiet. The birds weren't making any noise either. Both sat in their vehicles listening and watching. After several minutes, both climbed out and slowly moved to the steps on the porch. Bish tried the front door and found it was locked as he'd left it. He unlocked the door and, looking at TJ who indicated Bish was to go right, TJ would go left, Bish turned the knob and threw open the door. The two rushed into an empty cabin.

Instinct and training kicked in and Bish was first to speak up saying 'CLEAR' and TJ quickly followed suit saying the same. When it hit them that's what they'd done, both looked at each other and laughed.

"Ain't we a pair," Bish laughed out.

TJ just nodded. They looked around the cabin and nothing seemed out of place. Bish went and checked the backdoor – still locked. He turned to TJ and shrugged his shoulders.

"Don't think he, or they, came in," Bish said.

"What makes you think 'they'?" TJ asked.

"Two limbs."

"Ah…makes sense."

"Want some tea?"

"Nah, I should get back on the road. Your phone work up here?"

"Nope."

"Rats. We'll need to work that out with something, huh."

"Yeah, I suppose."

"You gonna tell Anita?"

"No and neither are you."

That got a chuckle from TJ. "Well, I'm gonna hit the happy trails," TJ said holding out his hand after holstering his sidearm.

Bish shook his hand and said, "Check six and keep it safe out there, my friend."

"Always," TJ said, turning for the door.

Bish walked him out and waived as TJ swung around and drove out. Bish stood on the porch for a bit and was about to go back inside when it struck him that the birds were making racket again. He thought it must have been the two vehicles that quieted them earlier. He chuckled and went inside.

Chapter 32

Bish had been at the cabin for eight days. The book was coming along nicely, according to him, and he felt he really had an accomplishment with his work. He knew he'd made the right decision to have power run out to his place, even though it had cost him. Between the electricity, water, and sewage, the bill was…almost hurtful. He shuddered, thinking about it.

The day was a beautiful one. No clouds. The wind was just a gentle breeze, and the birds were making a lot of noise this sunny morning. Bish had taken his break after writing for just over an hour, walking to the end of his lane and back to the cabin. Once back, he poured a cup of coffee and sat on the porch on the sunny side to enjoy the sunshine.

He was taking a sip of his coffee when the birds went quiet. He paused listening, and could hear a vehicle coming down his lane. He pulled his sidearm, ensured a round was chambered and held it down on his right side in anticipation.

It was a sheriff's vehicle, and as it drew closer, he could see Dave Malone at the wheel with a broad smile on his face. He stuck his arm out the window and gave a wave as he pulled into the small clearing in front of the cabin.

Bish jumped up, holstering his sidearm, and met Dave as he was getting out of the SUV. "How's it goin'?" he asked.

"I'm doing fine, Bish, how are you?" Dave asked.

"It's nice being out here, but I miss Anita something awful," he answered, then, "What brings you out?"

"My turn to patrol out here, Centennial, Albany, Woods Landing…you know, so I thought I'd stop by and say howdy," Dave said in answer.

"Glad to have you or TJ anytime. How's he doing?"

"Same old, same old. You know TJ, always on the move and not really getting anywhere."

Both chuckled.

"Fresh pot on, you want a cup?" Bish asked.

"You have to ask?" Dave said incredulously.

Another chuckle by both, then the two turned and went inside. Bish poured and handed a fresh cup to Dave and refilled his mug also. They went back outside and sat on the Adirondacks on the front porch.

Dave had just taken a sip of his coffee when he remembered something and said, "You remember that casting TJ took of that partial boot print?"

"Yeah, vividly, why?"

"We got a hit on the make of the boot, a Venezuelan combat boot no less."

"No way, really?" Bish asked, astonished.

"That's what the people say, a Venezuelan combat boot, one that is issued to their Special Forces people. You can get 'em on line at a few US outlets, but they're expensive as all get out. No way to check if anyone in the area has ordered a pair, but we're still looking."

"Wow, that's amazing that you could ID those from that print."

"It was the pattern of the cleats that did it. The pattern is very specific to their manufacturer, go figure."

"Still, someone hit a home run picking up on this. I bet you've already wondered the same things I'm wondering now, huh."

"I'm sure we have, like are we dealing with some Special Force dude from Venezuela, or just some wanna-be schmuck that Salinas has hired to look around your place."

"That's just for starters I bet. Makes me wonder how Salinas found out about this place since only a handful of people know."

"Probably had you followed one of the times you came out and you didn't notice the tail. It happens."

"Yeah, you're right," Bish agreed thinking. "I don't recall any particular vehicle or vehicles tailing me on the way out this time. I even had several stops in Cheyenne and Laramie before I came up here."

"Well, don't lose sleep over it. You'll burn your brain out thinking it over. Suffice it to say someone knows about your place now. Cann't really be sure who it is. Might just have been some Joe out for a hike, and decided to smooth his trail on the way out. Who knows…?"

"Eh…oh well. Wanna stay for a sandwich for lunch or you gotta get back out there?"

"Yes," Dave said, deadpanned. "Yes to the sandwich, but, sadly, yes, I gotta get back out there," Dave, said turning to go in and put his mug in the sink. When he came back outside, he moved to his SUV, Bish following, turned and gave Bish a handshake and said, "Take care out here and keep vigilant, kid."

"Kid, yeah, right…I'll be watchful," Bish promised. "You watch yourself out there and keep safe yourself."

"I promise," Dave, said turning to get in. He started his rig and pulled out, giving Bish another wave as he left.

Bish waved, too, and went back to sipping coffee on the porch. It wasn't long before the birds renewed their racket all around the cabin. Bish chuckled and stretched out in the Adirondack.

✻✻✻✻✻

Early the next morning, Bish put his fishing gear into the ATV and after locking the cabin, took off for a spot he knew up on the Rob Roy Reservoir. It took close to a half-hour to get there and the sun was just peaking over the trees. *Perfect* he contemplated. He got out, prepared his rod and reel, hooking a large Canadian earthworm on the hook, and sent the lure out about twenty-five yards or so. Now the fun part – waiting.

To help pass the time, he poured a mug of steaming coffee, set up his camping chair, and enjoyed the surroundings. It didn't take long for the cacophony of bird sounds to start and that made Bish smile.

His first catch was a nineteen-inch Rainbow trout. Nice fish to pan fry for dinner that evening. The second was fourteen inches and the third seventeen. He would eat well that evening. Before he'd left the cabin, he'd put out some of his frozen bread dough. It should be thawed by the time he got back so he could cut it and make it into at least four small loaves, maybe five. He would have the other loaves for breakfast the following day, the day he was to return to Cheyenne.

He field-dressed the fish, leaving the left overs for the local critters to clean up, which they always did. It was his way of thanking the Lord for the catch, leaving enough behind to feed some critter that needed it. He put the fish into his small cooler, loaded his fishing gear and camp chair, got in, and left for the cabin.

He would take care of the bread first, and then clean his gear. Afterwards, he would write for at least two hours, taking his break walking around the cabin and sitting on the porch. This was his last day to stay in the cabin, so he would also break out his bottle of scotch and have one shot. He'd promised Anita he'd only have one the whole trip and he knew she would grill him as soon as he got home in Cheyenne.

He got back to the cabin and did as he'd planned; first putting the fish into the small plug-in cooler, they had for the cabin. He cleaned and put away his gear, and then cleaned up himself before working on the bread.

He cut the loaves, placing them on a small, greased cookie sheet, and set the four small loaves aside to rise. He started a fire, got his camping oven out, and set it up to bake the bread. He'd done this on many occasions and knew just how much time to allow the bread dough to stay over the coals. The fish he would fry in his cast iron skillet. He would also have chilled carrot sticks with his dinner. Once everything was prepared, he sat at his computer and began to write, sipping the last of the ice tea he'd made.

*****

The ratty-looking Ford drove by Bish's home from east to west. No hesitation, no stopping, it went its way as if it was nothing. The two men inside knew different. They had once again followed Bish, and once again, surprisingly, not been perceived by him. The two were smiling as they passed the his home.

Five minutes later, they turned north on I-25, steering towards Wheatland. The report they would give Chogan Black Cloud would be well received. They deserved a rest after all they'd done.

As they pulled into the drive, the deputy observing the place took note and called the sighting in, also describing the ratty Ford, and most importantly, gave the license plate number.

Chogan met them at the door, asking, "Well, were you successful?"

"Yes indeed, Mister Black Cloud," the larger of the two answered. "We have everything required to make an attack on the place. We even drew up a map of the surrounding area."

Smiling broadly, Chogan said, "Wonderful…come in, come in, and rest. Are you hungry…thirsty?"

Sandwiches made and cold beer served, the two and Chogan sat at the dinner table and held an impromptu meeting about Bish's cabin and land. It lasted over an hour and Chogan was very satisfied with the pair's efforts.

"Take a week off and go wherever you desire," he told the pair. "I will relay your report to our benefactor and see what he wishes to do with the information. I especially like the two spots you've chosen to lie in wait so we can dart Bishop and his woman," ending that sentence with an evil continence.

"Thank you, Mister Black Cloud," the larger of the two said. "May we start by leaving tomorrow morning?"

"Yes, yes, certainly you may," Chogan answered. "Enjoy your afternoon and evening men."

"Thank you, sir."

Chogan turned for the hallway and after one-step, turned and looked at the larger of the two men with a stern face. Once he had eye contact, he said, "Make sure you take your burner phones with you tomorrow."

"Yes, sir, Mister Black Cloud, we'll have them," he answered.

✱✱✱✱✱

"Did they see you notice them?" Deputy Malone asked Bish.

"I don't think they did, buddy, not at all," Bish happily answered. "I'm sure they were clueless just like they figured I was."

"Okay. Our drone picked them up and followed them to the house up in Wheatland," David said. "The deputy watching the place confirmed that and added a description of the Ford along with the plates. Your PD ran the plates and they were stolen. The task force has already decided not to act on that, just keep an eye on the place and the Ford."

"Sounds good. My camera showed them driving by east to west after I'd gone inside," Bish told him. "If we need that, I'll save it."

"Yeah, I'd advise that, too. I'm sure the task force will want it when the time comes."

"So, we still on for the adventure?"

"TJ and I are getting ready. He's collecting…materials as we speak. Today and tomorrow are his weekend. He said he would store the items up at the spot."

"Good. I'll do my part here. I'll have three of each of everything along with more than enough supplies for each."

324

"That'll do. I'm actually a little pumped over this. They're never gonna expect it, huh."

"I think they'll be appropriately surprised."

Both laughed.

"Hey, I gotta go, you take care, and I'll see you when you give the green light."

"You be careful out there yourself, my brother. Talk to you later," and Bish hung up.

Bish sat back in the dining room chair and thought about what he and David were speaking of. TJ was acquiring two Ghillie Suits and a few more booby trap goodies. Bish was picking up three AR-15s and three Glock seventeens in nine-millimeter. He would have seven magazines for each firearm; the mags for the ARs will be twenty-round type, as the rifles handled better with those.

He would also fill the Jeep with food, as he didn't know how long the trio would be up there before the actual event. It was his task to devise some way of letting Salinas' men know he was heading for the cabin for another extended stay. It would be dicey after that, especially the waiting. His mind dwelled upon the waiting, the uncertainty, the doubt…yes, even doubt. Would they be successful? Would they be harmed or killed? Would Salinas' men even act? So many unanswered questions, ones that led to more questions.

Bish shook his head and stood, shaking off the thoughts, went into the kitchen and poured himself a glass of iced tea to take upstairs for his writing session. Before he sat down, he turned on his computer monitor, nudged the mouse so the screen would activate, set his clock for ninety minutes, and then sat down.

But, he didn't write. He sat staring at the screen, his thoughts returning to what the three called the adventure. He wondered again if they were doing the right thing. His doubt and uncertainty rising, he stood again, looking out the window and down below he could see several children playing in their yards, mothers close by, watching.

That did it. Seeing those children. He was a cop, albeit retired, but still a cop and thus charged with protecting the public and his coworkers. He had to succeed to protect others. No more deaths of his fellow officers.

His thoughts wandered to those already murdered – Nate and Trudy; Daniel Flores and his wife; Kevin and Barbara; Willie and Tim. His feelings led him to prayer, praying for the families of the fallen, and too, for their fellow officers still investigating. He prayed for the safety of all the LEs involved in this case, especially those that had dealings with the rescue. They were the targets. Their lives were the prizes Salinas wanted.

He heard laughter and that brought him out of his revelry. He looked out the window and it was the children, laughing, huge smiles on their faces. The innocents that didn't have a care in the world. That was his mission, to protect and to serve.

He sat back down and began writing, and a smile spread across his face. He was satisfied with what he had to do. And, he had two very good friends to help out. The three felt it was a good plan or they would not have begun the steps to implement it. He smiled and continued writing.

✱✱✱✱✱

Women. What was it about women that they could zero in on their man, knowing they were up to something even though a closely guarded secret…?

Bish was stunned when she came in that night and looked at him asking, "What are you up to?"

He looked at her with a confused look and said, "All I did today was write...and walk around some. Why are you concerned?"

"No, you have your '*spidy-sense*', I have a woman's intuition and I know you're up to something," she stated. "What is it? What are you up to?"

"Uh, chapter twenty-eight…" he sheepishly said with a shrug of his shoulders.

"Don't give me that crap, Bish," she flatly intoned. "What are you conniving with Gerill and that Malone deputy? What are you up to?"

Bish sat in his chair looking at her. She knew. He didn't know how, but she knew. 'Women's intuition'…yeah, right. He suddenly wondered if she had the house bugged and he quickly cast his eyes around the room.

"What are you looking for?" she asked, also looking around.

"Nothing."

"Again, Bish, what are you up to? Your planning something with the Albany County boys…what?"

He looked at her again for a moment, sighed, and said, "Close the door, please."

She did so and he got up and physically sat her down in his chair.

"Now, don't you go off on me now, ya hear," he started, looking in her eyes. She crossed her arms – not a good sign.

Bish stood up straight, collected his thoughts, sighed again, and began. He told her everything. It took almost thirty minutes, and all the while, she listened intently, not interrupting. Bish could see the wheels turning in her mind and when he was finished, he actually sucked in and held a big breath, thinking he was about to get smacked.

Anita watched him for a moment longer, and then her eyes lowered. She was looking at the floor, contemplating what she'd just heard. Bish stood there looking at her finally remembering to breathe again, and kept quiet, watching her think.

After a few more moments of quiet thought, she looked up at him and asked, "You're planning to capture them, not kill."

He nodded affirmatively.

It got quiet again.

Startling him, she asked, "How many know?"

"Just the three of us, and now you, so four," he said almost in a murmur.

She went back to thinking and he kept standing there.

After what seemed a lifetime to him, she looked at him and smiled, saying, "I like it. The bait will be that much more appealing with you and I there. I just bet we're the distinguished catch. I bet we're the reason for the revenge, the others are just the lead in to the grand finally, us."

He couldn't disagree with her reasoning.

"I really like this. We…Bish…," her eyes wide, "we're the reason behind all this. It makes sense. I led the rescue operation and you were directly involved in everything. No one else was, or had the dealings and knowledge that you and I had on that case. And the media sensationalized us so much that it probably drove Salinas mad."

He kept his mouth shut even though he wanted, even needed, to verbally agree with her. He watched as she hung her head and after a moment began quietly crying. He knelt and enveloped her in his arms, knowing what she had just realized. She was blaming herself for the eight murders so far.

"Oh, Bish, why…why?"

"They're sick, babe, just plain sick…that's all. But, we're gonna get 'em. This I promise."

She looked into his eyes and saw the determination…and the fire. "I'm in. No arguing. What are we doing now?" she asked, wiping her eyes.

"TJ is getting some specialized supplies – did you know he was a Ranger in the Army? Anyway, the stuff will include some booby trap materials and some other equipment. David is on food and camping supplies. I'm on weapons detail – and now that you're on board, I'll need to up the order so, excuse me while I make a call."

Bish tried to stand but Anita held him down in a bear hug. "You know, I love you, you big lug," she whispered then kissed him passionately.

"Wow, I love you, too, babe," he said just as quietly and kissed her back. He stood after the kiss, took his cell out of his pocket, and dialed a number from memory. Once answered, he said, "Update on the order…yeah…no problem on the money…up everything to four, we have another member. Yes on the additional mags. Yeah…yeah…that soon…yeah, I'll be there. I owe you big time – steak dinner with all the trimmings some place special? Yeah, that'll do. See you soon," and hung up.

"I'm not gonna ask…"

"Please don't, you really don't want to know."

"How much money are we talking about?"

"That's not part of your input so you don't need to know. The less you know until the event, the better, if you know what I mean."

"Yes, Bish, I understand. Should we call TJ and David and tell them the good news?

Chapter 33

Deputy David Malone was more than happy to have Anita as an addition to their plot. Deputy TJ Gerill, not so much. He was more reserved. Being an old-school Wyoming cowboy, he was just a tad chauvinistic when it came to women. He would rather have her stay home or in her own PD. But, he relented, setting his feelings aside, and welcomed her onto the team.

Two days after the pair of Albany County deputies had been told about Anita, Bish disappeared. No one knew where he had gone, as his Jeep was gone also. Anita assured everyone that he was most likely fine, but she too, didn't have a clue where he was. He must have shut off his cell phone as all calls and texts went to messaging.

What no one knew was Bish had received a call from his arms contact. His order was ready to pick up. After the transaction was complete, the contact assisted Bish with loading everything into the Jeep. It was quiet the haul, settling the little four-wheeled drive vehicle on its springs due to the load of ammunition – two-thousand rounds each of .556 and nine-millimeter ammo.

Just before Bish climbed into the Jeep to leave, he jokingly said, "Geeze, I hope the Jeep doesn't catch fire…if it does, I'm running for Montana." The dealer was not amused.

Bish headed for home. He noted the Jeep didn't hesitate much even though the load bogged the body onto the frame some. *Impressive* he thought to himself. Back at his home, he pulled the Jeep into the garage, covered the load with a tarp, leaving all of it in the Jeep. He then called TJ and said, "All the groceries are in the fridge."

TJ knew from that the weapons and ammo were in Bish's garage and safe for the most part. TJ had received his materials the day before and just happened to be home when Bish called, putting several of the booby trap devices together. He'd already had the ghillie suits out and made adjustments to both, adding faux foliage and strips of forest green, brown, and tan, cotton material he'd picked up at Hobby Lobby.

Nodding to himself, he was happy that their plan was coming together nicely. Everything was falling into place. Malone had put the extra food and camping items in the cabin. He had all of the materials he'd ordered, and now Bish had called with a completed order of his own.

The best part was that now the four of them would meet. It had been previously planned the four would meet for a dinner to finalize plans and pick a date for the actual operation to commence. The kicker would be getting the information on Bish and Anita's holiday to the cabin known publicly so the bad guys would get wind of it and act. They had chosen the *Wyoming's Rib & Chop House* in Laramie for their dinner, and would take place the Saturday following the call. The place had a great cuisine, which included salmon steaks, ribs, pork selections, and beefsteaks all cooked to one's order. Since Gerill knew the proprietor, a secluded booth would be reserved on the date selected, the upcoming Saturday night.

Gerill called the place, talked with his friend, the manager, and arranged everything. The team would meet at five on Saturday afternoon, and might have the booth for several hours. The manager said no problem at all, knowing Gerill and his friends would be shelling out some serious bucks for this dinner. He also knew to have a bottle of eighteen-year-old Macallan ready for their use. He was smiling already in anticipation of the tab on Saturday night.

After that call, TJ continued working on the booby traps, completing one and setting it aside to begin work on another. He had planned for twenty traps to be set out all around the cabin. They would disable, not kill. He smiled deviously, knowing that if someone sprung one of the traps, they certainly would be hurting, and most likely yelling. *Serves 'em right* he thought. He began whistling.

✱✱✱✱✱

Saturday came and the four were seated in the private booth near the back of the restaurant. The server told TJ about the Macallan, which was promptly requested, and poured. Even Anita joined in, giving a small cough after the first toast, which of course brought chuckles from the guys.

Their dinner orders taken, they settled in to start the discussion on the operation, from time-to-time sipping on the Mac. Most importantly for the operation, it would hinge on when Anita and Bish could get away for a week or so. That was the first order of business.

"You and I need to get together at home and discuss this, coming up with a viable reason for the two of us to take off at the same time," Bish said to Anita.

"Yeah and how we'll 'leak' it to the right people so Salinas gets the word," Anita added.

"You guys have somebody in mind to use to let the cat-outta-the-bag?" David asked.

"I think I have just the right pigeon in mind," Bish answered.

"Who?" Anita queried.

"You know, we've seen 'em twice at Perkins, I'll go there and have lunch with a certain official from the rodeo crowd," Bish told them. "I'm positive half the county will know within an hour of our breakfast."

Gerill chimed in with, "That means we'll have to have someone up there all the time after your announcement to keep watch. If Salinas' men show up before you arrive, we'll need to act quickly."

"Agreed," David, said. "I'll take the first watch as I have more leave time than you, TJ."

"I s'pect," TJ said, nodding.

"What do I get to do during all this?" Anita said.

TJ was quick to say, "Just look pretty and shoot straight, darlin'."

Laughs around the table.

They picked at the chips and dip while waiting for their main dishes to be served. The four were deep into thought when the server came out and said it would be another five minutes or so before their dinners would be served. She cleared the chips and dip bowls from the table and reset with hot dinner rolls, butter, and the spiked, garlic potatoes, a deep-fried appetizer that came with the dinner. Each took one spiked tater and all enjoyed the flavor.

Their main meal now served, they bent to the task and appreciated the food. It was indeed very well prepared. There was some small talk during the meal.

Anita commented on the sunrises lately.

Gerill saying they had a 'smattering' of snow up in the Snowy Range. But, snow in the Snowies was never news – it was expected, even in the summer months.

Bish laid out his book idea to David and TJ, with both nodding approval of the storyline.

Malone said his life was just work, work, work, for now. He said he enjoyed going to church, being with all the people and that he had the folks in a Bible study he attended, praying for an upcoming police operation somewhere in the state. God would know of whom they prayed for.

After their meal, another round of scotch was poured, the dishes cleared, and the server out of earshot, the foursome bent to the task at hand. Tactics and strategies were debated. Bish had made a copy of a map that showed his land. He'd drawn in his cabin and the two-track.

They discussed tactics in the terrain that Bish described. One of them, TJ or David, would be on the cliff in a Ghillie suit. If necessary, Anita and Bish would run his direction and David could take care of whomever followed.

Gerill said he'd found a nice depression seventy yards east of the cabin. He would settle in there in his Ghillie suit. Anyone upright in front of the cabin would be a nice target.

David said he'd come running if he heard gunfire at or near the cabin, and would set up somewhere to the south of it. He knew where the depression TJ would be using was and said he'd not fire in that direction.

TJ gave a small 'a-hem' and Bish asked, "What?"

"I've been able to acquire four hot-mike outfits for our use," TJ told the three. "They can be used several ways, but I feel the most important is we'll be able to leave them on when the time comes. That'll allow us to speak so that everyone on the net can hear and not have to use hands to transmit. It's an open-mike system that allows us to either use a mike button to transmit or set the switch and you'll be on an open-mike all the time. I figured we would need those."

"Boy, I'll say," Bish, said. "Those will really come in handy. I'm not gonna ask where they came from, but thank whoever is letting us use them, please."

"No problem, I've already thanked them enough," TJ said.

"I suddenly feel like the proverbial fifth-wheel around here," Anita said, morosely.

"I still think you're the prettiest bait I've ever seen," Gerill said, smiling.

"Hey," Bish intoned, "enough of that kind of talk. She'll be a gun and a half when the time comes. She's a better shooter than I, and I ain't bad."

"Any ideas you come up with, Anita, don't fret, we'll listen," Malone told her.

"Shoot, just listening to you three gives me the willies," she said to the men. "You've already got this figured out. So much so that I do feel like the odd person out. But you're doing great so I don't really need to add anything. I think you've covered all the bases. We'll just all need to be on our toes if they take the bait."

"Not if, Anita," Gerill commented. "They'll be there. There's no way they won't take the…bait," he said looking at her. "They'll want the big apples I'm sure."

"I agree with Tom," Malone said. "You know they'll feel like kids breaking into a candy store. They'll go outta their way for you two."

That statement sobered all four of them. They looked at each other somberly, knowing each were putting their lives on the line. It appeared as if this revelation hit them all at that moment.

Several moments passed with them deep in their own thoughts. TJ suddenly stood and said he'd be right back. Bathroom break. Anita got up also. Bish and David looked at each other and Malone shrugged his shoulders.

"Could get dicey out there," he said, looking at Bish.

"Yeah," Bish murmured.

Chapter 34

Unknowingly, Gerill's mention of 'a smattering' of snow up in the Snowies at their dinner in Laramie proved to be an understatement. September went out like a lamb…and that led to October. It was as if God saw an opportunity for some fun and threw a giant snowball at Earth, hitting squarely between Cheyenne and Laramie. From Elk Mountain, just west of Laramie about fifty miles or so, to the eastern border town of Pine Bluffs, Wyoming, an average of thirty-one inches of snow fell between October third and fourth. It paralyzed both Albany and Laramie Counties.

Every town in the two counties was closed for the most part. Both county governments had everything from plows to road graders and even bulldozers out moving snow. The storm caused nineteen deaths, with everything from ambulances unable to reach several residents that were having heart attacks, to stranded truckers dying from carbon dioxide poisoning.

It took several weeks to get both counties up and operational after the storm. It did snow two additional times, adding another five inches to the mess, but that was tolerable.

Bish, TJ, and David had made a trip one weekend up to the cabin to move snow on the Bishop's two-track. It took every bit of the two days they had to move it all, using a borrowed truck with a plow one of TJ's rancher friends had. It took another day - Bish had stayed behind to finish the work – for Bish to dig out the ATV. He attached the plow blade on it and was able to complete what he, TJ and David, had begun.

Two weeks later, the Chief of CPD, called a meeting of all the task force players in his conference room. "Alright, people, I want to know if there's anything new."

Silence was the reply.

"Any movement by the men in Wheatland?" he asked.

"Just normal everyday movement; to the store, to the gas station…stuff like that," an FBI agent told him.

"What's the word on Salinas?" the Chief asked.

"He's gone to Barbados again," Captain Carlisle answered and added, "We figure he's going to be there for most of the winter since he left when that storm hit."

"We still have eyes on his place in Colorado?"

"Yes, Chief, they're on a 24-7 rotation watching and nothing new there, sir," Anita told him.

"Okay, any new ideas from our side or thoughts on how to go on?"

Silence was once again the reply.

"So we have no new evidence to prosecute with…or plans or actions available on this?" he asked.

Silence again.

The Chief took a deep breath and slowly let it out. "Okay, people, get back to it. Come on, folks, dig, dig, dig. Let's get something we can use to prosecute. Find it!" He was just as frustrated as the whole task force was.

But Anita was holding her tongue, knowing she and her three amigos were holding an ace up their sleeves. With that in mind, as they were leaving the meeting, she caught Captain Carlisle's sleeve and asked, "Cap, since we're so stymied on this, would you consider allowing me to take a week vacation and spend some time with Bish?"

Carlisle looked at her for a moment and said, "Sure, I'll approve it. When do you want to take off?"

"I'll talk it over with Bish and let you know…and thanks, Daryl," she said, earnestly.

He looked at her, startled, and smiled. That was the first time she'd called him by his first name in all the time he'd known her. It actually made him happy.

✶✶✶✶✶

Bish called TJ and David, letting know they were looking at a calendar, and wanting their input.

"Sooner the better," from TJ.

"I agree, you just say when and we'll make it so," David said.

"Then I suggest two weeks from this coming Saturday," Anita said. "That way we can get any equipment we think of out there. Sound Okay?"

"Agree," from TJ.

"Agree," from David.

"We both agree also," Anita said. "So that's settled. I'll get the okay from the captain tomorrow morning."

There was a very pregnant pause as the four contemplated what they were about to do.

Bish jumped as David came across the speaker beginning a prayer for the four. TJ added his prayerful partitions, as did Anita and Bish. Anita was almost in tears.

"Gentlemen, we will go with God…bless you guys," Anita whispered over the phone.

No one could better that comment so TJ was the first to ring off, then David. Anita and Bish sat together holding hands and looking at each other.

"We'll be fine," Bish finally said, getting up and heading for the stairs.

"Where are you going?" Anita asked him as she watched him climb.

"To write some more," he answered.

She thought *nothing daunts that guy at all.*

But, as he entered his library, he drew in several deep breaths, leaning hard on his desk with both hands. He was terrified, his PTSD kicking in. He began a cold sweat. The shakes began. He closed his eyes tightly and concentrated on his breathing. He had a death grip on the desk.

He tensed even more when Anita gently placed her hand on his shoulder. She said, "Bish, we'll be fine. God's not going to let any of us suffer loss anymore with this, that's why we're gonna win."

He looked at her, sweat running down his forehead and cheeks, with tears intermingled with it all. He turned and embraced her as if she were his only lifeline to earth.

She felt him trembling and asked, "Bish, you want to call this off?"

He clung to her for several moments before answering with a quiet, but determined, "No."

The two stayed embraced. His trembling finally subsided and the sweat and tears stopped. He stood back and looking at her said, "I'm fine…it'll be okay…won't it."

Anita just nodded positively.

"I've never reacted to anything like this before," Bish stammered. "I…I don't know what to say."

"You don't have to say anything, Bish, I know what you're going through," Anita said. "I'm here for you. We'll get through this, ya hear?"

"Yeah, I got it," he answered. "But I think I'm gonna be a little shaky. I'm not afraid, just anxious."

"I know, Bish, I am, too," Anita said in a comforting voice. "I promise to be there for you if you're there for me."

"Always…always," and they embraced again.

Salinas entered the home in Colorado wanting a hot bath and his favorite mixed drink. "Have Chogan contact me as soon as possible," he told Allister.

"Will do sir," Allister answered, rushing to call Chogan, and then to prepare the bath and mixed drink for the boss.

Salinas went into his master bedroom, disrobed, and donned a terry cloth robe. He opened his luggage and retrieved a book he was reading. He would enjoy another chapter or two while soaking in the jet tub. He took the book into the bathroom, set it on the counter near the tub, opened a drawer, and took out a face cloth and a hand towel. He used these while in the bath, wiping sweat from his face.

He was smiling as Allister entered, handing Roberto the mixed drink and turning to start the water into the tub. Salinas went back into the bedroom. Allister set the towel and cloth in their place next to the tub, placed the book also, and covered it with another hand towel. He touched the water finding it just a tad too warm, added just enough cold water making the temperature a perfect one hundred-eight degrees Fahrenheit. When the tub reached the proper level, he started the jets and the heat pump, looked around the room deciding everything was in order and left.

Salinas went back into the bathroom, seeing Allister leaving, and took off the robe, setting it on the counter and eased into the hot, tumultuous water, and giving an audible sigh. After a few moments of savoring the heat and jets, he dried his hands on a towel, and began reading the novel.

An hour later, he answered a phone. It was Chogan, "Ah, Chogan, how are things in Wyoming?"

"Did you hear about the snow storm we had a few months back?" Chogan asked,

"Yes, was it a mess in Wheatland, too?"

"Not as bad, but we did get some snow," he answered. "What may I do for you?"

"Any actions while I was away?"

"No, el Jefe, none at all."

"So no targets of opportunity arose then?"

"None at all. We do have detailed mapping of the Bishop cabin in Albany, Wyoming. It might prove useful if we decide to hit them there."

"Very good. I should like to see a plan to that affect when you're down here next."

"It will be done, el Jefe."

"Good, good, now I must ring off as I'm in the tub relaxing after the long flight."

"I'll talk to you soon, el Jefe," and Chogan rang off.

Salinas hung up the phone and resumed his book reading and basking in the heated tub.

✶✶✶✶✶

"Hey, it's me, Gerill…yeah, the cabin's ready," he told Anita. "I put extra ammo in the locker and a dozen of those flash-bangs."

"Sounds great, TJ, thanks for letting me know," Anita thanked him.

"Good as we can get it I think," TJ told her.

"Well, I was thinking," she said with inflection.

"Uh oh, what are you thinking," TJ asked.

"You know they were using the air guns and darts to take folks down…I was just thinking…"

"Oh my goodness, girl, why didn't I think of that," TJ almost screamed. "We can get two of the things and as we lie in wait, hit 'em when they don't expect it. They'll go down in moments and we'll have 'em. Great idea, Anita."

"I think I can get a couple over here in Cheyenne," Anita told him.

"No, I got just the contact over here in Laramie, and she'll be thrilled to death to help us out on a real operation…you don't need to worry about a thing, I'll take care of it."

"Okay, TJ, you got it," Anita said, happily.

"I'll talk to you when we're ready, you take care," TJ said ending the conversation.

"We'll be fine…you, too," Anita returned and hung up.

"That is a good idea," Bish said as she hung up. "I can't wait to use it on them. We'll drag 'em into the cabin and have a talk with 'em when they wake up. I think we can dupe them."

"Dupe them…how so?" Anita asked.

"Tie 'em real good in a chair bolted to the floor," he said. "Arrange a table in front of them and spread some tools and things on it and cover it with a cloth of some kind."

"What kind of tools?" she asked confused as to where he was going.

"You know, clippers, needle-nosed pliers, vice grips, a ballpeen hammer or two, some rope, some needles…I got an old scalpel we can set there, just so they can see it. You know, make 'em real nervous. We can make up a strange story, maybe making you the bad cop in this game, telling them one of the murder victims was a good friend or relative of yours and you want some pay back. Talk you up good and then you come in. The three of us will quietly leave. They'll sing like canaries," Bish ended with a smile.

"Ah, I got it – torture – but not really. Just mentally."

"Yeah, you could tell us to tie ones' legs apart real wide and you could stare at his eyes while we're doing that, giving him a knowing half-smile. He'd load his britches I bet."

"They would sing, wouldn't they?"

"Um-humph," Bish said with an evil grin.

"We need to have dinner with the boys over in Laramie – you in the mood for some ribs?"

"Always, darlin', always."

✶✶✶✶✶

A week later, they were at *Rib n Chops* having a side of ribs with tots and salads all around. They were all laughing, as

David had hit 'em with a cop joke, something about why cops smelled bad, the punch-line being because they were on dooty. The meal went like that for some time.

When the bones were cleaned and cleared, the boys had a drink of some kind and Anita had a glass of white zinfandel. She would be driving home.

"We've got the air guns in the trunk along with the extra darts and the serum," TJ began, "enough to drop a small army. My contact, like I said, was more than happy to help out. I don't know how, but she knew Nate."

"I'm glad you have the guns," Anita said. "We've got news ourselves. Bish came up with an idea that I'm still laughing over since it's so perfect. Bish…"

Bish gave that little evil grin of his and bent low to the table to begin. Dave and TJ leaned in also.

After Bish had explained everything, the foursome burst into laughter as the plan made too much sense and was perfect in their eyes. Dave even said he would ask a nurse friend of his for some 'extra tools' to add to the table. He said he would ask her to get the most frightening looking things she could.

The four finished their drinks, collected tickets, so to speak, paid and left for home. It was a most profitable evening the four figured. Anita, driving, said, "I think David and TJ were thrilled with our little idea."

"No kidding," Bish answered. "I like the idea of Dave going to that nurse he knows and getting some doctor tools to help with the play. That'll give it credence."

"Yeah, I like that, too," she said giving him a sideways grin. "I'm going to like this adventure and I'm going to play it to the hilt."

"That's my girl," Bish said, patting her thigh. "They're gonna sing for sure. I'm gonna beef 'em up with a story about you and one of the victims, saying that you were in love or something and that in your grief, you want some righteous payback."

"I bet when I walk in and you guys leave, I won't even have to touch anything and they'll start spilling their guts," and her statement brought laughter from both. The rest of the drive home was like that – laughter.

Chapter 35

"You know, sometimes I think these weather prognosticators should open their windows and actually take a look outside," Bish complained.

Anita began to laugh uproariously. "It's only a little snowfall, Bish."

"Yeah, just enough to make things miserable, slick, sticky, and just plain…ugh," Bish replied.

"This may just be the weather we're hoping for, if you know what I mean," Anita said, giving him a stare.

His eyebrows went up in understanding.

"I'll check with the captain and see if he'll let us take some time off," she said with a grin. "You," she said pointing at Bish, "check the pass, and see if eighty is open," she told him, wondering if the I-80 pass was open. If the winds were up, then even a little snow could shut the pass down for hours on end.

She left the office and went to the captain's office. Once there, she was ushered right in by Tabitha, who left the door open just a crack as she left.

"Anita, what's up beside the snow depth?" Captain Carlisle asked her as he pointed to a chair for her to sit in.

"Not much, Cap, just wanted to ask you a question," she answered.

"Certainly, what do you need?"

"Time off," she answered sheepishly giving him a half-grin."

Without hesitation he said, "Sure, how much?"

She was stunned.

"Come on, Anita, you've been working you butt off, and for that matter Bish has as well," the captain told her. "If anyone needs time off, you do. Now how much time do you want?"

"Tomorrow through next Wednesday okay?" she once again asked sheepishly.

The captain thought a moment then said, "Tomorrow's Friday, I don't want to see you or Bish again until the Monday after next. Got it?"

"Sure, Cap, thank you," she answered quietly, with a surprised look on her face.

"You sound surprised. You deserve it. I'm making it time off with pay, not your vacation time. The only caveat I have is you need to be able to be contacted."

"Uh, about that, Cap, uh Bish bought some land over near Laramie, actually up in the mountains near Centennial, and built a cabin on it…there's no phone reception there," she said with reservation.

He looked at his desk and after a moment looked up at her and said, "Then take a radio with you and a charging bank – you do have power in the cabin?"

"Yes, sir."

He picked up his phone and called the supply room and said, "This is Carlisle; I'm sending Chief of Detectives Bishop down to you. I want you to issue her one of the long-range radio systems and a charging bank. In fact, make it two radios, one for her, and one for Mister Bishop. They'll be in an area without phone reception and I want them available for contact."

He hung up and said, "There. On your way out, stop by down in issue and get those radios and the bank – now get," he said with a smile.

"Thank you, Daryl," she thanked him.

"You two be careful on your way over – you know the pass – now get," he said pointing to the door.

She noted the open door as she left and wondered to herself about the mole…

348

As soon as she entered the office, she called Pete and Mike into a private conference, giving Bish a thumb up as she moved to a quiet corner of the office with the pair. Bish headed for the door with his coat. Mike and Pete understood and said so. Anita thanked them and went to her desk, grabbed her coat and purse, and with the bag with the radios and recharging bank, left the office.

She met Bish at the car and he already had it running. They would drive to the house first, pack lightly and leave. She got in and took out her cell phone, calling TJ. When he answered she said, "We're on," and hung up.

Those two words set TJ in motion. He called David and said they were a go and to pick him up soonest. The pair had already been approved for a leave of absence by the Sheriff. He knew when the two left that the game was on. The sheriff was the only other person on earth that knew about the operation and was just as sure the plan would work as the four people putting the plan into action.

TJ left and went home. He would change into his winter hunting clothing, adding the winter Ghillie Suit he had. It matched the one David would have. He loaded his weapons and ammo, grabbed his packed backpack, and waited at the door.

Eight minutes and David pulled up in his truck. TJ closed the door to his home and casually walked to David's truck, throwing his equipment into the bed and hopping in. It looked as if the two were going on a hunting trip – and they were.

Up on the mountain, David parked near a well-known bed and breakfast. The pair put their packs on, gathered the remaining equipment and began hiking almost due east, well away from where Bish's cabin was. They would enter a heavily wooded area in just a tenth of a mile, and turn towards the cabin after entering.

They were in luck as an elk herd had passed through the woods in front of the cabin sometime after the new snowfall. This effectively covered their tracks as they went into the cabin to prepare.

They donned their Ghillie Suits, loaded the air rifles with C02 cartridges, injected the horse serum into their darts, and waited. They were ready and waited for the Bishops to arrive.

Which they did; loudly, laughing and yelling about having a great time together. Bish backed the Jeep into its spot, climbed out, and retrieved their bags. The two happily entered the cabin after unlocking the door.

The four smiled at each other and Anita asked, "All set?"

"Yep, we sure are," David, answered.

"All set and ready to go," TJ added.

Bish asked the pair of deputies with concern, "You two gonna be warm enough out there?"

"We'll be fine, Bish, promise," TJ answered.

The four looked at each other, knowing this was an all or nothing maneuver. Anita was the first to move, giving first TJ then David a bear hug.

"We'll be praying for you while you're out there," she told them. "Let's pray together now."

The four gathered together and prayed for several minutes with each putting in a petition for their safety and positive outcome of this operation. When Bish said the final Amen, David and TJ headed for the door. Anita said, "Go with God my friends." They simply nodded to her and left, each going to their chosen spots to wait for…whatever.

Bish and Anita went about their business, building a fire, setting the pot for their hot water, even though they had a hot water heater now. They laughed nervously at each other's jokes and comments, knowing the hazards they could be facing. Bish sighed and threw another log onto the fire.

✶✶✶✶✶

Salinas was sitting by his own fireplace when his phone rang. It was his contact in Cheyenne, relating the Bishops had left for their cabin and was not to return until the Monday after next.

350

He smiled as he hung up. He destroyed the burner phone then yelled for Allister.

"Bring me another phone, quickly," he ordered Stevens.

Stevens ran from the room, quickly retrieving another phone for Salinas. He was dismissed with a wave of Salinas' hand after he'd passed him the phone.

Salinas quickly unboxed the phone and dialed Chogan Black Cloud.

"Black Cloud," Chogan answered.

"My contact in Cheyenne tells me the Bishops have gone to their cabin," Salinas began. "Have the men take action as soon as possible."

"Yes, el Jefe, it will be done," Chogan answered. The line went silent.

Chogan destroyed the phone, stood and looked out the window of the house in Wheatland. He watched the snowfall for a few moments and then went in and told the two men to go and do their work. He reminded them to film everything and to make it very painful for the two.

Both jumped up smiling and left the safe house.

✱✱✱✱✱

The Platte County Sheriff's Deputy noted the time of departure of two men from the house. They were in the van. He called it in to the sheriff's office and they, in turn, called it in to the Cheyenne PD, and informed them no one was following.

Captain Carlisle got the word about the two men a little later. He quickly stood. It didn't feel right. He was perplexed. Why now? Where were these two heading? He walked around his desk and slammed his door as he went by. He walked several laps around the desk and suddenly came to a halt – *Anita and Bish. They're going for them,* he thought. He opened his door, and flew to the communications room and tried raising Anita or Bish on the radio. He tried several times and after no response, ordered the desk officer to continue trying and why and what to report to Anita when contact was made.

Carlisle ran back to his office, quickly dialing the chief. After updating the chief on his suspicions, he ran back to the communications office and watched as the officer repeatedly tried to get in touch with the duo. Carlisle told another patrolman to contact the Laramie County Sheriff's Office and see if he could speak with either Deputy Malone or Gerill.

The captain was very much surprised when the Sheriff came on the line and asked what was up. Carlisle explained his suspicions and wanted to know if they knew where the cabin was. The sheriff apologized, telling the captain he did not know where the cabin was but would get in touch with both Gerill and Malone and update them.

Carlisle thanked him and hung up. He continued to listen in as the officer attempted to reach the Bishops.

*****

"Gerill, this is the Sheriff…you're hot," is all the sheriff said and stopped the communication.

TJ and David both heard the call and knew their plan was working. TJ knew he had time so he got up and warned the Bishops, quickly returning to his position.

Anita and Bish prepared by loading their M-4 rifles and ensured their side arms were loaded and ready to go.

This done, Bish threw two more logs onto the fire. Anita began cooking their dinner. They would attempt to appear as if everything was normal until action dictated otherwise.

Anita was setting the table when the call came in from Malone, "Car on the main road…stopping near your drive…two doors closing…I can hear footsteps…standby."

Gerill smiled and pulled the trigger. The dart flew out of the muzzle and hit the man just below his left gluteus maximus. The result was almost comical.

Malone's dart hit his target high in the right thigh with almost the same comical result as TJ's. Both of the men cursed and yelled about how mosquitoes should not be out in winter. Both dropped after that statement and were out cold.

"Got 'em," TJ said into his mike. "Come on out and help," he said chuckling.

Malone said, "I can't believe this was so easy. These two are going to freak here in just a while."

"Yes they are," Anita agreed as she and Bish walked up to assist in dragging the two up to the cabin, where they would be prepared for Anita's performance. It would be an award winning presentation they were sure.

It took nearly a half-hour for them to get the two where they wanted them. Bish had firmly affixed two chairs to the floor. The two were strapped, tied, and taped with duct tape, effectively making them immovable. Their heads were the only parts of their anatomy that could move. At this point, their mouths were gagged and their eyes covered.

TJ and David had set up the table with a red tablecloth no less. They set out all the 'implements' Anita would require, and covered the lot with another red tablecloth.

The four pulled chairs together and sat, waiting. They knew it would be close to an hour from the time they were hit to when the men would begin to wake.

It was an hour and ten minutes when the first attempted to stir. The man quickly realized he couldn't move. He tried to move the blindfold to see, but couldn't. He attempted to speak but all that came out was a muted sound that resembled an angry bear awaking from hibernation.

The four laughed. The man froze, his head coming erect, trying to hear.

"Don't try to move, you're not going anywhere," TJ said in a low, menacing tone. "You've split your britches bub. You and your friend."

The man tried to speak, emitting a guttural sound.

"Don't try to talk, you can't…well not right now anyway," TJ said. "You'll be speaking soon, I assure you. There's a lady outside – you murdered one of her friends – and she's pretty miffed by that. She brought a bunch of stuff with her and she's got it all on a table right here," he said and slapped the table.

The man jumped.

TJ and David laughed. Bish and Anita got up and eased outside.

TJ continued, "I hope you like pain, my friend, 'cause she's gonna light you up here in a bit. I was looking at all these tools she's got before you woke up, and I'm leaving when she gets started."

The second man woke and tried to move like the first. David and TJ laughed, making his head jerk up also. TJ told him what was going on, almost word for word like he told the first.

"You two are really in for a treat," TJ continued. "I'm sure you know who Anita Bishop is. She'll be here for you two in just a bit. She's the one who set up this table and I watched as she placed each tool and device just so. Scared me to death just watching her."

Malone put his hands over his mouth to prevent the laughter from coming out.

"What do you think she'll start with?" Gerill asked Malone.

"I figure she'll skin their legs first, maybe add a little salt afterwards…I saw her put that can of salt there."

"You think?"

"I don't really know for sure, but she did finger that scalpel there quiet a bit," Malone said. "I figure she'll start with that. Although, that funny looking round thing with the teeth looked interesting. Not sure what she'll do with it, but I don't want to be here when she does."

"Me neither, friend."

"You think she'll let 'em pray first?" David asked.

"Good question…maybe you two," TJ said giving the first to awake a slight kick, "should start praying now. I would."

That was the signal and a loud knock on the door came. Both of their heads lifted at the sound and the first one awake turned his head in that direction.

TJ and David had both left their winter balaclavas on and TJ said, "Well, it's time you two got to see who is coming to dinner…so to speak," and he stood and removed the blindfolds.

Both blinked rapidly in the light and the first thing they set their eyes on was the table covered in the red cloth. Eyes wide, both turned their heads as Malone rose and eased over to the door, opening it and seeing Anita standing there said, "Evenin' ma'am. These two are ready for you."

Anita entered the cabin and looked at the two, staring into their eyes. "You two can leave," she said.

Both TJ and David moved quickly out the door, slamming it as they left.

The smaller of the two men, the second to awake, began trembling.

✱✱✱✱✱

"Sheriff, you gotta get up here, these two are singing like you wouldn't believe," Gerill said over the secure comm link.

"It worked?" the sheriff asked.

"Like a charm, sir," TJ answered. "These two are telling us everything. You should of seen it, sheriff, when Anita took the top tablecloth off, they began screaming in their gags. Now they answer questions as fast as we ask 'em.

"I'll be there in forty-five," the sheriff said. "Keep 'em hot until I arrive."

"See you soon," TJ said and signed off.

Chapter 36

The task force met. What Anita, Bish, TJ Gerill, and David Malone had accomplished was considered a miracle. It would be a closely guarded secret, with nothing going to the press. The Chief of the Cheyenne PD asked if there was any new business for the force.

Anita raised her hand.

"Chief of Detectives Bishop, what have you got?" the chief asked.

"Sir, I believe I know who the leak is," she stated.

Members shifted in their seats at this news.

The chief looked at her and said, flatly, "Go on."

Anita explained what had happened in the Captain's office and about noting the door being ajar when she left. She further explained that the two captured in the cabin showed up less than four hours after she and Bish had departed for the presumed vacation.

The chief was staring at her and she suddenly felt uncomfortable. It was always a hard thing to do to accuse a coworker of criminal activity, but this was accessory to murder, murder of their own. "What would you like to do, Anita?" the chief finally asked.

"I'm sure she's using burner phones – I checked," Anita began. "Our phone records from that day show no outgoing calls from her desk. I'd like to set her up and make sure she's our leak."

✳✳✳✳✳

The two arrested at the cabin could not identify Salinas. They did finger Black Cloud and several others as accomplices to the murder ring everyone was sure run by Roberto Salinas. They needed to get another prisoner. They had more than enough to convict the first two captured, and again more than enough to imprison the two from the cabin for life plus. They could move now and arrest the others, but that would leave Salinas loose and a threat.

Several ideas were thrown around the room, one of which came from Detective Michael Hicks, who said, "Look, we have probable cause to go to Salinas' home in Colorado and do a search. I doubt we would find anything and just irritate the snake. We need to set up another ambush like the one they did at the cabin. If we can get someone to I.D. Salinas, and agree to testify, then we can move on him. I'm sure Colorado would extradite him to Wyoming, and with what we have and with a witness testifying, we could put him away for life…or worse."

"They'd balk at us using the cabin again," Anita said. "I'm sure they're wondering where their two men have gone. If I'm right on the leak, they'll know soon enough. That means they'll be cautious with anything we might throw at them."

The room was silent for several long minutes while the people thought about Mike and Anita's comments.

Sheriff Al Tomlinson from Albany County spoke up saying, "Then let's use their paranoia against them and they'll move."

The chief asked, "How so?"

"Your leak," Tomlinson stated. "Use that to the fullest. Anita can give a fictitious report for the captain to her. In that report, Anita can add something about moving the two prisoners somewhere or doing another sting operation some place, (this got a chuckle – sting, darts…cop humor). It should be loaded with information that would implicate Salinas, even though false. She would leak that information and possibly create another opportunity they would use to make a play to get their two men back – or even kill them, or to make another play for victims."

That statement regarding prisoner movement sobered everyone as that meant the officers driving the vehicle would become targets themselves. And no one wanted to see more officers hurt or killed.

"If we did a fake prisoner move," Sheriff Tomlinson began, "we would have to use extreme caution. We're not sure of the capabilities of these people – do they have explosives, such as rocket-propelled grenades or something worse. Do they have fully automatic weapons and if so how many and what caliber? Ultimately we would have to protect our people and not knowing exactly where they would be hitting the SWAT van..." he ended letting the statement hang.

"All good questions," the chief stated. "We'll have to look at these ideas further, discuss them, and make formidable plans for both, and then decide on the best operation to use. For now, I suggest we adjourn, go back to work, and workout both plans to the fullest. Detective Bishop, you have the bait plan and the fabricated report to build. I'll brief our SWAT Chief and get him on board for possible action if we use the prisoner movement. I want Donaldson and Hicks as his contacts with your team, Anita."

"Yes, sir," she quickly answered.

"Okay, everyone, if there is nothing further...thanks for coming in and we'll be in touch," the Chief said. "Please remember to contact everyone if you garner any new information. Thanks again," and with that he turned for the door, the meeting was over.

*****

"Any word on your two men?" Salinas asked Chogan over the phone.

"No, el Jcfc, it is as if they dropped off the face of the earth," Black Cloud commented.

"I have not received any word from my Cheyenne contact, so the mystery deepens," Salinas said, rhetorically.

"If I may suggest..." Chogan timidly asked.

"Yes, yes, go ahead."

"I would like to send two men to Cheyenne to take a look around, you know, visit bars and such frequented by police, and ask questions about the investigation into the murders," Chogan detailed. "They would be warned to be cautious with their inquiries."

"Yes, that could possibly benefit out quest…yes, yes, I like that so go ahead and send them."

"It will be done, el Jefe."

"Is that all?"

"Yes, my friend."

"Let me know immediately if you hear from or about your two men," Salinas ordered.

"Yes, el Jefe," Chogan answered into a dead phone as Salinas had hung up. Chogan shook his head and wondered if he would live through this.

Almost a month later, the task force had decided to attempt another sting operation. The prisoner movement ploy was judged to be just too dangerous to be put into action. It had been decided that Anita would create the false report, leaving it on Tabitha's desk, with information regarding the capture of the two men. She made it sound as if it was a chance capture, accomplished by Bish on one of his hikes around the property. She left out the part of Albany County Sheriff's Deputies taking part, and the use of the dart guns. She would add that the two men were remaining non-committal about speaking so nothing new had been learned. Anita would also leave a new vacation request for the captain's signature. It would give dates that Anita and Bish would be leaving for a real vacation to an as yet unknown location, but in Wyoming so they could keep in contact with the team.

Anita had conscripted Bish to be her recorder and scribe on the project. They were keeping as much information from the others as possible by order of the chief. The pair hated to do that to their team, but orders were orders and the team understood.

"We need to go have dinner with TJ and Dave again," Bish mumbled.

"What?" Anita asked, looking at him.

Bish looked up at her and said it again, "We need to go have dinner with TJ and Dave again."

She looked at him blankly, and finally asked, "Why?"

"So we can plan this again. They might know a place where we could go for our 'vacation' (he used his fingers to quote the word). Some place quiet, out of the way and remote so that we would put the fewest folks in danger. They just might know a place over in Albany County that fits the bill."

Now her wheels were turning, her eyes squinting.

He knew he had her. He just wanted an excuse to go the *Rib's n Chops* place again for another rack of ribs.

She looked at him and said, "Call 'em and make the arrangements, for this weekend if we can."

He turned for the phone.

"What did they say," she asked when he'd hung up.

"Saturday was best for all of us," Bish answered. "TJ said he'd arrange it, but we're going to a place in Centennial called The Old Corral. Said they had the best steaks in Albany County"

"Ohh sounds delicious, and I'm in the mood for a good hunk of meat."

Bish got a smile on his face and started to say something but she held up a finger, shushing him. He smiled demurely.

"Reel it in, darlin', we're working," Anita ordered, smiling herself.

The pair continued working, casting stealthy looks at each other from time-to-time, and both still smiling.

Detective Hicks walked by and quietly said, "You two need to go get a room."

Anita and Bish both broke out into laughter, as did Hicks.

However, the pair continued working on the project. Anita was sure the report and the vacation request would turn the tide.

After Bish finished the report and prepared the vacation request, Anita called the captain on his private cell and told him she was ready to deliver. He needed to be out of the office so the ruse would work by leaving the report and request on Tabitha's desk.

"Tabitha!" Carlisle yelled.

"Yes, sir," she answered, startled that he had yelled her name.

"I gotta go see the chief; I'll be back in an hour or so," he told her as he went by.

She didn't have a chance to respond so remained quiet, watching the door close to the stairwell. She shrugged her shoulders and went back to her task.

Twenty minutes later, Anita walked up and asked if she could see the captain.

"Sorry, Anita, he's been called to the chief's office, but should be back in less than an hour – I can let him know you were here," Tabitha told her.

"Nah, I just need to drop off this report for him and this vacation request," Anita said, smiling. "Bish and I still need some time off."

"I'd give my right arm for some time off," Tabitha said, taking the proffered report and request. "I'll give these to him as soon as he comes back. Can I do anything else for you?"

"No, thanks, I'll talk to you later, Tabitha," Anita said in a friendly manner.

"Okay, Anita, see ya," Tabitha said, placing the papers into the Captain's In Box.

*****

Saturday afternoon at two o'clock, the foursome met in Centennial. TJ had once again arranged for a private area for them to use. The meal was as TJ said, superb, the steaks being perfect. The meal completed, more sweetened iced tea was poured, and the four left alone.

"So," TJ began, "what is it you want to talk about, Anita?"

"We've gone with another sting operation and for that, we were wondering if you guys knew of another place over here in the mountains somewhere we could use," Anita said.

Dave and TJ looked at one another, and then bowed their heads in thought. Both were deep into cooking brain cells, so Anita and Bish kept quiet, sipping their tea.

Finally, Dave spoke up saying, "I know a guy over near Saratoga, has a cabin on the southwest face of Elk Mountain…he might let us use it."

"I know a guy, too, has a place near Foxpark…he might let us use it," TJ said. "What do you have in mind? Something like before?"

"Sorta," Bish answered. "Main focus will be not putting others in danger, just those on the sting, so we're looking for remote, outta the line-of-site of other homes and stuff."

"That leaves Foxpark out," TJ said. "Homes all around that place."

"Elk Mountain is good," Dave said. "Nearest place is about a half-mile away to the east, last time I was there anyway. Good, heavy forest, too. I can call him if you want."

"That would be nice," Anita said. "He'll be well compensated, too. The governor assures the task force he had money available for us."

"Money…now that brings something else to mind," Dave said, looking at his glass of tea.

"What…?" TJ asked, looking at him.

Dave looked at TJ and said a name, "Chester Wilcox."

TJ sat up straight and a crafty smile crossed his face. "Yeah, Chester would even want to load up his Colts and help out."

"Who's Chester Wilcox?" Bish asked.

"You remember the Confederate treasure hoard that was found a few years back?" Dave answered.

"Yeah, who doesn't," Anita said.

"It was on his ranch, the Bar W…very remote and he doesn't let anyone on it uninvited," TJ added. "He'll love this and would probably finance the whole thing just for the fun of being involved. His place is perfect," he ended looking at Dave.

"Yeah, it would be, wouldn't it?" Dave asked with a devious grin of his own.

"You know," TJ said looking at his hand, "I bet he'd invite Light Horse."

Dave's eyes lit up, "Oh, yeah, and his people…" Dave said dubiously.

"Who's Light Horse?" Bish asked.

"He's an American Indian," Dave answered. "A very serious American Indian. Some say he's Cherokee or Shoshone, but no one's really sure. We met him up there along with about twenty-five of his people as he calls them. They all had rifles and handguns and helped us with that firefight we were in. They cleaned house, and we didn't even know they were there until the action started. It was as if they just…showed up."

"Very spooky that was," TJ agreed. "Those folks move through the woods and you won't even know they're around. Mister Light Horse, his first name is Thomas, scared the tar outta me one time. I was standing in this little clearing, it was about fifteen feet around, all alone, by myself, no one else around…and suddenly he was just there, like Scotty had beamed him in or something. I didn't see or hear anything…he was just there." TJ squirmed just a bit and added, "I still get goose-bumps when I think about that."

"Yep, that's the way the guy and his people are so I really think if Chester lets us do this up on his place, and he invites Mister Light Horse, whoever comes on the Bar W won't have a chance," Dave said.

"We want 'em alive," Anita insisted.

"Sugar," TJ, said, "…that won't be a problem. We'll give the air guns to Light Horse's people and they'll deliver 'em to you hog-tied and ready for transport." He's said that while smiling.

"I'll give Chester a call right now," Dave said, getting up and pulling his cell phone.

Anita and Bish watched him leave. Bish looked back to TJ and asked, "You're really serious about these folks…?"

"Absolutely! I'll take Mister Light Horse and his people any day. They are that good…scary good."

"TJ, you really think they would help us out with this?" Anita asked.

"All we can do is ask, politely," TJ said, and then followed up with, "They'll want to meet you first, especially Mister Light Horse. Chester'll give you a bear hug you'll never forget," he said with a chuckle. "He's quite the character, and I love him. He's a wonderful man and a fine Christian. He's an old-school cowboy/rancher so when he says something, it's etched in stone. His word is his bond and he'll certainly let you know it. His handshake is as good as a written contract in his eyes, so remember that. When it comes to business, when he says something or shakes your hand, you'd better comply with your part."

"Sounds like the kind of man I want to meet," Anita, said smiling. I hope he agrees to help out."

Dave came back right then, sat down and said, "I bet he's already wearing the Colts…he's in and can't wait to meet you two. He said he'd read everything about the rescue and thinks you two are real heroes. I gotta warn you though he's very serious when he wants to be."

"Yeah, we get that since TJ's been telling us about him and Mister Light Horse," Bish commented.

"You agree with what TJ tells us about Wilcox and this Light Horse guy?" Anita asked.

"In spades," Dave answered seriously. If we have those two, and for that matter, Light Horse's people, on our side, Salinas is toast."

"That's good to know," Anita said, still somewhat doubtful.

"Anita, we're serious about Chester and Mister Light Horse," Dave said. "They're real and can be real dangerous when the need arises. Chester really does have a pair of Colt .45's that he wears on occasion, and he really does know how to quick draw and use 'em – he could shoot a pencil outta your hand from a draw. If they agree to help us out, I'll say we're ninety-nine percent sure to come out of it unscathed."

Both Bish and Anita looked at him disbelievingly.

"You sound confident saying that," Anita stated.

"That's because I am that confident in their abilities, abilities I've seen firsthand and have been saved by," Dave said with conviction.

"You two sound doubtful…look, we both understand," TJ said indicating Dave. "These people saved our lives – twice. Both times we didn't even know they were around until it was all over." He paused for a moment, looking at the pair, and then said, "Look, I was a Ranger in the Army. Folks say we could sneak up on a sleeping rattler, thump him on the head, and be gone before he knew what happened. These people can do the same except they'd turn the snake over onto its back and leave without it even knowing. Mister Light Horse scared the tar outta us more than once just showing up."

"That's a fact," Dave agreed shaking his head. "I'll never forget the first time I saw him. He just appeared on a ridge above the ranch, to the southwest. Chester pointed him out to me. But, that's not the eerie part. I was walking back to camp and he just…well he was just there. Scared me silly. Almost drew my weapon on him. And he smiled at me and motioned for me to go on by. I waved as I went by, and a few steps later turned to see if he was following and he was gone. I'm like TJ and still get goose bumps just thinking about that."

Anita looked at Dave for several moments and knew they both were telling the truth, or at least believed what they had seen. Bish still looked dubious.

"Okay," Anita began, "I'll buy off on this since Mister Wilcox already agrees to help out. What county is that place in?"

"Wapiti County," Dave answered.

"Okay, we'll have to coordinate with their Sheriff's Office. I'll talk it over with the captain and the chief and see if they would approve the operation and get the sheriff up there to buy off on it. If they all do, I'll let you know and we'll get together again, in Cheyenne this time, and formulate a plan. Maybe Mister Wilcox can come down, at my expense, and join us. We'll need maps of his place and the county where it actually is so we can view it on the satellite program we have."

"No problems on any of that," TJ said, bringing up an app on his phone and showing Anita where the Bar W was located up in Wapiti County.

They talked for almost another hour before finally stopping the get together. Hugs and handshakes all around as they neared their vehicles. They departed knowing they just might have the upper hand on Salinas and his men again. It was a good feeling.

Chapter 37

The Bar W Ranch was a sprawling place almost centered in Wapiti County, Wyoming. The county itself was made up of prairie lands on the east, rolling hills in the middle, and mountains and valleys on the south and western sides. Wapiti County was formed in the 1888 split of Albany County, and encompassed almost two and a half million acres of mostly wilderness, prairie, and, high desert lands.

Chester Wilcox's ranch was made up of mostly prairie grasslands and rolling hills. The canyon, *Crashed Wagon Canyon*, where the gold and silver hoard was found, was on the southwest section of the property.

Chester was waiting at the gate when the foursome arrived. He was all smiles and waived the team through the gate, closing it as they passed. He jumped into his old rattletrap truck and yelling at the top of his voice told them to follow to the main house.

"Everybody got their seatbelts on?" TJ asked. A chorus of yesses rang out. "Good 'cause it's gonna get bumpy here real quick."

Dave was driving and did his best to keep up with Chester, but Anita was begging for mercy in no time. The two-track into the Bar W's main house and complex was not smooth to say the least. Anita wondered if Chester had ever had the track graded.

"Has this track always been like this?" Bish asked, bouncing around despite being tied in with the seatbelt.

"Yep, and this is the smooth part," Dave exclaimed.

It wasn't too long, however, until they pulled into the main complex's drive, which was asphalt-paved. The home, rebuilt after the find, was beautiful. The line of small cabins to the south, just as lovely, surrounded with Aspen trees. A barn and corral were to the north and a large outbuilding was to the west, probably holding vehicles and such.

Dave pulled in front of the cabins and parking, undid his seatbelt and jumped out, running over to Chester's truck. TJ did the same.

"I'm not sure I've finished bouncing," Bish commented, eliciting laughter from Anita and a comment about the same.

"I don't think my bladder will ever be the same," she jokingly said. Bish now laughed.

They unbuckled and got out, moving slowly towards the truck, watching as the trio of men shook hands and slapped each other on the back. It looked like old-home week or something.

"Chester," TJ said, "…this is Mister and Missus Samuel Bishop, otherwise known as Chief of Detectives Anita Bishop, and Author Samuel Bishop."

Chester held his hand out to Anita first, who flinched at the rawhide-like feeling the hand of the Bar W Ranch owner had. He did have a gentle shake for the lady, however.

For Bish, the handshake was a grasp, with the old man looking at Bish's eyes and not seeing any flinching or appearance of pain.

"You'll do," Chester said and gave him a slap on the back that did produce a flinch. "Now for my hug," Chester said, and turned, grabbing Anita in a bear hug.

Dave and TJ began laughing and TJ said, "I told you so."

"I ain't had a pretty lady up here since Mary and Jim was up here a few weeks back," Chester said, stepping back and giving Anita the once over look. "My, she is good lookin'. You boys were right," Chester said looking at Dave and TJ.

"Hey, this one's mine," Bish said moving up to Anita's side.

"Protective, huh," Chester said with a sideways glance. "Better be or I'll take her off yer hands, youngster."

"Chester, settle down," Dave said putting a hand on Chester's shoulder. "How 'bout a cup of your cowboy coffee?"

"Now yer talkin' boy, come on into the house y'all, and we'll have a cup or two or three," he said turning for the home.

Inside, Anita and Bish marveled at the woodworks, the collection of rifles and shotguns in racks along the front wall, and another rack of handguns, one spike holding a pair of Colt .45s in a dual western holster outfit, the extra shells gleaming in the light.

"Y'all come on in and sit at the table," Chester just about ordered. He busied himself with fixing the coffee and once it began to brew, sat with the team.

"What you two did for those little girls was a real hero's action," Chester began. "I read everything I could and watched the news for weeks afterwards. That was really something. I read how that one guy sent you two on a honeymoon to Barbados. That was real nice of him. Did you have a good time down there?"

"Yes, sir, it was a swell time," Anita answered.

"You was still hurt if I remember right, wasn't you?" Chester asked Bish.

"I was still recovering from the gunshot wound, yes, sir," Bish said rather sheepishly.

"Nothin' to be ashamed of, sonny, I'm just glad you're alright now. You are, aren't you?"

"Yes, sir, I'm doing just fine," Bish answered.

"Don't let him fool you, Mister Wilcox," Anita said. "He still has his moments with pain."

"Can't them doctors do something about that?" Wilcox asked.

"Already doing everything they can, sir, and I'm really doing quite well," Bish explained. "I do have a twinge from time to time, but it's because I've moved wrong or something."

"I got throwed from a bull one time and got busted up some and I still hurt from that thing," Chester said. "I know what pain is, too."

"Chester," TJ interjected, "…you really up for this little operation of ours?"

"You betcha, TJ, I'm ready," Chester said shaking his head. "I got old Indian Tom lined up, too. He'll probably bring in some of his people fer this one. Y'all be seein' him pretty soon I s'pect. Don't freak out when you see him. You boys let 'em know how he is?"

"Yes, sir, we briefed them," Dave answered. "Told them how cantankerous you were, too."

Chester burst into laughter with that, stood up and went to pour a round of coffee for everyone.

Once everyone was served, Chester sat back down and looking at Anita and Bish, sincerely said, "Welcome to the Bar W Ranch. My home is now yours. I'm hopin' we can bust these guys like you want and I think we got a pretty good shot at doin' this, 'specially with Old Tom and his people on hand. They'll never know what hit 'em," and he began laughing again.

"This coffee is great," Bish said. "What brand is it?"

"Cowboy coffee," Chester said. "Ain't got no brand, just coffee."

"Where do you get it – I'd like a can or two to take home," Bish asked.

"I get fifty pound bags of the beans from an outfit in Peru, the country in South America," Chester explained. "Once I get it, I use my grinder and grind up a couple a pounds of the beans. That lasts a while. I'll grind up a few pounds for you before you leave."

"That's swell, thanks a lot," Bish said, taking another sip of the strong brew.

"This is very good, thanks," Anita told Chester.

"Chester, you sure Light Horse is okay with helping out?" Dave asked, attempting to move the conversation back to the task at hand.

"Oh yeah, he actually smiled, and you know how hard it is to get a smile outta him," he answered.

"Yes, sir, I do," Dave answered. "That is a good sign isn't it?"

"You betcha, sonny," Chester said.

"Do you have any idea how many men he'll have with him?" Bish asked.

That got smiles from TJ, Dave, and Chester. "As many as he needs I s'pect," Chester said. "He could have anywhere from a few to several hundred and we wouldn't know it."

"I understand that from what Dave and TJ have told us," Bish said. "They tell me they get around pretty quietly."

That statement produced another round of laughter from the trio of men.

"Boy, I'll say," Chester, said between laughs. "Old Tom's scared the tar outta me on more occasions than I can count. Does it on purpose I think, just to see the reactions I have."

"I agree with that," TJ said, smiling.

"I tell ya, you'll just about jump outta your skins the first time he gets you," Chester said, laughing all the more. "It'll be a sight fer sure."

A light knock rapped on the front door. Chester looked up, surprised, and asked if they were expecting anyone else. Negative answers were given. He got up, went to his Colts, drew one, and turned for the front door. He heard several slides being moved on handguns behind him and knew he had backup.

He opened the front door, let out an audible sigh, and said, "Thomas, you gave us a fright."

Thomas Light Horse entered the house without being invited. He looked at the people at the table and nodded to TJ and Dave. Anita and Bish just got a stare.

"Come on in, Tom, and let me introduce you to the new folks," Chester said, giving a wave of his hand towards the table.

Light Horse walked over to the table and stood in front of Bish, looking him in the eye. Bish returned the stare.

"This here's Detective Samuel Bishop, retired, and his lovely wife, Chief of Detectives Anita Bishop…Anita, Bish, this here's Thomas Light Horse," Chester said introducing everyone.

Bish held his hand out and Light Horse gripped it, his hand like Chester's, similar to shoe leather…the bottom of the shoe. Light Horse turned and gave Anita a light shake, then sat where

Chester had been sitting, forcing Chester to retrieve another chair for the table.

"You want some coffee?" Chester asked Light Horse.

"Yes," was the one syllable reply, and Chester brought him a cup.

After Chester sat, the room became very quiet. Anita and Bish looking Light Horse over, Dave and TJ watching for their reactions, Chester looking at everyone, and Light Horse looking at his coffee.

"Too quiet in here," Chester said.

So Bish took the initiative and said, "It's a pleasure meeting you, Mister Light Horse, we've heard so much about you from TJ and Dave. We thank you very much for any assistance you might give us on this case."

Anita jumped in with, "Yes, sir, nice to meet you, and we very much appreciate your assistance.

"Good," Light Horse replied.

That brought a moment of uncomfortable silence. Good that Anita and Bish said something or the coffee was good.

"You old rattlesnake," Chester said to Light Horse. "What's good – the coffee?"

"No, good to meet new people," Light Horse commented. "Coffee horrible as usual."

That brought a tension relieving laughter from the group.

"What'd ya mean my coffee's horrible," Chester complained, bringing more laughter from the group.

They talked well into the evening, taking a break to cook up some burgers on the grill. After dinner, they talked more about preparations for the upcoming operation. Anita and Bish telling Light Horse about the specialized air rifles they'd brought and the drug infused darts. Anita stressed they wanted these people alive if at all possible. Light Horse maybe said ten words all evening.

✶✶✶✶✶

Salinas read the report for the tenth time. His contact in Cheyenne had emailed him a copy with two attachments, one being the report from Detective Bishop, and the other a vacation request. He smiled at the vacation request and noted a blank box where destination should have been written. They had not made up their minds yet. He would know soon enough.

The report was interesting in that it happened to be a chance encounter that got the two men arrested for trespassing, and a few other charges, including a weapons charge. They were being held in the Cheyenne Police Department's holding unit in the basement of the complex in Cheyenne.

His contact had come through once again. She was a valuable resource of information, and he showed his appreciation by adding another handsome sum to her offshore bank account in the Cayman Islands for the information he now held.

After transferring the funds, he picked up the report and reviewed it once again. How simple it all seemed. A chance encounter in the middle of nowhere led to the arrest of his men. He shook his head. *Unbelievable* he thought. He shook his head, tossed the thing on his desk, got up, and left the room. He was frustrated, as it now seemed that nothing was going his way and that was not acceptable.

He went into the living area and picked up a burner phone, dialed a number from memory and when the party answered, he said, "Chogan, my friend, I need you here as soon as you can,"

"Yes, Jefe, I'll be on my way shortly," Chogan responded.

Salinas hung up and went outside on the back deck of his home.

Chogan destroyed the phone, and left shortly thereafter in the Camaro.

The Platte County Deputy called it in and Captain Carlisle was notified eight minutes later. He called the detective's office and Mike Hicks answered. "You and Tony available?" the captain asked.

"Yes, sir, what's up?" Mike asked.

"You two get in an unmarked car and go up to the north side and keep an eye out for the yellow Camaro. It's heading south. Follow it until you can't."

"Yes, sir, on it," Mike answered motioning for Tony to get his coat. They left in a hurry after briefing the 'kids' on what was going on.

Mike and Tony watched as the Camaro went by, doing sixty-four in a sixty-five speed zone. They got on I-25 and followed the Camaro to the Colorado/Wyoming border, called the captain and reported.

"Okay, get on back here," the captain, ordered.

"On our way, Cap," Tony said.

*****

Allister met Chogan in the drive, taking the Camaro to the garage after Chogan got out and ran inside to meet with Salinas.

"Ah, Chogan, so good of you to join me…scotch?" Salinas offered.

"No thank you, Jefe, I'm fine," he answered. "What may I do for you?"

Salinas handed the report to Chogan and said, "Read this and tell me what you think."

After several minutes, Chogan handed the report back to Salinas and said, "Most unfortunate, Jefe, a chance encounter like that."

"So, you feel this is real?" Salinas asked with a crooked smile.

"Real…I don't follow, Jefe," Chogan said, confused.

"Do you think the report is real or a fabrication?" Salinas asked again.

Chogan motioned for the report again and after reviewing it said, "I believe it to be real," he said matter-of-factly and handed the report back to Salinas.

"I find it hard to believe myself, that two of our men could 'by chance' be arrested like that on private property. The more I read this (holding up the report) the more I do not buy it."

"Why would the police fabricate a false report like this?" Chogan asked rhetorically.

"My question exactly."

The seeds of doubt planted, Chogan looked at his boss in consternation and wondered to himself about the report.

Light Horse had called in a few of his people and they were given the air rifles and instructions on their use. They, and Light Horse, left Chester's home. The four watched as they melted into the landscape to the east, towards the ranch entrance.

Chapter 38

Bish's contact with the Colorado police had called him the moment the yellow Camaro had pulled up to Salinas' home. She also told him it was Chogan that had gotten out. She assured Bish that they would keep watching and she would call him the moment anything new happened. He asked if she would put in a formal contact report on this for the record. The contact would be used in court when the time came.

*****

Anita had called Captain Carlisle and told him where she and Bish were staying for their vacation. He put on a good show, sounding very happy for the two and that he would add the location to their request. After hanging up, he walked out of his office to Tabitha's desk and asked her for Anita's vacation request form, saying how happy Anita had sounded on the phone.

Carlisle wrote in the location on the form, and gave it back to Tabitha. "I bet those two have the time of their lives up there," Carlisle told Tabitha. "She said they were going to get a tour of that canyon where all that treasure was found."

"That sounds exciting, Captain," Tabitha said.

"Yeah, I'd love to be with them, that would be a swell tour to be on," the captain replied going back into his office. He turned on his computer and began going over the Daily-Dailies, knowing full-well Tabitha would be relaying the Bishop's location to Salinas any minute. The computer I.T. guys had figured out how she was contacting Salinas, and were now watching everything she did on her system.

The FBI had been notified and after some work, their I.T. team had found her offshore account and had been watching the deposits arrive shortly after she transmitted material to Salinas. When the time came, she would be spending a very long time in a Federal Penitentiary for women, probably in the supermax for women in Colorado.

✳✳✳✳✳

"Chogan, please come in," Salinas told his friend and comrade. "I have news from my contact in Cheyenne. It seems the Bishops have gone on vacation to the Bar W Ranch in Wapiti County, Wyoming. They are staying in a cabin as guests of one Chester Wilcox, the owner. It is a very remote part of Wyoming."

"I have heard of this place," Chogan said. "It's where that treasure was found."

"Yes, the Confederate gold and silver hoard was found there," Salinas verified. "I want immediate action on this. The Bishops and anyone else at the Bar W Ranch are fair game. I want you to leave as soon as possible. And Chogan," Salinas said laying a hand on Chogan's shoulder, "…I want no mistakes this time, no chance encounters. I want you to take the entire crew with you and take care of this personally. Do you understand?"

"Yes, el Jefe, it will be as you say," Chogan answered.

Salinas removed his hand and gave a little nod of his head, sending Chogan away on his mission.

✳✳✳✳✳

"Bish, Chogan's leaving in the yellow Camaro right now," Bish's Colorado contact told him on the phone.

"Thanks, darlin', I owe you a big steak dinner with all the trimmings," Bish said.

"And I'll hold it to ya, ya big lug…give Anita a hug for me and you two be careful," she told him.

"We'll be careful and I'll certainly give Anita that hug," Bish said, smiling. "Hey, again, I really appreciate all the work you've done for us. Thanks."

"Don't worry, you'll pay for it," she said and hung up.

Bish hung up and grabbed Anita in a bear hug, saying, "That was Colorado, Chogan is in the Camaro and she thinks he's heading back this way."

"Let me go, bruiser, I gotta call the captain," Anita said, struggling to get away from Bish.

"But I promised to give you a hug from her," Bish said, hanging on.

"That didn't include smothering me now did it?" Anita said breaking free at last.

Bish laughed and said, "We owe her a huge steak dinner somewhere."

"Figured that…now be quiet." Anita dialed the captain and when he came on, said, "Cap, Chogan's heading back north, Colorado just called."

"Alright, get everything ready and kick some butt when they get there," Carlisle said, giving a knowing smile. "You all be careful up there, you hear."

"We will Daryl, I promise," Anita told him.

"Anita…" Carlisle's emotions were breaking.

"I know Daryl, we'll be careful. We got this, Cap. I'll give you a call when it's done."

*****

When Anita briefed Chester, he drew one of his Colts, went to the front door, and fired one round into the evening sky. This was the prearranged signal that everyone needed to be on their toes until this thing was over. He went back inside, reloading the Colt as he entered and discarding the spent casing.

"I'm brewing a big pot of cowboy coffee if anyone's interested," he said heading for the kitchen.

"I bet we'll need it," Anita responded with a smile. "When it's ready, yell and I'll come get a mug."

"Darlin' when it's ready I'll bring you a mug," Chester said over his shoulder.

Bish shook his head and continued cleaning his M-4 carbine. As he cleaned the rifle, he prayed he wouldn't need to use it or his side arm. But, both would be ready to go if the need arose. He'd already cleaned Anita's for her and made sure both were fully loaded and ready for action.

TJ and Dave had done the same earlier. Both would be stationed outside beginning at dark, with Dave in the barn loft watching with night vision equipment, and TJ would be in the house attic, doing the same. Dave had opted for a police shotgun that held nine rounds of double-ought buckshot. TJ had his M-4.

Other than the dart guns, they had no clue what Light Horse's people would be carrying. The five weren't sure if they wanted to know either. What was important was the fact that these folks were there to help. It was a wonder to Anita and Bish, the others taking it in stride. As Chester put it, this was their land, even though he owned it, and they had free-reign on it. That was his agreement with the tribes in the area. They were even authorized to take up to ten cattle a year for their meat. If more than that were needed, they would just ask and Chester always agreed.

When he spoke of it, he said it in quiet tones, as if he were ashamed for some reason. And as far as Anita and Bish knew, he had never spoken of why. They had watched him after talking about it and he'd had a faraway look in his eyes and had looked sad. Neither pried.

TJ came in and said, "Its dark. I think we outta pray together before we split up."

"I agree sonny," Chester said and began praying.

The others gathered into a circle and prayed together. When TJ said the Amen, they all hugged each other and shook hands. Grim but determined looks on their faces. Dave was first to leave, heading for is position in the barn. TJ was next, climbing the stairs to the attic. Anita and Bish gave Chester one last hug and left for their cabin – they were the bait. Chester poured himself another mug of cowboy coffee and readied his Colt pistols and Henry rifle, both the same caliber so used the same ammunition. Anyone coming on the ranch this night would be taking their lives into their own hands.

✱✱✱✱✱

The fourth night brought a cold drizzle. Dave swore some of it was snow. The wind amplified the coldness so much he had to walk around in the barn's loft just to keep warm. He was tired. He had never liked night shifts. He always seemed off for a while after a run of night shift and it seemed to take longer for his body to readjust to daytime living.

They had not seen a thing out of Salinas' men since Tabatha had sent the message to Roberto. No other communication between the two had taken place, however the FBI reported to the chief that another hefty deposit had been made in the Cayman's account. This information he relayed to Captain Carlisle. His ire for his secretary mounted. He would ensure she would spend many, many years behind bars. He wondered why she was doing this, not knowing she and Salinas had attended college together and had dated.

Dave continued to walk around the loft, stopping to scan the surrounding area with his night vision goggles before making another lap. Chester had brought a thermos of cowboy coffee earlier and it helped somewhat. Dave sipped the steaming liquid, savoring the heat it produced going down.

He was scanning the area when he saw Light Horse standing in the thick cover of a stand of pines. Old Tom was looking right at him, and once he knew Dave was looking, signaled that four men were on the property.

Dave activated his throat mike and said, "On your toes folks, Light Horse just signaled there are four unwelcome guests prowling about. Watch yourselves and get ready for anything."

He didn't hear anything but knew four other people, TJ, Anita, Bish, and Chester, were ensuring weapons were loaded and ready to go. He knew TJ would be donning his night vision goggles to watch from the attic.

What none of them knew is that Light Horse's people already had two of the men down, hog-tied, and gagged. They were out like a light just seconds after being darted. The other two were about a quarter mile from the complex when Light Horse's friend James tonudvhna Nashoba (the Cherokee name translated to English means Silent Wolf), fired his dart gun, hitting the third man, who took two steps and fell face down in an Aspen stand.

The fourth man, Chogan, heard his partner fall and wondered if he'd tripped. He waited, unmoving, listening. Not hearing anything else, thinking his man had very quietly risen, and continued on, Chogan moved forward. He could see the home through the trees. He was raising his rifle to peer at the place through his scope when he had a stinging sensation in the middle of his back. He squirmed a little thinking something had gone down his neck into his shirt. That happened to be his last thought as the horse sedative quickly took affect and Chogan Black Cloud crumpled into a sleeping heap.

*****

Late the following morning, a very warm and refreshed Deputy David Malone, stepped out of the hot shower, dressed and left his cabin for the main house. He met TJ along the way and they knocked on the door to Chester's place.

"Come on in!" they heard Chester yell.

The two entered, wiping their boots first, and were assailed by the smell of fresh-brewed cowboy coffee, bacon frying, and eggs cooking.

"'Bout time you two got up," Chester said as he busily moved around the kitchen. "Sit and I'll bring you a mug of joe."

No arguments from the two as they sat and thanked the old timer when he brought their coffee.

"You boys want the usual?" Chester asked the pair.

"Yes, sir," both answered.

"Mornin' you two," Anita said.

"Yeah, mornin'," Bish echoed.

"Morning to you, too," Dave said smiling after his first sip.

"Those four still out?" TJ asked.

"Oh yeah," Bish said smiling. "Light Horse and his team have 'em trussed up very well. I can't wait for 'em to wake up."

"Shouldn't be long," Anita said, finishing her breakfast. "Chester, I got the dishes."

"Why thank you, ma'am, that's much appreciated around here," Chester said with a huge smile. He had loaded two plates with bacon, eggs, home fries, and toast, and set them in front of TJ and Dave, who promptly prayed and dug into their breakfast.

Bish dried as Anita washed. "I cannot for the life of me figure out why that went so well last night," Bish commented.

"Yes, it did appear rather easy," she added.

"Rather…?" Bish said smiling.

"Well, it was."

"Yeah, too easy to me."

"We'll find out here in a bit when we go out to the barn and see if our captives want to talk about anything."

After they'd eaten, TJ and Dave went out to the barn, Chester in tow, to set up Anita's table again. Chester leaned against the barn door with a sprig of grass hanging out of the corner of his mouth, watching the two deputies.

When they'd finished and finally draped the red tablecloth over everything, of course while the four captives watched, Chester asked, "What's all that stuff fer?"

TJ waived at him to follow the pair and as they got out of earshot, TJ and Dave explained what had gone on with the previous captives.

Chester laughed so hard he was wheezing, finally choking out, "That's the dad burndest thing I ever heard of. Them boys are gonna load their pants fer sure," and laughed just as hard as they entered the house.

"What's he laughing at?" Bish asked Dave.

"He asked what was with the table…we told him about Albany and he's been laughing ever since," Dave explained.

"Wish I could be there when you do that to 'em, lady," Chester said, hugging Anita.

"How about from the back side of the loft," TJ said, looking at Anita.

"Sure, just have to remember to be quiet," she said. "If you get to laughing, that will bust us," she said pointing to Chester.

"Yeah, maybe I'd better stay in here…it'd be better if I did," Chester said morosely.

"Did you guys talk me up out there?" Anita asked.

"Oops, forgot to do that part," Dave said and he and TJ headed for the door.

"Talk you up…what's that mean?" Chester inquired.

"They'll tell 'em mean things about me, and good things about Bish," Anita explained. "Bish will go in first and ask some questions, friendly like, and since he probably won't get any answers, the three of them will split the captives up into different rooms, leaving one near the table, and let them know that I'll be talking to each of them one at a time out where the table was."

"You know, you shoulda asked Night Horse to help with this part," Chester said with a faraway look. "He and his people have been known…"

And that's when Anita ran to the front door and yelled for TJ and Dave to get back inside. Once in, she poured everyone a mug of coffee and had them sit at the table.

"Chester had a great idea and I like it," she began.

Bish smiling, said, "Me, too."

After she'd explained, TJ and Dave liked it, too. Chester got up, drew one of his Colts, and opening the front door, fired one round into the morning sky.

Twenty minutes later Thomas Night Horse knocked quietly on the front door.

✶✶✶✶✶

Night Horse was all smiles as he got up from the table. He went to Chester's phone and dialed a number from memory, and when answered talked in his native language for several minutes. After hanging up, he sat back down with everyone and slid his empty coffee mug towards Anita.

"Sure thing," she said with a smile and got up to refill his mug. Several other mugs slid her way and she refilled them.

"Nashoba coming," Night Horse said to Chester. "He's bringing more tools," saying this with an evil grin.

"You're gonna love this ain't cha," Chester commented.

That got him a sideways glance from Old Tom.

It wasn't too long before they heard James' old Ford truck sliding to a tire-squealing stop on the asphalt out front. One door slammed and someone could be heard coming up the steps out front. The knock was loud compared to Night Horse.

Chester opened the door and said, "Come on in, James, glad you could come."

"Are you kidding, I wouldn't miss this for the world, man," James said almost laughing. "This is gonna be great. I ain't had a chance to scare a white man like this in a long time – no offense there," he said to Chester.

"None taken, feller, just glad to have you help out," Chester said sincerely. "I'm sure these folks appreciate your help, too."

"Yes indeed," Anita agreed, getting up and shaking James' hand. "Coffee?"

"Yes, ma'am, and I hope you folks don't take offense to the white man comment either," James said.

"None at all," Bish answered, shaking James' hand also. "Like Chester said, we're very glad you two have joined us. This is going to be a day to remember."

TJ and Dave shook hands with James also, and commented on the day's events. Anita had started another big pot of cowboy coffee, and turned, looking at the men speaking together and gave a little ahem.

The men turned their attention to her and she said, "We need to get busy. I want to start with that young one, and I want Chogan last," she said with a wicked look.

TJ and Dave, with mugs in hand, left for the barn. Night Horse motioned for James to follow him and they too, went outside to parts unknown. Chester, Anita, and Bish waited. TJ and Dave knew to talk up Anita, Night Horse, and James to the hilt.

In the barn, the two deputies dragged three of the four to tack rooms around the barn, put earplugs in them, covered their eyes, and made sure the gags were still secure.

The youngest one…well, they dragged him to a center position in front of the table. TJ commented, "I can't believe she got the Indians to come help her with this." The kid's eyes got big.

"Yeah, that was a change," Dave said. "She's never done this before. These guys don't stand a chance, do they?"

The kid's head flew to TJ.

"I recon not…I don't know what they'll do, but it's gotta be worse than what she does with this stuff," he said, pointing at the table, the kid's eyes following his finger.

The young man had begun to sweat, beads running down his forehead into his eyes.

"Well, you better put that blindfold on him or she'll be ticked," Dave said.

"Oh, yeah, I got it right here," TJ, said, pulling a kerchief out of his back pocket, and blindfolding the kid.

"That on tight?" Dave asked.

"Yeah, it'll do," TJ, answered. "I hope you answer her questions, man, 'cause if you don't…well it's gonna hurt some."

They could tell it was pleading coming from the gag, the kid's head shaking. TJ removed the gag and the kid began spilling his guts. Dave was writing furiously as the kid spoke.

That's when Night Horse and James came in, bringing in all manner of implements for use in getting people to talk.

The young man was screaming now…NO, NO, NO… He was crying. TJ and Dave lifted the tablecloth and Night Horse and James arranged their tools beside the rest. Night Horse hesitated, looking at the kid, and reached back and picked up what looked like a smaller version of a jawbone tomahawk, the jawbone portion from some small animal with very sharp teeth. He turned with it in his hand, and pointed it at the kid and said something to TJ in his native language.

"What'd he say?" TJ asked James.

"He wants to know if we can keep the parts we take off of these men to feed his cats," James politely answered.

"What do you want to know…I'll tell you anything…I'll tell you everything…," the kid yelled with spittle flying.

That's when Anita entered. She walked up to the table, looked at the kid, then at Night Horse, and said, "So, you've begun?"

TJ answered saying, "No, not really, he's just asked a question, that's all."

"What question?" Anita asked, the kid looking from face to face as they spoke.

"He," TJ said indicating Night Horse, "…asked if they could keep the parts they took from these men to feed their cats."

Anita almost lost it and it was everything she could do not to bust a gut right there. She was having a time of it keeping the smile from forming. However, she kept her composure and said, "I don't mind…get that bucket over there for them, and then you can go."

Dave chimed in then, "He's already started talking. I got everything I could here," he said handing Anita the pad and pen. "He'll probably tell you anything you want."

TJ delivered the bucket, placing it right in front of the kid, whose eyes bulged out and he began crying and trembling again.

"I'll tell you anything, just ask," he cried out.

"You two leave now," Anita ordered and TJ and Dave headed for the door. Anita selected a tool from the table and the kid began screaming. Loudly enough the other three, even with the earplugs, could hear him.

****

That evening at the dinner table, Anita, Night Horse, and James all related the conversations they had with three of the four. After Anita had finished with the kid, they took him into another room blindfolding and gagging him.

The next two players had talked just as much as the kid. Why? James had killed one of Chester's chickens, which was baking in the oven right then, and had dribbled the blood on some of the tools and around the ground where the kid had been. They spoke rapidly when Night Horse proffered the bloody tomahawk.

Anita said she couldn't write that fast and had to slow them down a time or two. She said if they went quiet about something, James or Night Horse would select something from the table and they'd talk faster and faster.

"We have enough to send Chogan Black Cloud and Roberto Salinas to prison for ever. We didn't even need to talk to Chogan. The oldest of the three told us where a bunch of paperwork and burner phones with Salinas' number already programmed, are located in the Wheatland house. I've already called the Platte County folks and told them to get a search warrant and go in and get it."

"We've got him now," Bish said.

Chapter 39

The Captain was once again beside himself with glee. His people along with the Native American Indians and the ranch owner, Chester Wilcox, captured four henchmen without firing a shot and no one got hurt. Save for the pin pricks each of the four received and the chicken they had for dinner.

The information they supplied would be more than enough for an arrest warrant for Salinas and anymore of his men that might be around. It would be a great day.

He did however arrange a special thank you from the Governor to the Cherokee and Shoshoni peoples and another to Chester Wilcox of the Bar W Ranch of Wapiti County. Both were delivered by the four officers that ran the sting operation.

Next on the list of things to clean up, the captain, Anita, and the FBI Agent in Charge showed up at Tabitha's desk on Monday morning, first thing. The FBI Agent began, "Tabitha Crowell, you're under arrest for suspicion of aiding and abetting first degree murder, accessory to murder in the first degree after the fact, releasing privileged information according to the Privacy Act Laws, and releasing information of Law Enforcement Personnel in violation of the Private Records Act. *'You have the right to remain silent. Anything you say can and will be used against you in a court of law. You have the right to an attorney. If you cannot afford an attorney, one will be provided for you. Do you understand the rights I have just read to you?'* The FBI Agent read from her Miranda card.

Tabitha softly said, "Yes, I understand."

Anita turned her around and cuffed her, rather roughly, and said through gritted teeth, "With these rights in mind, do you wish to speak with me?" as she turned her around to face her.

Head down, tears running down her cheeks, she said, "I'll remain quiet for now."

The FBI AIC took charge of the prisoner and led her away. Carlisle and Anita looked at each other and the captain said, "That was harder than I thought. I'm glad you talked me into letting the AIC do it. I probably would have smacked her around a little. Thank you."

"I'm sorry we had to do that, boss, but she is an accomplice after all," Anita said. "In quite a bit actually. The Feds have grabbed all the offshore account monies and they'll be dispersed to the families of the fallen after the trials are completed. She, the FBI AIC, told me that a while ago."

Another FBI Agent walked up right then and said, "I need to block this area as evidence, please."

The captain and Anita went into his office and watched as the agent wrapped Tabitha's desk in yellow FBI crime scene tape, and sealed the drawers and computer with sticky tags. He pulled the mouse and keyboard and placed them into an evidence bag, along with everything else that was lose on top of the desk. After sealing and annotating the bags of evidence, he took those and left the area.

Carlisle closed his door and sat heavily in his chair. Anita plopped into one of the guest chairs. He pulled out a key, unlocked his lower desk drawer, and pulled out two glasses and a bottle of Glenfiddich scotch, poured a healthy amount into both glasses, proffered one to Anita who took it and watched as the captain tossed his back.

Anita took a healthy sip of her scotch and gave a little cough as it went down. "Strong stuff," she said.

Carlisle poured himself another shot and sat back in his seat, and said, "Yeah," and took another sip.

They sat in silence for a while, sipping their scotch, neither looking at each other nor saying a thing. It went on like that for quite a while.

Anita was first to break the spell, reaching forward with her empty glass and motioning for another shot, which Carlisle gladly poured. She sat back, took a sip, and said, "They're gonna put her away for a long time, aren't they."

"Yeah, they are," Carlisle, agreed. "She'll never get out I'm afraid. What she did…well, it ain't right, that's all."

"Yeah, Cap, it ain't right," Anita, agreed. "I kinda feel sorry for her."

"NO!" Carlisle yelled. "No sympathy for her. She did something despicable…horrible in my view. She'll be lucky to get life several times over. I'd just as soon take her out and hang her publicly."

Anita, startled, kept her mouth shut. She'd never seen this much emotion from the captain.

"There better not be anyone else involved with this in my department or with the CPD for that matter. I'll kill 'em."

"I'm sure a bunch of us will want to help you," Anita commented. "The firing squad would be distinguished I'm sure."

"The way our people died, a firing squad is too fast. I want 'em to die slow like our people did. Hanging…that's what I'd do. Hang 'em all."

Anita hung her head, took a sip of her drink, and then said a quiet prayer for the captain. He was too upset and making statements that he shouldn't. She felt sorry for him also. She was having mixed emotions, wanting the same as the captain, but the Christian in her was taking charge. She knew what she wanted to do but knew in her heart she wouldn't. She vowed to pray more and let God do His thing.

The captain's phone rang and he quickly answered, curtly, saying, "Carlisle…yes, chief…yes, chief…yes, sir. The FBI have already sealed her desk and taken evidence. They said someone would be by for the computer, and the stuff in the desk drawers. Yes, sir…yes, sir I'll get right on it."

Carlisle hung up the phone and looked at Anita, "He's really ticked. He wanted to be here for the bust. I didn't know that. Oh well, water over the dam."

"What's he want you to do?" Anita asked.

"He wants a complete inventory of her desk items - didn't say why - and I'm to ask the FBI to provide that as soon as possible," the captain answered. "I guess he wanted to see her face or something. Maybe grill her a little."

"Yeah, I'd love to do that myself," Anita said with emotion.

Daryl looked at Anita and quietly said, "Anita, I'm sorry about my outburst earlier. It was uncalled for and outta line."

"No, I don't think it was, Daryl," she said. "I appreciate the apology, but we're all going through some rough emotions right now. I'm a Christian and I'm fighting with both sides inside right now. I want to do the same things you do, but the Christian side of me trumps those feelings. You know what I mean?"

"Yes, Anita, I do," Daryl answered. After another moment of contemplation, the captain said, "Go on back up to your people. You all take the rest of the day off. If I need you, I'll call so no arguments. Take Bish out to dinner or something. I think we can relax a little now. I'll see you all in the morning. We'll have a meeting first thing, okay."

"Thanks, Cap, we'll all appreciate it I'm sure," Anita said, getting up and turning for the door.

"Anita," the captain said, stopping her in her tracks, "Don't let your hair down too much out there tonight. "I'll see you in the AM."

Chapter 40

It was a Monday morning. Skies were clear, the sun just peaking up over the horizon to the east. A huge flock of geese flew to the south, right over Anita's SUV. She and Bish both looked up to see the sight.

"I love hearing those things as they fly over," Bish said.

"Yeah, me, too," Anita said.

The radio cackled and everyone was told to move into position. Anita started the cruiser and followed the lead FBI vehicle.

After two weeks of grilling Tabitha, the FBI called the task force together for a meeting. They had invited a contingent of Colorado FBI agents and state troopers since the bust would be made in Colorado.

The briefing had lasted over four hours and when the force adjourned, the decision had been made to make the bust on this Monday morning.

It was just past six in the morning. Eight FBI vehicles, ten Colorado State Trooper vehicles, five Wyoming CPD, Laramie County, and Albany County Sheriff's office vehicles, all moved into position around Salinas' place in Eldorado Springs, Colorado. The night before, several FBI tactical agents traversed the mountain north of the place, covering the back. Once they were in position, a radio call had been made and that is what started the action.

The law enforcement agencies involved expected a blood bath. However, the surprise was complete and not a shot was fired.

Roberto Salinas was led out of his mountainside chalet with his hands cuffed behind him. Allister Stevens and Renaldo del Monte, along with four other men, were led out in the same manner. All were placed into separate vehicles and taken to the FBI holding cells in the Denver Federal Building.

✶✶✶✶✶

"Not a drop of blood spilled," Bish said, amazed. "I figured we'd be in a battle royal like the rescue."

"Me, too," Anita said, climbing back into her SUV. "Since we're down here, let's call your Colorado contact and have a nice steak dinner somewhere."

"Oh, I couldn't agree with you more," Bish, said, getting out his phone, and making the call. The contact readily agreed and said to meet her at the *Buckhorn Exchange* just south of the Lincoln Park. Bish said he knew where the park was and they were on their way.

All three had steaks with all the trimmings, with Bish opting for the high plains buffalo prime rib, the sixteen-ounce version, with sautéed mushrooms, onions, and green pepper spears. They had a hearty red wine, actually two bottles. The evening was a smashing success with the main topic of conversation the bust earlier in the day.

When the trio broke, after Bish paying the bill, Anita and Bish said their farewells and thanked her quite a bit for her assistance. Neither Bish nor Anita could really drive back to Cheyenne, so they opted to stay in a local hotel for the night. Both slept soundly.

The following morning found Bish driving through the Denver and Fort Collins traffic, which was as usual atrocious. They had to stop twice for vehicle accidents. Back in Cheyenne, Anita went to the Captain's office while Bish went upstairs to check in with the team.

Carlisle said he'd figured she and Bish had stopped for dinner. When Anita told him about the contact, he said it was for the better and that they had used their heads and stayed in a hotel instead of driving under the influence.

"What would you like us to concentrate on today, Cap?" she asked him.

"Golly, I hadn't really given it much thought until right now," he replied. He smiled and said, "I suppose you can give your crew some time off it they want it. I'll sign all the requests – they deserve it."

"Yes, they do, Cap," Anita, agreed.

"I think you and Bish ought to go up to that cabin of yours and veg out for a week or so."

"No, he's wanting to get back to writing and I agree," she said. "I want to get back to normal myself and have some work I need to catch up on. Any ideas on what they'll do with Salinas and his people?"

"Yeah, the FBI AIC called and the trial will be here in Laramie County, with Albany County taking part, specifically Malone and Gerill. Those two were a gold mine for us, huh."

"You bet, and Bish and I still owe them a steak dinner. We're taking them to the Old Corral in Centennial again. We want you and the missus to tag along with us on that one, our treat."

"I'd like that…and I know she will, too."

"I'll let you know so you can put it on your calendar. Hey, speaking of that, when are you getting a new secretary?"

"Funny you should say that as I hired a nice young Christian lady this morning. She'll start her processing Monday. I think she'll be a winner."

"How do you know she's a Christian?"

He chuckled and said, "She was digging her paperwork out of her bag and a Bible came out with it, falling on the floor. I asked her what she was reading and she said it was the Bible. That's when I said I was a Christian and read my Bible daily. We hit it off after that."

Anita laughed and said, "That's a neat story. I'll have to invite her to our Bible study at our place sometime."

"You do that…now get. I'll let you know when I hear anything on the Salinas case."

Anita left his office and went back to hers. The team was hard at it, doing catch up paperwork on cases that had taken a backseat to the Salinas case, but it went silent as soon as she came in, all eyes turned to her.

"We did great," she began. "And because of that, the Captain has given us *Carte Blanch* on vacation applications so if you want, fill out a form, and give it to me. He wants to sign 'em so I'll take 'em up. You all deserve it and I'm thinking a bunch of commendations will be coming down the pike pretty soon also."

She stood there looking at everyone and smiling and asked, "Anything else for me?"

The silence hung in the air for a few moments, and then Mike Hicks stood and began clapping. It was no time at all and everyone were on their feet clapping. Anita was stunned and her emotions got the best of her.

✶✶✶✶✶

The trials lasted for months, but when all was said and done Salinas received the death penalty. Of course, there would be an appeal and everyone expected it.

Chogan Black Cloud also received the death penalty. He too, would appeal, but since he was a direct part in the killings, he would not be granted any concessions on the appeal.

Renaldo del Monte was give life without the chance of parole. He was remanded into the FBI's custody and taken to the supermax near Pueblo, Colorado.

Isabella was charged with accessory to murder in the first degree after the fact and another thirty years was added to her sentence. She would never be free again.

Allister Stevens being almost completely unaware of what was transpiring in Wyoming was given parole with time served while awaiting trial. No one was given bail. He would remain in Colorado until his parole time was over, and then move to Wyoming like he wanted.

The other men directly involved in the murders received the death penalty. The other three men were charged and found guilty of multiple charges, and sentenced to thirty or more years in the Wyoming prison in Rawlins.

✳✳✳✳✳

When Salinas' execution date finally arrived, several thousand people showed up at the Rawlins facility. Of course, they weren't let in. Captain Carlisle, Anita, and Sam Bishop were among those invited. This was the first hanging in Wyoming since the nineteen-nineties. The families of those murdered opted not to attend the execution. Dave Malone and TJ Gerill had been invited and were on hand and sat with Anita and Bish.

Those attending were sequestered in a room behind one way, mirrored glass. They could see the execution, but no one in the execution enclosure could see them. Inside that room was the judge, a priest, giving last rites, the FBI AIC and one other agent, a doctor, and three other men.

These three men were all dressed exactly the same, in black suits with white shirts and black ties. The kicker was these three all had black velvet face covering that hung to their chests. These coverings did have slits for their eyes. They were the executioners. They stood to the side of the gallows, each grasping with their right hands, a roped lever. One of those levers released the prisoner to his death. None knew which lever was the actual one. This allowed the executioners to have a doubtful escape from knowing they had executed someone. They stood waiting

At exactly ten o'clock that night, the judge gave a nod of his head. The three men pulled in unison the three levers, and Roberto Salinas dropped to his death. Those inside the room heard the crack of the vertebrae as it snapped. Those on the other side of the glass did not. They did, however, see Salinas drop and sway for a moment.

After a fifteen minute wait, they lowered the body onto a gurney. The doctor went over, removed the hood from Salinas' head, and for a full minute checked for a carotid pulse. Finding none after that long minute, the doctor pronounced Salinas, dead at ten-nineteen that evening. Salinas had never made a sound through the process. The Salinas family was no more.

✱✱✱✱✱

Chogan Black Cloud however was a different story on his execution day. He yelled and begged to be jailed for life. His hood was wet with sweat and tears and the onlookers could clearly see he was trembling with fear. When the rope went over his head and tightened, he screamed in fear.

Again, the three men waited for the judges signal, and precisely ten o'clock that evening, he nodded. Chogan Black Cloud dropped, screaming, to his death. The doctor also pronounced him dead at ten-nineteen that evening.

✱✱✱✱✱

The other four hangings all went similarly to Chogan's execution. Wyoming was the only state in the union to use hanging as a form of execution in almost fifty years. Every left-wing organization in the states complained and Wyoming left 'em all hanging, so-to-speak, not commenting at all.

✱✱✱✱✱

Captain Carlisle was considering retiring and secretly doing the paperwork for Anita Bishop to take his place. She was the

400

only logical replacement. He was recommending Mike Hicks as Chief of Detectives. And the captain's new secretary would reveal nothing to anyone.

Connie Dominguez was promoted to rookie detective. So too, was Andrew Nelson. Clint James and Tom Alton went back to patrol and found that life very boring after the time they'd spent with the detectives.

The Chief received a huge check from the FBI, which was used exclusively for the survivors of those murdered. The money had come from Tabitha and Salina's accounts, those that the feds could find. The survivors would never want for anything save the love of their fallen family members. The money was really no consolation.

*****

Anita and Bish finally took some time and vacationed in their cabin, hiking their property, going to Rob Roy and fishing and hiking up there. Bish had his laptop with him and did write some. He was almost finished with his book. Anita…relaxed and watched the animals. She loved sittin' up on the cliff above the creek and watching the animals come and go. She and Bish liked taking naps up there, as the noise from the creek was soothing.

One morning, Anita had fixed a nice breakfast and they were eating out on the front porch. They had just finished when they heard a vehicle coming down their lane. Both had weapons handy, Bish his Benelli twelve gauge, and Anita her AR-10.

It was TJ and Dave, and TJ said as he got out of the vehicle, "All that's missing is banjo music." All four bust a gut laughing.

Anita got up and poured coffee for the two and Bish got two more deck chairs for them. They sat for hours drinking coffee and telling stories. Anita and Bish both wanted to hear a detailed briefing on the *Crashed Wagon Canyon* treasure case the two had been on. That was something to hear.

TJ and Dave wanted to hear the couple's real version of the *Ladies of Cheyenne Rescue*. The four couldn't believe they were part of the son's revenge campaign. Both TJ and Dave asked a load of questions about Bish's time in the hospital and his recovery from the gunshot wound.

After all the stories, they got up and made dinner. Dave had brought out steaks and potatoes for the four, and Bish and TJ went to work on them right away. Anita concentrated on the salad and the drinks, which Dave delivered...regularly.

Other Books by James W. Murphy

I'm Tired of Zombies Series 1-4

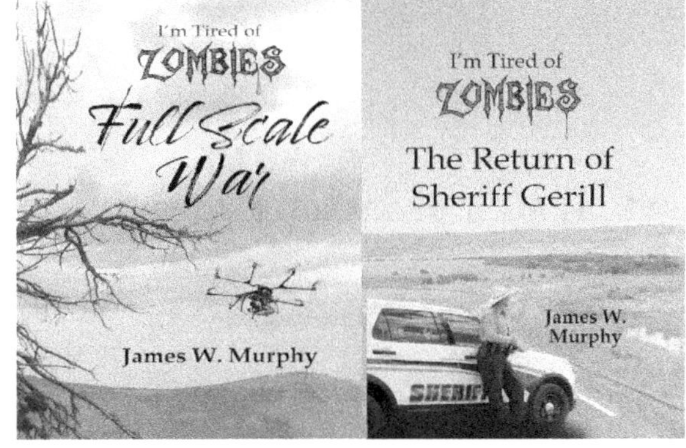

Crashed Wagon Canyon

Abducted: Book 1 of Bishop Series

About the Author

James 'Jim' Murphy was born in Rabat, Morocco, North Africa. After a few years, the family moved to Louisiana, then to Puerto Rico. There, he found Jesus and was baptized at age seven, and shortly afterwards became an American citizen in San Juan in 1960. In 1969, the family moved to Bunker Hill, Indiana. This is where God led James to his soul mate, Jean. They became high school sweethearts, and were married in 1974, and have been happily married since. They have three grown daughters, eight grandchildren, and three great grandchildren.

James served his chosen country, The United States of America, for over twenty-three years in the Air Force. He was a medic specializing in Aerospace Medicine. He has an Associate's Degree in Science from the Community College of the Air Force, an undergraduate certificate in Biblical Studies from Colorado Christian University, and is currently enrolled in the Dallas Theological Seminary, with a course of study in Biblical Studies. He and Jean moved to Cheyenne, Wyoming, in 1996, and have resided there since on the Nickle 'J' Ranch.